SHORT STORIES FROM THE SECOND WORLD WAR

SHORT STORIES
FROM THE
SECOND WORLD WAR

Chosen by Dan Davin

OXFORD UNIVERSITY PRESS
1982

Oxford University Press, Walton Street, Oxford OX2 6DP

London Glasgow New York Toronto
Delhi Bombay Calcutta Madras Karachi
Kuala Lumpur Singapore Hong Kong Tokyo
Nairobi Dar es Salaam Cape Town
Melbourne Auckland
and associates in
Beirut Berlin Ibadan Mexico City Nicosia

Introduction and selection © Dan Davin 1982

British Library Cataloguing in Publication Data

Short stories from the Second World War.
1. Short stories, English
I. Davin, Dan
823'.01'08[FS] PR1309.S5
ISBN 0-19-212973-2

Set by Western Printing Services Ltd
Printed in Great Britain
at the University Press, Oxford
by Eric Buckley
Printer to the University

Contents

Introduction

IN selecting the stories for this anthology, I have tried to follow two principles not always easy, as it proved, to reconcile: on the one hand I wanted to include stories which represented as many aspects as possible of the British at war in the years 1939 to 1945, stories which would cover life on the home front as well as life in the armed forces; on the other hand, I wanted to apply a standard (ultimately subjective, of course) which would ensure that each story merited inclusion by its own literary right. My original aim was to provide, as it were, a fictional companion to the history of World War II, or rather the part played in it by Britain and the Commonwealth: something which would bring home, as only imaginative writing can, the human anguish, the individual fate, that lies behind the historian's necessarily objective and largely generalized narrative of events as they affected nations and peoples rather than particular persons; for there is a sense, even in terms of truth, where imagination is superior to chronicle, and the facts present a version of reality that is less veritable than fiction.

Unfortunately, inescapable restrictions of overall length forced me to modify this no doubt excessively ambitious scheme and I had to impose on myself a degree of sumptuary ordinance. So I have been obliged to omit stories sometimes which I would in principle have been glad to include: usually because their theme or background duplicated that of another which seemed to me to be marginally superior in interest and quality. So fine have been the distinctions in the final stages of selection that only decisions which I should be hard put to rationalize finally allayed the pangs of editorial hesitation and the tormenting strain of finding pretexts, often almost frivolous if not aleatory, for exclusion as against inclusion.

Some rules of thumb, reluctantly adopted, did ease the task. I decided to confine my choice to stories published in the United Kingdom during the war or not long after it, hoping that the gain in immediacy would make up for any loss of maturity. I also excluded all stories not originally written in English, on the ground that my centrally British brief excused the parochialism. And for the same reason I have made no attempt to represent writing from the United States.

In practice also, I found that I was excluding contributions from Canada and South Africa. During the war, in various campaigns in the Middle East and Italy, I fought alongside troops from both these countries and conceived the greatest admiration for them. But, though I hardly doubt that good stories about the war were written by both South African and Canadian writers, I could not find anything in my intensive and extensive, but not exhaustive, reading of the books and periodicals published in England during the relevant period which seemed to me near enough to what I was looking for. This absence is a shortcoming of which I am very conscious and which I find embarrassing but it ought not to be taken as a slight either on the part these countries played in the face of the common enemy or on the contribution their writers have made to the common stock of literature that deserves to be remembered.

For whatever reason, stories from Australian and New Zealand writers were easier to find but exigencies of space again restricted my choice to those which complied with the criteria of inclusion I have already explained. For the fact that New Zealand is represented only by myself I must blame these same criteria, the advice of friends, and – all too probably – the partiality of my own judgement.

Considerations of bulk compelled one further and rather arbitrary canon of acceptance. I was anxious to represent as many sides of the war, and as many theatres, as possible. This meant that I had to fix an upper length of about 10,000 words and on the whole I looked for stories much shorter than that. Wherever I have included stories of more than 5,000 words it is because they were the only ones I could find which were both good in themselves and representative of a campaign or a service which might otherwise have gone by default. It would have been easy, for example, to find other and shorter stories by Alun Lewis than the ones I have chosen: but his 'Private Jones' seemed to me to illustrate better than anything else the early days of the war on the home front seen through exceptionally sensitive eyes; and his 'Ward "O" 3 (b)' seemed to me to cover the war in the East better than any other story that I could find room for.

It is not always easy to date stories by their composition, even where subject, content, and date of publication make inference justifiable. Nevertheless, I have tried to arrange the collection roughly in the chronological order of their probable date of composition or of the events to which they refer. Within that approximate arrangement by period I have tried to juxtapose the stories in such a way as to set them off against one another or to balance them in relation to the arm of the service or part of the home front with which they are concerned.

So much by way of explanation of how this anthology has been put together. But perhaps something should be said by way of accounting for its being prepared at all. The short answer is that no comparable collection of short stories about World War II is known to the compiler. One is reluctant to accept that the war should be recalled only in the comedy and caricature, however enjoyable, afforded by *Dad's Army* and the like; or by films and flashbacks to the Blitz, Churchill, Dunkirk, Colditz and so on which present a heroic myth, perhaps necessary to the nation's sense of itself but none the less myth for that and, as such, a departure from reality which in due course is bound to provoke a wholesale scepticism in generations who were spared the experience of the facts and are bored or challenged by venerable reiteration.

True, a number of excellent novels have emerged and will by their truthfulness continue to command credibility; and the poetry of men like Alun Lewis, Sydney Keyes, and Keith Douglas will stay with us. Ronald Blythe produced for Penguin an excellent anthology of verse and prose, *The Components of the Scene* (1966), and Robert Hewison's *Under Siege* (1977) gave a valuable account of how the world of British art, in all the senses of that word, was faring in embattled London. And, more recently still, *Return to Oasis* (1980), edited for the Salamander-Oasis Trust, was a gathering together of poetry and prose pieces by servicemen in the Middle East which reveals to this narrow island that, in the early years of the war, the place where most of the fighting was done was also the source of some excellent writing that was too little known. All that has been done, then, and all that has not been done emboldens one to think that there is a good case for a collection devoted entirely to the short story of the period, the more especially since this literary form proved to be one of the hardiest blooms to survive in a time of devastation and weeds.

II

According to the late Cyril Connolly, in his editorial to *Horizon*, Number 49 of 1944, 'War-writers are disappointing, either because they submit too bare a reportage or derivative *pastiches* by Hemingway'. And he goes on, '"Horizon" will always publish stories of pure realism, but we take the line that experiences connected with the blitz, the shopping queues, the home front, deserted wives, deceived husbands, broken homes, dull jobs, bad schools, group squabbles, are so much a picture of our ordinary lives that unless the workmanship is outstanding we are against them.'

One shares, of course, Connolly's distaste for 'bad schools' and 'group squabbles' as subject-matter; but, in spite of the cautious covering phrase about 'outstanding workmanship', he is here virtually declaring that the life he was living – along with millions of others – during the war was not a subject for creative fiction; whereas, in my view at least, life is always a proper subject, wherever and however and whenever it is lived. Connolly's fastidious rejections are interesting mainly for the inference that the 'enemies of promise' had now come to include himself, that he was fretting against the sterility and barrenness which invariably supervene when the aesthetic sense hypertrophies at the expense of creative vitality.

Much more acceptable, it seems to me, were the editorial principles, implicit mostly but sometimes more explicitly glanced at, which supported the more eclectic and also more humane and representative editing of John Lehmann's various collections and especially *Penguin New Writing*. Connolly judged the health of literature by his own pulse and temperature. Lehmann studied the charts of others, attended the clinics, as it were, and patrolled the wards. It was this wider sympathy and receptiveness that made *Penguin New Writing* the most truly representative of all wartime publications, the one most hospitable to talent from all over the world, whether already famous or still obscure.

Although *Horizon* and *PNR* were the most sustained and notable wartime outlets for literature, it would be shabby not to mention in this context the work of other courageous editors who sustained periodical publications like *Modern Reading*, *Penguin Parade*, *Writing Today*, *Bugle Blast*, and *Life and Letters Today* or, from Cairo, *Personal Landscape* and *Citadel*. The obstacles were formidable: paper shortage, unreliable communications and a far-flung authorship, the anxieties and setbacks inevitably attendant on any enterprise not directly geared to the war itself and very often depending on only a secondary share of the time of those responsible. These editors, and indeed their publishers, did good service to the cause and those who were fighting for it, and to the continuity of civilized letters.

Wartime difficulties, of course, were not exclusive to editors and publishers. Jenkins, in Anthony Powell's *Valley of Bones*, remarks: 'Whatever inner processes are required for writing novels, so far as I was concerned, war utterly inhibited.' One may reasonably assume, for once, that here a novelist's character is voicing the feelings of his creator. It is true that in the third volume of his autobiography, *Faces in My Time*, Powell says in his own person: 'Even if the war had left a kind of jet-lag there could be no doubt one had been advantageously shaken up as a writer.' But the two statements are by no means incompatible: each is true for the time of which it speaks. And what was true for Powell, as for most novelists in active service, was only less true for the writer of short stories to the extent that the short story, in principle at least, needs less time both for preliminary reflection and for the actual composition.

The chief deterrent was indeed, even with this qualification, the lack of uninterrupted leisure for meditation and concentration. It is part of military folk-wisdom that the army can make you do anything except have a baby – this particular formulation of course antedates the time when women were also members of the forces. The tradition might be extended to suggest that the army is also well placed for the abortion of anything except the product of the military art. For there is much truth in that other soldier's commonplace that war is an alternation of long periods of boredom and short periods of terror. Or, as Alun Lewis put it, speaking of army life in India, an alternation of 'periods of spiritual death, periods of neutrality, periods of a sickening normality and insane indifference to the real implications of the present, and then for a brief, wonderful space, maybe every six weeks, a nervous and powerful ability wells upward in me'.

Periods of terror, if survived, may provide material for subsequent imaginative use. But boredom tends to be sterile, both at the time and in retrospect. Moreover, boredom does not necessarily imply idleness, let alone leisure. To have an hour or two in hand is not to be guaranteed against interruption. The free moment is threatened by every signal, every buzz of the telephone, by every casual intrusion, and by the imminent whims of people who command your time as well as yourself and who may at an instant's notice deflect you from thought into some petty task or meaningless action. Nor is it an escape to be in command of others, since they have first claim on your solicitude and attention. Your time, in short, is not your own.

Nor is there privacy. You are a unit in a world of units, a member of a demanding family and of a commanding hierarchy. To want, or at any rate to take, the solitude which the act of imaginative writing requires is to betray the system. 'Who wants imagination, anyway?', as a character in one of Julian Maclaren-Ross's stories remarks. So, when you have the right feelings, the situation for expressing them is wrong; and, when it is right, as like as not you are in the wrong mood. In fact, from the moment you join the army – and the army can stand representative in this respect for any of the services – a determined attempt is made to turn you into a standard bundle of predictable reflexes, a closed circuit system of reactions and responses.

In action there is no time to reflect on anything but the desperate issues immediately at hand. Before and after action, the daily routine ensures that when the day's or night's work is done an immense lethargy ensues, a physical, moral, and mental exhaustion which can be refreshed only by the sleep of reason, the cessation of all thought except for rest and food and the relaxations of ordinary comradeship. Nor are brief spells of leave or furlough long enough to allow creative recovery, however helpful, essential, they may be towards your recuperation as a soldier. The soldier's perils, as Bacon somewhere remarks, do commonly demand to be paid in pleasures. He was not thinking of the pleasures of the study or of the pen.

On the other hand, war – as distinct from soldiering – is a great intensifier. It concentrates the mind wonderfully on first and last things, the eschatological. Its extreme experience was felt as a necessity to many writers, once committed. Thus Alun Lewis wrote to a friend, 'I want to run the gamut'. He saw it as providing 'the true story and the proper ending'. And for Keith Douglas 'the experience of battle was something I must have. Whatever changes in the nature of warfare, the battlefield is the simple, central stage of the war; it is there that the interesting things happen.' But this sense of battle as the absolute experience, without which the truth of war could not be fully known, meant that for the writer – as for everyone else – the here and now dominated the foreground: the past, however recalled, regretted or vainly longed for, became unreal and totally cut off, with letters from home coming from another world, a lost world; and the future, if the soldier were unwise enough, against Sydney Smith's injunction, to take long views, seemed even more remote both in time and possibility, whereas its inevitable sequel, death, had to be strenuously ignored, because of its unpleasant proximity. So, far more than in the piping times of peace, it was the present moment that counted. War, in fact, was life speeded up.

For those whose reflective or creative turn of mind was sufficiently stubborn and who had enough energy to overcome or avoid the enervations of routine, the luck to survive the exacting excitements of battle, and the gift of extrapolating themselves from the intrusive and levelling pleasantries of comradeship, war can have the advantage of heightening perceptions, enhancing appreciation of a vast variety of people whom one would not otherwise have known. It affords the opportunity of correcting one's own conceit by the standard of other men's modesty and unselfishness and overcoming the intellectual's occupational disease of over-valuing literateness at the expense of moral character and physical courage. There is nothing like the continual sense of an imminent ending to give one an acuter sense of the value of men and of life.

Again, if time and privacy can be found, war is favourable in another way to the writer, and particularly to the writer of short stories. The threat of death or maiming or separation is so omnipresent that there is available to him a pervading tension of background. In times of violence the solution of tangled plot by the death of dispensable characters is made more plausible. War abounds in extreme situations swiftly enacted and if the writer can transpose them into art rather than merely transcribe them he need never be at a loss for narrative. There will be problems of professional jargon, ephemeral slang, matter and motive not at once clear to a civilian reader, but these problems are a challenge to technical skill rather than a real obstacle to achievement. The true problems of the short story are the same in war as they are in peace: because of the need for brevity, every comma, colon, full stop, paragraph, every word must be made to count. The narrative and theme must be fundamentally simple, however large or subtle the implications. If there is to be chiaroscuro or moral it must be through suggestion or by means of a conclusion which the reader can infer but which the writer should not formally express. There is no room for extravagance. The writer must be frugal and able to draw on the resources of the implicit. He must, above all, have something to say but never forget that it has to be said through the medium of narrative, not homily.

III

In our war, then, as in the Great War, writing somehow got done. On the whole, as one might expect from the conditions which I have sketched, it took the form most compatible with brevity of occasion – the lyric or the short story. It has to be admitted that some of Connolly's animadversions on mere reportage were justified. In traversing all the contemporary material I could lay hands on I could not help being struck by how often the authors of stories were writing too close to their experience, without the time perhaps to reflect that to record an experience is not necessarily to convey its full meaning to another. Strict adherence to the facts too often had produced the material for a story rather than the story itself. The writers were indeed writing from intense experience – more intense, at least in externals, than peace would normally provide – but they were for the most part young men, untrained in writing but desperately aware of how little time might be left to them; and so in too much of a hurry to be able to give their matter an enduring form. For reasons such as these much of the contemporary writing has faded like the cheap paper of the little magazines in which they were printed, or like the photographs in old wartime albums, meaningful only to those who shared the experience they recall and incapable of transmitting it to those who did not. I have done my best to select from the exceptions.

DAN DAVIN

12 February 1982

Men at Work

RICHARD SKATE had taken a couple of hours away from the Ministry to see whether his house was still standing after the previous
night's raid. He was a thin, pale, hungry-looking man of early
middle age. All his life had been spent in keeping his nose above
water, lecturing at night-schools and acting as temporary English
master at some of the smaller public schools, and in the process he
had acquired a small house, a wife and one child – a rather precoci-
ous girl with a talent for painting who despised him. They lived in
the country, his house was cut off from him by the immeasurable
distances of bombed London – he visited it hurriedly twice a week,
and his whole world was now the Ministry, the high heartless
building with complicated lifts and long passages like those of a
liner and lavatories where the water never ran hot and the nail-
brushes were chained like Bibles. Central heating gave it the stuffy
smell of mid-Atlantic except in the passages where the windows
were always open for fear of blast and the cold winds whistled in.
One expected to see people wrapped in rugs lying in deck-chairs and
the messengers carried round minutes like soup. Skate slept downstairs in the basement on a camp-bed, emerging at about ten o'clock
for breakfast, and these imprisoned weeks were beginning to give
him the appearance of a pit-pony – a purblind air as of something
that lived underground. The Establishments branch of the Ministry
of Propaganda thought it wise to send a minute to the staff advising
them to spend an hour or two a day in the open air, and some
members did indeed reach the King's Arms at the corner. But
Skate didn't drink.

And yet in spite of everything he was happy. Showing his pass at
the outer gate, nodding to the Home Guard who was a specialist in
early Icelandic customs, he was happy. For his nose was now well
above water: he had a permanent job, he was a Civil Servant. His
ambition had been to be a playwright (one Sunday performance in
St. John's Wood had enabled him to register as dramatist in the

Central Register), and now that the London theatres were most of them closed, he was no longer taunted by the sight of other men's success.

He opened the door of his little dark room. It had been built of plywood in a passage, for as the huge staff of the Ministry accumulated like a kind of fungoid life – old divisions sprouting daily new sections which then broke away and became divisions and spawned in turn – the five hundred rooms of the great university block became inadequate: corners of passages were turned into rooms, and corridors disappeared overnight.

'All well?' his assistant asked: the large-breasted young woman who mothered him, bringing him cups of coffee when he looked peaky and guarding the telephone.

'Oh, yes, thanks. It's still there. A pane of glass gone, that's all.'

'A Mr Savage rang up.'

'Oh, did he? What did he want?'

'He said he'd joined the Air Force and wanted to show you his uniform.'

'Old Savage,' Skate said. 'He always was a bit wild.'

The telephone rang, and Miss Manners grasped it like an enemy.

'Yes,' she said, 'yes, R.S. is back. It's H.G.,' she explained to Skate. All the junior staff called people by initials: it was a sort of social compromise, between a Christian name and a Mr. It made telephone conversations as obscure as a cable in code.

'Hello, Graves. Yes, it's still standing. Will you be at the Book Committee? I simply haven't got any agenda. Can't you invent something?' He said to Miss Manners, 'Graves wants to know who'll be at the Committee.'

Miss Manners recited quickly down the phone, 'R.K., D.H., F.L. and B.L. says he'll be late. All right, I'll tell R.S. Goodbye.' She said to Skate, 'H.G. asks why you don't just put Report on Progress down on the agenda.'

'He will have his joke,' Skate said miserably. 'As if there ever is any progress.'

'You want your tea,' Miss Manners said. She unlocked a drawer and took out Skate's teaspoon. No teaspoons had been supplied in the Ministry after the initial loss of 6,000 in the opening months of the war, and indeed it was becoming more and more necessary to lock everything portable up. Even the blankets disappeared from the ARP shelters. Like the wreck of a German plane the place seemed to be the prey of relic-hunters, so that one could foresee the day when only the heavy Portland stone structure would remain, stripped bare, scorched by incendiaries and pitted with bullet-holes where the Home Guard unloaded their rifles.

'Oh dear, oh dear,' Skate said, 'I must get this agenda done.' His worry was only skin deep: it was all a game played in a corner under the gigantic shadow. Propaganda was a means of passing the time: work was not done for its usefulness but for its own sake – simply as an occupation. He wrote wearily down 'The Problem of India' on the agenda.

Leaving his room Skate stood aside for an odd little procession of old men in robes, led by a mace-bearer. They passed – one of them sneezing – towards the Chancellor's Hall, like humble ghosts still carrying out the ritual of another age. They had once been kings in this place, the gigantic building had been built to house them, and now the Civil Servants passed up and down through their procession as though it had no more consistency than smoke. Long before he reached the room where the Book Committee sat he heard a familiar voice saying, 'What we want is a really colossal campaign . . .' It was King, of course, putting his shoulder to the war-effort: these outbreaks occurred periodically like desire. King had been an advertising man, and the need to sell something would regularly overcome him. Memories of Ovaltine and Halitosis and the Mustard Club sought an outlet all the time, until suddenly, overwhelmingly, he would begin to sell the war. The Treasury and the Stationery Office always saw to it that his great schemes came to nothing: only once, because somebody was on holiday, a King campaign had really got under way. It was when the meat ration went down to a shilling; the hoardings all over London carried a curt King message: 'DON'T GROUSE ABOUT MUTTON. WHAT'S WRONG WITH YOUR GREENS?' A ribald Labour member asked a question in Parliament, the posters were withdrawn at a cost of twenty thousand pounds, the Permanent Secretary resigned, the Prime Minister stood by the Minister who stood by his staff ('I consider we are one of the fighting services'), and King, after being asked to resign, was instead put in charge of the Books Division of the Ministry at a higher salary. Here it was felt he could do no harm.

Skate slid in and handed round copies of the agenda unobtrusively like a maid laying napkins. He didn't bother to listen to King: something about a series of pamphlets to be distributed free to six million people really explaining what we were fighting for. 'Tell 'em what freedom means,' King said. 'Democracy. Don't use long words.'

Hill said, 'I don't think the Stationery Office . . .' Hill's thin voice was always the voice of reason. He was said to be the author of the official explanation and defence of the Ministry's existence: 'A negative action may have positive results'.

On Skate's agenda was written:

1. Arising from the Minutes.
2. Pamphlet in Welsh on German labour conditions.
3. Facilities for Wilkinson to visit the ATS.
4. Objections to proposed Bone pamphlet.
5. Suggestion for a leaflet from Meat Marketing Board.
6. The Problem of India.

The list, Skate thought, looked quite impressive.

'Of course,' King went on, 'the details need working out. We've got to get the right author. Priestley or somebody. I feel there won't be any difficulty about money if we can present a really clear case. Would you look into it, Skate, and report back?'

Skate agreed. He didn't know what it was all about, but that didn't matter. A few minutes would be passed to and fro, and King's blood would cool in the process. To send a minute to anybody else in the great building and to receive a reply took at least twenty-four hours: on an urgent matter an exchange of three minutes might be got through in a week. Time outside the Ministry went at quite a different pace. Skate remembered how the minutes on who should write a 'suggested' pamphlet about the French war-effort were still circulating indecisively while Germany broke the line, passed the Somme, occupied Paris and received the delegates at Compiègne.

The Committee as usual lasted about an hour – it was always, to Skate, an agreeable meeting with men from other divisions, the Religions Division, the Empire Division and so on. Sometimes they co-opted another man they thought was nice. It gave an opportunity for all sorts of interesting discussions – on books and authors and artists and plays and films. The agenda didn't really matter: it was quite easy to invent one at the last moment.

Today everybody was in a good temper: there hadn't been any bad news for a week, and as the policy of the latest Permanent Secretary was that the Ministry should not do anything to attract attention, there was no reason to fear a purge in the immediate future. The decision, too, eased everybody's work. And there was quite a breath of the larger life in the matter of Wilkinson. Wilkinson was a very popular novelist who wanted to sound a clarion note to women, and he had asked permission to make a special study of the ATS. Now the military authorities refused permission – nobody knew why. Speculation continued for ten minutes. Skate said he thought Wilkinson was a bad writer and King disagreed – that led to a general literary discussion: Lewis from the Empire Division, who had fought at Gallipoli during the last war, dozed uneasily.

He woke up when they got on to the Bone pamphlet. Bone had been asked to write a pamphlet about the British Empire: it was to be distributed, fifty thousand copies of it, free at public meetings. But now that it was in type, all sorts of tactless phrases were discovered by the experts. India objected to a reference to Canadian dairy herds, and Australia objected to a phrase about Botany Bay. The Canadian authority was certain that mention of Wolfe would antagonize the French-Canadians, and the New Zealand authority felt that undue emphasis had been laid on the Australian fruit-farms. Meanwhile the public meetings had all been held, so that there was no means of distributing the pamphlet. Somebody suggested that it might be sent to America for the New York World Fair, but the American Division then demanded certain cuts in the references to the War of Independence, and by the time those had been made the World Fair had closed. Now Bone had written objecting to his own pamphlet which he said was unrecognizable.

'We could get somebody else to sign it,' Skate suggested – but that meant paying another fee, and the Treasury, Hill said, would never sanction that.

'Look here, Skate,' King said, 'you're a literary man. You write to Bone and sort of smooth things over.'

Lowndes came in hurriedly, smelling a little of wine. He said, 'Sorry to be late. Had to lunch a man on business. Seen the news?' 'No.'

'Daylight raids again. Fifty Nazi planes shot down. They are turning on the heat. Fifteen of ours lost.'

'We must really get Bone's pamphlet out,' Hill said.

Skate suddenly, to his own surprise, said savagely, 'That'll show them,' and then sat down in humble collapse as though he had been caught out in treachery.

'Well,' Hill said, 'we mustn't get rattled, Skate. Remember what
the Minister said: It's our duty just to carry on our work whatever
happens.'

'Yes, I didn't mean anything.'

Without reaching a decision on the Bone pamphlet they passed
on to the Meat Marketing Leaflet. Nobody was interested in this, so
the matter was left in Skate's hands to report back. 'You talk to 'em,
Skate,' King said. 'Good idea. You know about these things. Might
ask Priestley,' he vaguely added, and then frowned thoughtfully at
that old-timer on the minutes, 'The Problem of India'. 'Need we
really discuss it this week?' he said. 'There's nobody here who
knows about India. Let's get in Lawrence next week.'

'Good chap, Lawrence,' Lowndes said. 'Wrote a naughty novel
once called *Parson's Pleasure*.'

'We'll co-opt him,' King said.

The Book Committee was over for another week, and since the
room would be empty now until morning, Skate opened the big
windows against the night's blast. Far up in the pale enormous sky
little white lines, like the phosphorescent spore of snails, showed
where men were going home after work.

1940

The Deserter

THEY brought him in the night I was on guard. They brought him
into the guardroom around about one o'clock, when I was trying to
sleep before my second shift. He was long-haired and unshaven, but
I could not see much of the way he looked by the light of the single
oil-lamp in the guardroom. He simply stood there in silence in an
attitude of utter weariness, while the guard commander took down
particulars for his report.

He had deserted the day war broke out. He hadn't turned up with
the rest of his Territorial unit, and the police had been looking for
him pretty well ever since. Finally they had traced him, and they
had brought him in that night I was on guard. That was about
eleven weeks after the beginning of the war.

It was bound to be a court-martial case, of course. We all knew it
was bound to be a court-martial case, but we reckoned it wouldn't
be so bad. The old-timers gave him a couple of months CB, all
found. It wouldn't be a prison case. Some of us wondered if it
wouldn't be better for the poor devil if they did make it a prison
case. Maybe that was what he was hoping for, they said, so he
wouldn't have to go to the war.

They didn't court-martial at once. For the time being they made
him a regular mess-orderly in the men's mess, and confined him to
barracks. This would go on until the court martial, they told him;
but they could not say how soon that would be.

So he was there in the mess the next day. He was shaven now, but
his hair was still uncut, and he was still dark around the chin. He
was the sort of chap who would never look shaven, however close
he had shaved. He was very dark altogether, and his eyes were dark
too. They were big eyes, dumb, and I suppose you might have said
like a dog's, though I would have shuddered to see a dog with those
eyes. Every now and then some of the men stopped to talk to him
and ask him how it was going, and he would grin back at them
slowly, and not say very much. He didn't say very much ever, but

just grinned in that slow way of his, whenever anyone stopped to talk to him. He went about his work in the mess slowly but methodically. He did not in any way try to arouse sympathy, by his look or the way he went about his work, but most of the men were sorry for him. I reckoned he was past caring about sympathy.

For a few days people talked about him from time to time. Someone said once: 'It's a bloody shame. They shouldn't let a chap like that into the Army. Plumb scared of war, that's his trouble. It's a bloody shame keeping a chap like that in the Army.'

'Why in hell did he join the Army?' someone else asked.

'His girl wanted him to.'

'Oh, hell.'

Then we talked about him being plumb scared of war. We were all plumb scared of war, we reckoned. But it seemed to be different with this chap. He couldn't stand anything to do with war. He couldn't stand all the men in uniform and the routine and the rifles. It killed him inside and he went about in misery and awful fear. Everything he saw and smelt and heard made it worse, and some of us began to wonder if it would slowly drive him mad.

He stuck it for ten days. For ten days he went around the tables serving out tea, and standing around in the mess, generally unshaven, and always untidy, until he became a part of the place, as much a part of it as the tables and the benches and the smell of stale food. He hadn't any friends, but everyone was decent with him, and he seemed to be getting along. Anyone who didn't feel sympathetic left him alone. You couldn't make jokes at him. You wouldn't have got anything out of it.

But I doubt if any of us realized how unhappy a life it was for him. We did not know the sort of chap he was, and at best that mess was a godless place. The unit was in improvised quarters at the time, and the men's mess was in the disused part of a cotton-mill. It was a grey shabby building, square as a prison, but neglected and decaying too, and you felt cold looking at it. It was the same inside. I have never known anything so wrapped in gloom as that empty ill-lit machine room, where the mess-tables were laid out. The whitewashed walls were cracked and grey now and came away in flakes, if you brushed past, and made you cough. The damp ceiling hung with ancient cobwebs, and only a sickly wan light found its way through the small dust-caked windows. Here and there would be a pane missing, but it was not enough to make any difference. Some of the space was taken up with pieces of broken twisted machinery, flung together and rusting, like the wreckage of a bombed town. It was all right, of course, when the men were there, packed together, banging the tables and yelling for the orderlies and across at each other to make themselves heard: though even then there were men who would confide in you that the place got under their flesh.

The deserter was here nearly all the day. After the men had gone, he would be there still, in the empty gloom, going around the tables, collecting basins and bread-baskets and sweeping up the refuse and slops over the rough damp floor. Four times during the ten days that he stuck it the electricity plant failed, so that in the evenings he had not even the comfort of the few electric bulbs hung from the steel girders that spanned the machine-room. Instead they brought up oil-lamps, which made awful flickering shadows in the corners of the room, and turned the pieces of twisted machinery into fantastic surrealist shapes.

Even when his work was over, there was no escape from the mill. Between six o'clock and tattoo at ten-thirty he had to report every half-hour in the guardroom. There was no escape for him. His work might be over by half-past eight, but there was no relief. He could not go out like the other chaps and sit over a pint of beer in the comfort of a warm taproom. There was no sense in it, if you had to be up and out every half-hour to go to the guardroom.

So he stuck it for ten days. On the eleventh day he deserted again. Someone saw him go out after he had finished work in the evening, and then he failed to report to the guard when his half-hour was up.

Over a week went by and he was still missing. When we talked about him, it generally finished with someone looking at the ground or not quite at you and saying they'd find him in the river one day soon. I remember one of the chaps saying one day, as we were driving up in a lorry to the field, where we paraded: 'Ay, he were a queer chap. I reckon he's done himself in all right. He were just the kind of chap to do himself in. Queer bloke. There's something wrong with a chap, what gets like that.'

'Ought never to 've been in the mucking Army,' someone else said.

I didn't join in the talk this time, but listened in the dimness of the lorry.

'Nuts from the start, 'e were.'

'Bloody queer way 'e 'ad of looking at you.'

'Remember 'ow 'e used to stand around up in the mess there? Not looking at bloody anything. Oh, Christ. Gave me the bloody creeps.'

'Only one thing to it, though. He was plumb scared of war. Come to that, so am I.'

'Who the bloody hell isn't?'

Then we reached the parade ground.

I suppose it might have been a week later, when I was on guard-duty again. I had a stripe now, so I was junior NCO of the guard and did not actually mount guard myself. In the corner of the guard-room lay a brown suitcase and a pile of blankets and a palliasse. The corporal of the Regimental Police, who was on duty during the day and came off when the guard mounted for the night, came into the guardroom. He was an aggressive kind of chap. I didn't like him much. Nobody liked him much, but an RP has to face that. Nobody forced him to be an RP, anyway. He jerked his head towards the suitcase and the bedding.

'For Christ's sake nobody touch them things,' he said 'Let 'em alone, see? Them's the deserter's. They not got to be touched.'

Corporal Hanley, who was guard commander, looked up from going through the late-pass lists and report sheets.

'Don't tell me they're bringing that bastard in again tonight,' he said.

'They got a line on him,' said the RP.

'Just my luck, if they brought him in tonight.'

'Police know where he is,' said the RP. 'But I reckon you're safe tonight. Only don't nobody touch them things.'

'That's all right.'

'Do they reckon he's alive?' I asked.

'Couldn't say. If you ask me, I reckon they ought to drag the mucking river.'

The RP lowered himself on to a bench. I could see he was going to talk.

'Proper bastard, he were,' he began. 'Real proper bastard. We been through his stuff there. Been advertising in the mucking papers, he had. Said he was lonely. You know. Lonely 'eart seeks friend. Cor blimey. Proper soft bloody bastard.'

He paused. Corporal Hanley nodded, busy writing.

'You'd only got to look at him,' he said. 'Hey, what's the name of that mucker out there on guard now? I got to fill in this report.'

One of the other members of the guard went over and spelt him out the name. The RP went on: 'I'll let you have a look,' he said, speaking to Corporal Hanley. 'He was a queer bloody bastard all right. You can have a look, too,' he said to me.

He went over and fetched the case and slumped it down on the table.

'Orl right, orl right,' he ordered. 'Can't have everybody mucking around. You other bastards muck off. This ain't a bloody sewing party.'

He opened the case and took out a bundle of papers and drew a letter from the bundle.

'Here, look at this,' he said, handing it to me.

'What is it?'

'Answer to his bloody advert. Some kind of a tart he got hold of. Rare bloody couple they must've been.'

I took the letter and read it. It was a rotten thing to read the chap's letters, but I wanted to read it. I wasn't going to snigger over it, anyway.

It was quite a short letter, written in a very neat, copperplate hand, dated about eight months back. The girl wrote that she was lonely, too, and described herself a little, not her looks so much as the sort of girl she was, and ended with rather pathetic formality, saying she hoped this might be the beginning of a happy friendship. It wasn't a funny letter. It was tragic, not funny at all.

'Want to keep her address?' asked the RP.

I grinned at him.

'No, you keep it for yourself,' I said. 'I'm off women.'

'You got the right angle,' said the RP. 'You mark my words. That's where this mucker went wrong. Women. If he'd 'ave laid off women, he'd 've been sweet and pretty. He'd be sitting here the same as you and me, and nobody'd 've known the difference. Here's the advert he had put in the paper, what started all the shemozzle.'

I could not help smiling at the notice he had sent in to the local paper. 'Young man (rejected lover) . . .', it began. I could not help smiling at the style and that tense novelettish cliché, although I guessed it was sincere.

Along with the notice to the paper he had sent a long letter, in which he had poured out his soul. He wanted them to believe he was sincere and that his notice was not a joke. In an even undeveloped round hand, absurdly unsuited to the passionate words it formed, he had bared his soul before them. There were four good-sized pages of it, and there was not a single mistake of grammar or spelling. I reckoned he had been hours over it. At the end he asked if they would please let him have an answer to the letter, even if it were only acknowledgement. He sent money for the notice to be inserted three times.

It was the hell of a letter. You did not need his protestations of sincerity. No man, who had not been nearly mad with loneliness, could have written it. With all its clichés and the absurd sedate handwriting, you had set out for you in that letter, naked and unvarnished, the awful tragedy of loneliness.

I handed the letter back to the RP.

'Let the Corporal have a dekko,' he said.

Corporal Hanley ran his eye over it.

'Oh, God, I can't read this,' he said.

The RP took it and put it back with the rest of the papers in the case, and then shut the case and put it over in the corner again.

'Now don't let nobody touch that, or there'll be hell to pay,' he warned. He looked at his watch. 'Christ, I'm going to be late for my date. Good-night, you muckers,'

'Good-night, mucker.'

It was bloody cold in the guardroom that night. There was a howling wind outside, and the rain came in under the door and made a great pool in the middle of the guardroom floor. The tank and wick were missing from the oil-stove, and we had no heating. We played a few rounds of pontoon, but nobody seemed to want to play, and we didn't talk much. I think most of us had the deserter on our minds. In the lulls, when the wind dropped for a few seconds, we could hear the river roaring under the bridge and past the mill. I wondered what kind of a girl she had been, the one that answered his notice. I wondered if they had made out all right together, and I sort of thought it wouldn't be so bad, if they had been happy and stopped being lonely. I guessed it had been all right, when he first joined his unit in peacetime. She would never have wanted him to join, if she had known war was coming. Whichever way you looked at it, it was the war breaking out that had smashed everything. I remember him standing around in the mess, and his dark melancholy eyes, and the way he looked at nothing and then grinned slowly, when you spoke to him. I wondered why some people seemed to be predestined for tragedy, so that whatever happened it always ended in tragedy. I hoped very much that he had known for those last few months what it was like to be happy instead of tragic. I suppose I thought about it for hours. It was as cold and wild a night as I ever remember, and I kept my greatcoat on all the time.

I know that, as far as I was concerned, the tragedy was played that night. Three nights later, when I heard they had dragged him from the river some sixty miles away in a town I had never heard of, it did not mean anything to me at all.

The Voice

A MESSAGE came from the rescue party, who straightened up and leaned on their spades in the rubble. The policeman said to the crowd: 'Everyone keep quiet for five minutes. No talking, please. They're trying to hear where he is.'

The silent crowd raised their faces and looked across the ropes to the church, which, now it was destroyed, broke the line of the street like a decayed tooth. The bomb had brought down the front wall and the roof, the balcony had capsized. Freakishly untouched, the hymn-board still announced the previous Sunday's hymns.

A small wind blew a smell of smouldering cloth across people's noses from another street where there was another scene like this. A bus roared by and heads turned in passive anger until the sound of the engine had gone. People blinked as a pigeon flew from a roof and crossed the building like an omen of release. There was dead quietness again. Presently a murmuring sound was heard by the rescue party. The man buried under the debris was singing again.

At first difficult to hear, soon a tune became definite. Two of the rescuers took up their shovels and shouted down to encourage the buried man, and the voice became stronger and louder. Words became clear. The leader of the rescue party held back the others, and those who were near strained to hear. Then the words were unmistakable:

> Oh Thou whose Voice the waters heard,
> And hushed their raging at Thy Word.

The buried man was singing a hymn.

A clergyman was standing with the warden in the middle of the ruined church.

'That's Mr Morgan all right,' the warden said. 'He could sing. He got silver medals for it.'

The Revd Frank Lewis frowned.

'Gold, I shouldn't wonder,' said Mr Lewis dryly. Now he knew

Morgan was alive he said: 'What the devil's he doing in there? How did he get in? I locked up at eight o'clock last night myself.'

Lewis was a wiry, middle-aged man, but the white dust on his hair and his eyelashes, and the way he kept licking the dust off his dry lips, moving his jaws all the time, gave him the monkeyish, testy and suspicious air of an old man. He had been up all night on rescue work in the raid and he was tired out. The last straw was to find the church had gone and that Morgan, the so-called Revd Morgan, was buried under it.

The rescue workers were digging again. There was a wide hole now and a man was down in it filling a basket with his hands. The dust rose like smoke from the hole as he worked.

The voice had not stopped singing. It went on, rich, virile, masculine, from verse to verse of the hymn. Shooting up like a stem through the rubbish the voice seemed to rise and branch out powerfully, luxuriantly and even theatrically, like a tree, until everything was in its shade. It was a shade that came towards one like dark arms.

'All the Welsh can sing,' the warden said. Then he remembered that Lewis was Welsh also. 'Not that I've got anything against the Welsh,' the warden said.

The scandal of it, Lewis was thinking. Must he sing so loud, must he advertise himself? I locked up myself last night. How the devil did he get in? And he really meant: How did the devil get in?

To Lewis, Morgan was the nearest human thing to the devil. He could never pass that purple-gowned figure, sauntering like a cardinal in his skull cap on the sunny side of the street, without a shudder of distaste and derision. An unfrocked priest, his predecessor in the church, Morgan ought in strict justice to have been in prison, and would have been but for the indulgence of the bishop. But this did not prevent the old man with the saintly white head and the eyes half-closed by the worldly juices of food and wine from walking about dressed in his vestments, like an actor walking in the sun of his own vanity, a hook-nosed satyr, a he-goat significant to servant girls, the crony of the public house, the chaser of bookmakers, the smoker of cigars. It was terrible, but it was just that the bomb had buried him; only the malice of the Evil One would have thought of bringing the punishment of the sinner upon the church as well. And now, from the ruins, the voice of the wicked man rose up in all the elaborate pride of art and evil.

Suddenly there was a moan from the sloping timber, slates began to skate down.

'Get out. It's going,' shouted the warden.

The man who was digging struggled out of the hole as it bulged under the landslide. There was a dull crumble, the crashing and splitting of wood and then the sound of brick and dust tearing down below the water. Thick dust clouded over and choked them all. The rubble rocked like a cakewalk. Everyone rushed back and looked behind at the wreckage as if it were still alive. It remained still. They all stood there, frightened and suspicious. Presently one of the men with the shovel said, 'The bloke's shut up.'

Everyone stared stupidly. It was true. The man had stopped singing. The clergyman was the first to move. Gingerly he went to what was left of the hole and got down on his knees.

'Morgan!' he said, in a low voice.

Then he called out more loudly:

'Morgan!'

Getting no reply, Lewis began to scramble the rubble away with his hands.

'Morgan!' he shouted. 'Can you hear?' He snatched a shovel from one of the men and began digging and shovelling the stuff away. He had stopped chewing and muttering. His expression had entirely changed. 'Morgan!' he called. He dug for two feet and no one stopped him. They looked with bewilderment at the sudden frenzy of the small man grubbing like a monkey, spitting out the dust, filing down his nails. They saw the spade at last shoot through the old hole. He was down the hole widening it at once, letting himself down as he worked. He disappeared under a ledge made by the fallen timber.

The party above could do nothing. 'Morgan,' they heard him call. 'It's Lewis. We're coming. Can you hear?' He shouted for an axe and presently they heard him smashing with it. He was scratching like a dog or a rabbit.

A voice like that to have stopped, to have gone! Lewis was thinking. How unbearable this silence was. A beautiful proud voice, the voice of a man, a voice like a tree, the soul of a man spreading in the air like the cedars of Lebanon. 'Only one man I have heard with a bass like that. Owen the Bank, at Newtown before the war. Morgan!' he shouted. 'Sing! God will forgive you everything, only sing!'

One of the rescue party following behind the clergyman in the tunnel shouted back to his mates: 'I can't do nothing. This bleeder's blocking the gangway.'

Half an hour Lewis worked in the tunnel. Then an extraordinary thing happened to him. The tunnel grew damp and its floor went as soft as clay to the touch. Suddenly his knees went through. There was a gap with a yard of cloth, the vestry curtain or the carpet at the communion rail was unwound and hanging through it. Lewis found himself looking down into the blackness of the crypt. He lay down and put his head and shoulders through the hole and felt about him until he found something solid again. The beams of the floor were tilted down into the crypt.

'Morgan. Are you there, man?' he called.

He listened to the echo of his voice. He was reminded of the time he had talked into a cistern when he was a boy. Then his heart jumped. A voice answered him out of the darkness from under the fallen floor. It was like the voice of a man lying comfortably and waking up from a snooze, a voice thick and sleepy.

'Who's that?' asked the voice.

'Morgan, man. It's Lewis. Are you hurt?' Tears pricked the dust in Lewis's eyes and his throat ached with anxiety as he spoke. Forgiveness and love were flowing out of him. From below the deep thick voice of Morgan came back.

'You've been a hell of a long time,' it said. 'I've damn near finished my whisky.'

'Hell' was the word which changed Mr Lewis's mind. Hell was a real thing, a real place for him. He believed in it. When he read out the word 'Hell' in the Scriptures he could see the flames rising as they rise out of the furnaces at Swansea. 'Hell' was a professional and poetic word for Mr Lewis. A man who had been turned out of the Church had no right to use it. Strong language and strong drink, Mr Lewis hated both of them. The idea of whisky being in his church made his soul rise like an angered stomach. There was Morgan, insolent and comfortable, lying (so he said) under the old altar-table, which was propping up the fallen floor, drinking a bottle of whisky.

'How did you get in?' Lewis said sharply, from the hole. 'Were you in the church last night when I locked up?'

The old man sounded not as bold as he had been. He even sounded shifty when he replied, 'I've got my key.'

'*Your* key. I have the only key of the church. Where did you get a key?'

'My old key. I always had a key.'

The man in the tunnel behind the clergyman crawled back up the tunnel to the daylight.

'OK,' the man said. 'He's got him. They're having a ruddy row.'

'Reminds me of ferreting. I used to go ferreting with my old dad,' said the policeman.

'You should have given that key up,' said Mr Lewis. 'Have you been in here before?'

'Yes, but I shan't come here again,' said the old man.

There was the dribble of powdered rubble, pouring down like sand in an hour-glass, the ticking of the strained timber like the loud ticking of a clock.

Mr Lewis felt that at last after years he was face to face with the devil and the devil was trapped and caught. The tick-tock of the wood went on.

'Men have been risking their lives, working and digging for hours because of this,' said Lewis. 'I've ruined a suit of . . .'

The tick-tock had grown louder in the middle of the words. There was a sudden lurching and groaning of the floor, followed by a big heaving and splitting sound.

'It's going,' said Morgan with detachment from below. 'The table leg.' The floor crashed down. The hole in the tunnel was torn wide and Lewis grabbed at the darkness until he caught a board. It swung him out and in a second he found himself hanging by both hands over the pit.

'I'm falling. Help me,' shouted Lewis in terror. 'Help me.' There was no answer.

'O God,' shouted Lewis, kicking for a foothold. 'Morgan, are you there? Catch me. I'm going.'

Then a groan like a snore came out of Lewis. He could hold no longer. He fell. He fell exactly two feet.

The sweat ran down his legs and caked on his face. He was as wet as a rat. He was on his hands and knees gasping. When he got his breath again he was afraid to raise his voice.

'Morgan,' he said quietly, panting.

'Only one leg went,' the old man said in a quiet grating voice. 'The other three are all right.'

Lewis lay panting on the floor. There was a long silence. 'Haven't you ever been afraid before, Lewis?' Morgan said. Lewis had no breath to reply. 'Haven't you ever felt rotten with fear,' said the old man calmly, 'like an old tree, infested and worm-eaten with it, soft as a rotten orange?'

'You were a fool to come down here after me. I wouldn't have done the same for you,' Morgan said.

'You would,' Lewis managed to say.

'I wouldn't,' said the old man. 'I'm afraid. I'm an old man, Lewis, and I can't stand it. I've been down here every night since the raids got bad.'

Lewis listened to the voice. It was low with shame, it had the roughness of the earth, the kicked and trodden choking dust of Adam. The earth of Mr Lewis listened for the first time to the earth of Morgan. Coarsened and sordid and unlike the singing voice, the voice of Morgan was also gentle and fragmentary.

'When you stop feeling shaky,' Morgan said, 'you'd better sing. I'll do a bar, but I can't do much. The whisky's gone. Sing, Lewis. Even if they don't hear, it does you good. Take the tenor, Lewis.'

Above in the daylight the look of pain went from the mouths of the rescue party, a grin came on the dusty lips of the warden.

'Hear it?' he said. 'A ruddy Welsh choir!'

WILLIAM SANSOM · 1912–1976

The Wall

IT was our third job that night.

Until this thing happened, work had been without incident. There had been shrapnel, a few enquiring bombs, and some huge fires; but these were unremarkable and have since merged without identity into the neutral maze of fire and noise and water and night, without date and without hour, with neither time nor form, that lowers mistily at the back of my mind as a picture of the air-raid season.

I suppose we were worn down and shivering. Three a.m. is a meanspirited hour. I suppose we were drenched, with the cold hose water trickling in at our collars and settling down at the tails of our shirts. Without doubt the heavy brass couplings felt moulded from metal-ice. Probably the open roar of the pumps drowned the petulant buzz of the raiders above, and certainly the ubiquitous fire-glow made an orange stage-set of the streets. Black water would have puddled the City alleys and I suppose our hands and our faces were black as the water. Black with hacking about among the burnt up rafters. These things were an every-night nonentity. They happened and they were not forgotten because they were never even remembered.

But I do remember it was our third job. And there we were – Len, Lofty, Verno and myself, playing a fifty-foot jet up the face of a tall City warehouse and thinking of nothing at all. You don't think of anything after the first few hours. You just watch the white pole of water lose itself in the fire and you think of nothing. Sometimes you move the jet over to another window. Sometimes the orange dims to black – but you only ease your grip on the ice-cold nozzle and continue pouring careless gallons through the window. You know the fire will fester for hours yet. However, that night the blank, indefinite hours of waiting were sharply interrupted – by an unusual sound. Very suddenly a long rattling crack of bursting brick and mortar perforated the moment. And then the upper half of that five-storey building heaved over towards us. It hung there, poised for a timeless second before rumbling down at us. I was thinking of nothing at all and then I was thinking of everything in the world.

In that simple second my brain digested every detail of the scene. New eyes opened at the sides of my head so that, from within, I photographed a hemispherical panorama bounded by the huge length of the building in front of me and the narrow lane on either side.

Blocking us on the left was the squat trailer pump, roaring and quivering with effort. Water throbbed from its overflow valves and down its grey sides into the gutter. But nevertheless a fat iron exhaust pipe glowed red-hot in the middle of the wet engine. I had to look past Lofty's face. Lofty was staring at the controls, hands tucked into his armpits for warmth. Lofty was thinking of nothing. He had a black diamond of soot over one eye, like the White-eyed Kaffir in negative.

To the other side of me was a free run up the alley. Overhead swung a sign – 'Catto and Henley'. I wondered what in hell they sold. Old stamps? The alley was quite free. A couple of lengths of dead, deflated hose wound over the darkly glistening pavement. Charred flotsam dammed up one of the gutters. A needle of water fountained from a hole in a live hose-length. Beneath a blue shelter light lay a shattered coping stone. The next shop along was a tobacconist's, windowless, with fake display cartons torn open for anybody to see. The alley was quite free.

Behind me, Len and Verno shared the weight of the hose. They heaved up against the strong backward drag of water pressure. All I had to do was yell 'Drop it' – and then run. We could risk the live hose snaking up at us. We could run to the right down the free alley – Len, Verno and me. But I never moved. I never said 'Drop it' or anything else. That long second held me hypnotized, rubber boots cemented to the pavement. Ton upon ton of red-hot brick hovering in the air above us numbed all initiative. I could only think. I couldn't move.

Six yards in front stood the blazing building. A minute before I would never have distinguished it from any other drab Victorian atrocity happily on fire. Now I was immediately certain of every minute detail. The building was five storeys high. The top four storeys were fiercely alight. The rooms inside were alive with red fire. The black outside walls remained untouched. And thus, like the lighted carriages of a night express, there appeared alternating rectangles of black and red that emphasized vividly the extreme symmetry of the window spacing: each oblong window shape posed as a vermilion panel set in perfect order upon the dark face of the wall. There were ten windows to each floor, making forty windows in all. In rigid rows of ten, one row placed precisely above the other, with strong contrasts of black and red, the blazing windows stood to attention in strict formation. The oblong building, the oblong windows, the oblong spacing. Orange-red colour seemed to *bulge* from the black framework, assumed tactile values, like boiling jelly that expanded inside a thick black squared grill.

Three of the storeys, thirty blazing windows and their huge frame of black brick, a hundred solid tons of hard, deep Victorian wall, pivoted over towards us and hung flatly over the alley. Whether the descending wall actually paused in its fall I can never know. Probably it never did. Probably it only seemed to hang there. Probably my eyes only digested its action at an early period of momentum, so that I saw it 'off true' but before it had gathered speed.

The night grew darker as the great mass hung over us. Through smoke-fogged fire-glow the moonlight had hitherto penetrated to the pit of our alley through declivities in the skyline. Now some of the moonlight was being shut out as the wall hung ever further over us. The wall shaded the moonlight like an inverted awning. Now the pathway of light above had been squeezed to a thin line. That was the only silver lining I ever believed in. It shone out – a ray of hope. But it was a declining hope, for although at this time the entire hemispherical scene appeared static, an imminence of move-ment could be sensed throughout – presumably because the scene was actually moving. Even the speed of the shutter which closed the photograph on my mind was powerless to exclude this motion from a deeper consciousness. The picture appeared static to the limited surface sense, the eyes and the material brain, but beyond that there was hidden movement.

The second was timeless. I had leisure to remark many things. For instance, that an iron derrick, slightly to the left, would not hit me. This derrick stuck out from the building and I could feel its sharpness and hardness as clearly as if I had run my body intimately over its contour. I had time to notice that it carried a foot-long hook, a chain with three-inch rings, two girder supports and a wheel more than twice as large as my head.

A wall will fall in many ways. It may sway over to the one side or the other. It may crumble at the very beginning of its fall. It may remain intact and fall flat. This wall fell as flat as a pancake. It clung to its shape through ninety degrees to the horizontal. Then it detached itself from the pivot and slammed down on top of us.

The last resistance of bricks and mortar at the pivot point cracked off like automatic gun fire. The violent sound both deafened us and brought us to our senses. We dropped the hose and crouched. Afterwards Verno said that I knelt slowly on one knee with bowed head, like a man about to be knighted. Well, I got my knighting. There was an incredible noise – a thunderclap condensed into the space of an eardrum – and then the bricks and the mortar came tearing and burning into the flesh of my face.

Lofty, away by the pump, was killed. Len, Verno and myself they dug out. There was very little brick on top of us. We had been lucky. We had been framed by one of those symmetrical, oblong window spaces.

ALUN LEWIS · 1915–1944

Private Jones

DAFIS the post came down the lane to Siencyn's cottage earlier today than usual. He walked his bicycle through the stone muddy ruts, ringing his bell to call them out. Siencyn was still in bed, but Marged, his wife, had been up a couple of hours, feeding the wild chickens that nested in the apple trees and gorse bushes and mixing some swill for Granny the sow.

'It's come, Marged fach, it's come,' Dafis shouted, his excitement at a gleeful pitch. 'Siencyn's notice is come.'

He brandished a small brown envelope.

Marged straightened her heavy body, wiped her wet hands in her sack apron, showed nothing.

'Diw mawr,' she said to herself, thinking that something important was happening inside her.

'Siencyn!' Dafis called, leaning his bicycle with its tied-on parcels against the crumbled wall of the cottage. 'Your calling-up notice I got for you. Look alive, boy.'

Siencyn poked his long head out of the tiny bedroom window, his hair the colour of swedes. He was in his flannel night-shirt.

'Coming now, Dafis,' he said cheerily and withdrew. He pulled his trousers and clogs on, and came downstairs buckling his leather belt across a handful of trousers, very excited.

Dafis opened the letter, Marged looking over his shoulder. She was twice his size.

'Printed matter,' Dafis said. 'There for you. Instructions, look. Railway travel voucher. Free trip, see?'

'In the train?' Siencyn asked.

'Third class,' Dafis said. 'From Cardigan station, Great Western Railway, to Talcen station, ditto. East Wales Fusiliers it is for you, Siencyn bach, poor dab. Plenty of VC's they got already. Watch out, you.'

'East Wales Fusiliers, is it?' Siencyn repeated. 'Well, well. Third class?'

'When is it?' Marged asked.

'Friday next, 21st inst.,' Dafis said. 'Take your identity card, Siencyn bach, don't forget that, now. Or it's CB you'll be right from the word go.'

'Jawch,' said Siencyn, 'there's a lot to remember, Dafis. Where's my identity card, Marged? In the poe in the spare room, is it?'

'And your birth certificate is there,' she said, knowing where to put her hands on things. 'You'll have to find somewhere else to keep your things from now on, Siencyn bach.'

'Aye, that's true,' he said, rubbing his tangled hair. 'Well, I better go round and tell everybody.'

'Don't trouble,' Dafis said. 'I'll tell them on my round. Stay you, my boy. I'll come down tonight and give you a bit of wisdom, see? Four years of it in the last war I had, and no more for me thank you.' He looked at his right hand, from which three fingers were missing. 'German sniper did that,' he said proudly, and then screwed up his red bunioned face into a wink. 'Held it up above the parapet, see, Siencyn, and got a nice little blighty. But there, you don't know what a parapet is yet, I don't doubt.'

'I'll learn,' Siencyn said, with all the good will in the world.

'You will,' Dafis said, speaking with the sardonic finality of experience. 'Solong both.'

'Solong Dafis, thank you,' Siencyn said.

Dafis pushed his bicycle off, the cycle clips pulling his small trousers up nearly to his knees. He wore a straw boater all the year round, Dafis did.

The third winter of the war was just relaxing its grip on this closed corner of Cardiganshire; six weeks of frost had held up the winter ploughing and the spring sowing, and Siencyn had been having a soft time of it, lying in bed in the mornings, chopping a bit of firewood, mending a few broken scythes and shafts, patching up the cowsheds of his employer, cutting enough hay for the dray-horses, and a pint or two some nights. He had been medically examined and registered a whole year back, but his call-up was deferred for the summer harvest and the autumn trapping – Siencyn was the official trapper of the parish and sent four hundred and thirty-seven rabbits to Cardigan station, Great Western, in five weeks – and then the winter ploughing. He had got tired of waiting, restless and unable to merge himself in his work and the weather and the requirements of the horses and of Marged. He was a good-natured man, but out of patience with things. He had quarrelled with Marged a lot of this winter, beating her once, leaping out of bed on a Sunday morning when the cracked church bell was tolling, and beating her for calling him an idle heathen. And she used her tongue on him for that. Said that people were saying things about them. What things? She shrugged her shoulders. Once he'd cleared out of the way, they were saying, perhaps they'd discover before a year was out whose fault it was there were no babies coming in their house. Well, that wasn't a nice thing to say, and it says a lot for Siencyn's good nature that he only shrugged his shoulders and said pity they hadn't got more important things to think about than that. She didn't use the rough edge of her tongue on him again, but she was very secretive and moody all the winter. He didn't worry about her; he'd go and she'd stay behind; she was his wife; there you are; nobody is indispensable; she wouldn't want to leave the place she'd been born in, whether he went or not. It was different with him. He wanted to see the world. Lots of the boys from round about went into the merchant navy; either the sea or the land it was with all the boys. And he held it a grudge that his widowed mother had kept him home to work at odd jobs instead of letting him go to sea. His father must have been an old soft, too; he wasn't wounded and he wasn't ill in the last war. He just died. Ran home three times from the Army, and then died in detention barracks. Heart-broken, his mother said. Well, what a compliment for a man!

Nobody had a bad word for Siencyn, except that he was idle and fond of his drink and irregular as a Christian and not reliable for doing a job or fetching you something from market or being prompt at the chapel concert rehearsals. So, when he went round to say solong, everybody was sorry to see him go and genuinely hoped the Army would make a man of him before it got him killed. Old Mari Siop, who had a soft spot for anybody in trousers, said she thought strong men like him ought to stay at home in case the Irish attacked us. And he had a real good walk-round, ending up at the Ship hotel, saying goodbye and drinking basin after basin of tea in the cottages and then a pint all round on the house. This was on his last night, and you wouldn't believe the offers he had to knit comforts for him, and old drovers and flannel vests fetched out of the cupboards where they had lain since their wearers had died. He took them all, and all that he didn't drop on the way down from the pub he carried into the kitchen where Marged was sitting doing nothing by the wood fire. She was cross with him for taking them; they'd be saying now she couldn't look after her husband's pants even. She was always seeing the worst side of everything these days. She was almost fit to cry with desperation over a little thing like that.

So they had a bit of bread and milk for supper, not saying anything at all. Then he fetched the money from under the bed upstairs and counted it out, five pounds thirteen and four, and divided it into two piles, three pounds thirteen for her and two pounds for himself. And then he got up and very clumsily and hesitantly smoothed her hair back. She was vexed, and said what a mess she was, all untidy and fat-getting, and she bent her head forward as if she was feeling bad; and she was all white and her eyes were yellow and suffused with watery blood. He was shifting from one foot to the other, uneasy about what to do, and she wouldn't say a thing one way or the other. Dumb she was.

And he was thinking how happy everything and everybody had been when he went round the farms this afternoon, and now Marged spoiling it all. But when she looked up at him, raised her head to him slowly as if there was a millstone round her neck, and then stood up with her arms raised a little, and said that Welsh word to him that she hadn't said since they were courting, then he knew it was a million times better to feel black and torn in pieces like this than to be laughing and drinking tea and saying the Germans wouldn't last long now he was in it too. He picked her up, and she wasn't heavy any more; and carried her up the creaking stairs as if she was a young virgin. Only she was better than a virgin, her fine big body which his big shivering hands slowly divested of the red jersey and thick skirt and woollen stocking and flannel vests that she wore on it winter and summer. The moon was out and the river ringing on the stones and the old jollyboy owls crying goodywhoo in the wood, and he knew he'd been waiting for this for a whole year, to say goodbye to Marged like this. And she lay warm and silken and trembling under his huge hands and she heard neither the river nor the owls but only him grunting and breathing in her mouth and in her ears and something gentle at last opening inside her, like a baby begging her to receive it in.

Onions she boiled for his breakfast the next morning, and two hard-boiled eggs and a whole small loaf uncut for his pocket, and off he set, six miles to walk to Cardigan station. Dafis the postman had forgotten to bring him some stamped addressed envelopes, but he had found a letter in the grandfather clock with their address on it. He didn't know how to write the address himself, but somebody would copy it off this old letter for him when he got there, no doubt. So everything was alright. Plenty of wood left for the fire and Marged walking to the crossroads with him, and the weather crisp and young, the cockerels crowing all the way in to Cardigan station, and Dai Pencwm passing him on the road giving him the benediction of the big pew. His heart was like a feather, walking like this through his own countryside, seeing the sea through gates in the sandy hedges, and singing Dr Parry's *Jerusalem* to himself which was this year's test piece at the Eisteddfod, and feeling a free man, as if he owned the place and no need to pick up a shovel nor a scythe nor the handles of the plough. . . .

There were other men like him on the train the last part of the journey, from Swansea. But they were different to him, smoking cigarettes and wearing posh navy suits and pointy shoes, with white silk scarves and grease on their hair. He sat a long way from them and he felt hot and uneasy. But when they got there it was all in together and fags out and form up in threes with a soldier showing you how with a silver-knobbed cane, and march through the streets into the barracks. Then he lost direction and control, there were so many things and people. He knew how to sign his name, S. Jones, where they told him, but they wouldn't give him enough time to do it in, and he had to keep on signing in every room they went into, whereas he had never signed his name more than twice a week before, on the dole that was. But he was doing pretty well out of it; same as last night everybody was giving him things – mug, knife, fork, spoon, blankets, bag for straw, khaki suit, leggings, boots, cap, and lots of straps that he didn't know what for. And then a rifle and a bayonet. You didn't take long to become a soldier, for a fact. Then they had a good meal in the cookhouse, with girls in khaki doing for them, and then the most of them went out for a booze, and cursing everything they were when there were no corporals about. But Siencyn didn't open his mouth, and he was frightened a bit because he'd lost count of what was happening, and he wanted to lie down and sleep, being suddenly very weak and shaky and yawning all the time. As for Marged and all them at home, they didn't exist any more. It was all up with them, there was no doubt.

'You're looking buggered, Jack,' a dark man said, sitting on the floor cleaning his rifle in the empty barrack-room.

Siencyn, like a frightened animal, watched him suspiciously. 'Yes,' he said. 'Yes.'

'It isn't worth worrying about this lot here,' the man said. 'They don't count in this war. They're all peacetime soldiers. They don't know what the war's about, they only want to stay here and shout on the square and take the tarts out. You keep your head up. Don't pay any attention to them.'

'Yes,' said Siencyn not understanding much except that the man was friendly, 'that is so for a fact.'

The man began cleaning his buttons with a button stick and Silvo. 'I'll learn you how to do things,' he said. 'They don't mean anything, all the things they do here, but you might as well do them properly, just to show them there's nothing in it, and then get on out somewhere where there *is* a war.'

'You been a soldier before, is it?' Siencyn asked, friendly with him now, like a dog that barks first, then growls, then wags its tail and sidles up.

'Not in this army, mate. I fought two years in Spain, though. Seen a bit of it then, like.'

'For a living, is it?' Siencyn asked, shifting up, willing to listen.

'No, not for a living,' the man laughed. 'A collier I am for a living, when the pits are open. Collier, stay-in striker, party member, anything's better than keeping a greyhound, chum.'

'Spanish they speak in Spain?' Siencyn asked.

'No, not much now. German and Italian they speak there now. But it doesn't matter much there now.'

'*This* war will do for me alright,' Siencyn said. 'Farm labourer I am, see, and trapper.'

'That's right. You keep to the plough, mate. It's only a knife in your back or a few years in jail or no work and no friends you'll get if you start doing what you believe in. I've never had time to marry a wife, and yet I've never done nothing I can show.'

'I'm married,' Siencyn said. 'It isn't very much of a thing; only down our way you got to get married if you want any peace, see.' The man smiled, and Siencyn smiled back, and then sat thinking of the thing he'd just said.

'No girl in the valleys would take me on,' the man said. 'They want a steady man, see. I'm an anarchist. I won't go and live in two rooms and feed my kids on bread and dripping and make them sell the *Football Echo* and read the race results in the paper and shout hooray in the park on Labour Day.'

Well, well, thought Siencyn, this is a different life to mine, and what it all is I don't know. But I wouldn't like to be on the wrong side of this man, because he is like the prophet Ezekiel, and he can kill people by seizing their wickedness in his hands and squeezing it till they choke.

And Siencyn became devoted to this man, and he wasn't afraid of all the things that happened to him in the next few weeks.

Well, Siencyn became 283749551 Private Jones, S., before you could look round, and the nickname he went by was Timoshenko, which was something like Shenkin, his own name. And the first morning he wore his battledress he had to take it all off and lift his shirt and cough and bare his arm and have a needle in it, all in a whirl, walking round the room with all the others because there was no time to sit down and no furniture, not like waiting for the doctor at home. And then they all walked past a man in a white apron standing on a stool and they had to open their mouths for him and when he looked in Siencyn's mouth, he said 'Christ! Take the lot out. Top and bottom plate for this man. Ever used a toothbrush?' Siencyn said yes, because he'd used one in the infants' school, but he wasn't a kid any more so of course he hadn't used one since. He was a married man now. Jawch!

He was very bad after that, with a big swelling under his arm, and he crawled into his bunk like a sick animal and lay there till he was better, which was a day later. And then he had all his top teeth out, and his new boots were hurting something wicked, and he didn't have a handkerchief to wipe his bleeding mouth which was dripping into the tin of potatoes he was scraping, and the sergeant called him a dirty something and the next morning he was marched into a room and the officer looked fierce at him and said '283749551 Jones, S. Is that your name?' And he was told by the officer to get a shake on and wake his ideas up and not to come back to him again or look out. And Siencyn said he didn't want to come back to him again, not likely, and then he saluted the way he'd seen them do it, and he'd have smiled just to show there was no ill feeling, only his mouth was full of blood. And when he got back to his bunk and they asked him how he got on, he grinned – because he'd spat the blood out on the way back – and said 'The bastard!' And that made everyone laugh and slap his back and say he was a bloody good soldier already, calling the OC a bastard like that. And he always called everybody a bastard after that if they said anything rough to him, which was nearly always, and he felt better straight away then.

After he'd been there a fortnight and getting on famous with the boys and not too bad with the sergeants, and knowing how to slope and present, and halt and start up again, and fix bayonets and standing load, and unload, and two weeks wages, ten shillings a time, a telegram came for him, and that made him hot and excited and the centre of every eye, as you might say. But it was only Marged wanting to know if he was alright, because on account of forgetting to bring Dafis's stamped addressed envelopes he hadn't written home, not liking to ask any of the boys to copy the old address out for him; and no news is good news, isn't it? But the OC sent for him again and asked him if he had quarrelled with his wife or what, and told him it was bad for civilian morale not to write regularly and tell them you was getting on fine. So he confided to Daniel Evans from Spain and Dan wrote a letter for him in two shakes and addressed it and they posted it together on the way to the Naffy, and Dan said why hadn't he asked him before, it was nothing to him and he'd write Siencyn's letters regular for him. If he wasn't such a good man and a good scholar and knew everything about fighting and mining and unemployed and capitalists, Siencyn would have grabbed him by the waist and wrestled with him same as they used to do in the country when they was boys in school and big friends.

And at the end of three weeks the whole issue of them was sent off by train to the east coast of England to finish their training in a battalion that was short of men and wanted them handy in case of invasion. And in this new place it was the same as before only worse if anything. They had a new sergeant-major who shouted like a bull and you could smell his breath when he shouted. He came up close and shouted in your face, so you could only *think* he was a bastard, he was too near for you to mutter it. But their sergeant didn't like the sergeant-major and told the boys that he was separated from his wife for stripping her and thinking out dirty things to do to her, and he was only shouting like that because he wanted to keep in with the colonel. So Siencyn didn't bother about the sergeant-major shouting, now he knew there was no religion in him. But some of the boys that you'd have thought wouldn't care a bit – boys always boasting about what they'd done, big breaks in billiards, supper in married women's houses and that – they became like shivering wet rats after a bit and the sergeant-major used to pick on them all the time and shout at them till they shivered all over, only with Siencyn and Spain he never bothered at all. And as for the sergeant, well, he couldn't keep a straight face on parade with Siencyn. And when Siencyn caught a rabbit one day out on an exercise by putting his hand in a hole where he knew a rabbit was, and gave it to the sergeant to give to the grass widow he was always telling them about, the sergeant was always kind to him after that. Siencyn couldn't remember all the names on the bren-gun and the mortar and the 36-grenade and the anti-tank rifle and war gases and all that. So the sergeant never asked him the names when they were being tested.

The only fly in the ointment was the officer in charge of them. Not the young one, he was alright, nobody bothered about him; but the one with three pips that walked around all day looking at everybody; and when he stopped in front of you on parade he grunted and muttered to himself and then told you what a bloody army you were to be sure. Siencyn didn't like the smell of him, and he didn't feel strong in front of him the same as with the other sergeants and officers.

Everybody was frightened of him, yet they all said he didn't know his job and ought to be sacked. And there were lots of stories about what he did in the nights with his spare time, but still Siencyn couldn't stand up to him. Not even when he found out that the colonel could make the captain shiver like a rat the way the captain did to those under him. And one day, when their training was over and they were taking part in brigade schemes and defending aerodromes and building dannert fences and laughing at the Home Guard like hardened regulars, the captain sent for Siencyn and said 'I hear you're a country bumpkin, Jones.' And Siencyn said 'I live in Penyrheol, Cards, sir.' And the Captain said, 'I hear you were a poacher, Jones?' And Siencyn said 'Trapper, sir.' And the Captain said, 'I'm putting you to work in the Officers' Mess, to catch rabbits and partridges for dinner, and you will be my batman; and if there's any Silvo on my uniform or you get caught with a dead partridge trespassing, I'll break your bloody spine, do you understand?' And Siencyn wasn't brave enough to say no, so he said 'Yes, sir.'

So he became a batman for a change, and it was as bad as he feared, because when he woke the captain in the mornings it was like shaking a nest of adders; he always had a liver and a white tongue and never pleased with anything. But sometimes Siencyn got away on his own, three times a week, after rabbits and pheasants, and then he was as happy as could be. When the captain was shouting for him to clean his Sam Browne or fetch some hot water because the hot water had gone lukewarm on account of him not getting up when he was called, Siencyn felt as bitter and cynical as Dan Evans Spain, who was always sneering at the talk in the papers about fighting for freedom and decency and our children's futures. But when he was lying in the ferns watching the way the pheasants went for grubs, or setting a snare in a rabbit's run, then Siencyn really felt as if he were fighting for freedom and the right of a man to live his own life. Anyway, it was no good looking at things the way Dan Evans did. No doubt it was true all he said about the coal owners taking all the profits and the children without a decent pair of boots or a warm coat, and about the men in London exploiting the natives in Africa and India, and about the *Daily Worker* being banned like in a Nazi country; and when he put it to you you did find it queer to wonder why the poor women and babies suffered themselves to be bombed in the slums in Swansea and London when they wasn't getting anything out of it that you could see. Siencyn didn't have anything against the Russians, but all the same he didn't think it much sense wishing you could be one; and it was easy to see that nothing was the way it ought to be these days if you went by what it says in the Bible. But Dan was only making it hard for himself, refusing a stripe and barely civil to the captain and the sergeant-major and both of them with their knives in him, and it was a pity he was always getting daunted by what he read in the papers, or by what he said about the Army being unprepared and untrained and unarmed to fight a war with tanks and dive-bombers like they'll have to. But all the same, if it came to a fight, Siencyn wouldn't think twice whose side he was on. Dan's side he was on. Dan Spain was a man and he'd like anyone to deny it.

Every now and again he got a letter from Penyrheol, written in Dafis the postman's copperplate hand, with bits dictated by Marged in it and grandiloquent flourishes of Dafis's invention embossed on it, giving him the news as it left them at present and hoping he was in the pink. The first two or three letters had nothing abnormal, except that the sow had been up to the boar and was expecting, and the latch had fallen off the back door and she had tied it with string till he came home, and her marriage book had come and she had to walk to the post office every week to draw her twenty-eight shillings, and she was putting some of it by to buy black-out curtains so she could have a light in the house after dark for a change. Then came a different letter, very brief, and not written in Dafis's hand at all, but in pencil by Marged, and it said: 'Siencyn bach, wen coming back are you i am being sick in the mornings and the doctor jest been an sed i am in for a baby hopping you are not angry yewer loving Marged.'

Siencyn sat with this for a long time, and then he began laughing to himself, and got up feeling like the lord of creation, and went to look for Dan Spain to tell him and see what he said. And he didn't want to tell anybody except Dan, although he was just bursting with the news. So he went out of the guardroom where he was on guard and across the farmyard and through the sheds looking for Dan. But Dan was out on the cliffs the other side of the wood laying some mines, so Siencyn went after him, forgetting he was supposed to be on guard. And just as he came out of the woods and could see the grey North Sea and the black stubby shapes of a convoy jinking southwards in the middle seas, zoom-woof-scream, down came a big two-engined Dornier 215 for you, straight for the soldiers working in the minefield, straight out of the clouds over the sea. Somebody shouted and a couple made a run for it, and a few more fell on their faces, but most of them just looked up at it. And Siencyn looked at it with great interest, not having seen a Swastika before, and then it opened fire and swept past him only just above his head. One of the boys who was running staggered and clutched his guts and went sprawling, and Siencyn said 'Diw Mawr, too bad,' and ran out of the woods to pick him up. The plane had zoomed up over the trees behind him and was climbing in a great ellipse, going seawards, but Siencyn was only concerned to fetch the boy who was hurted, because he was one of the rest of them, and he was hurted. It was Nick Powell Tonypandy as it happened, and he was a mate of Siencyn's, they'd been on a charge together for putting Naffy buns in their respirators and he was going to get married to a butcher's daughter next leave, so his prospects were too good to waste by a bit of bad luck. And Siencyn picked him up and carried him fireman's lift, like in PT, to the shelter of the woods. Nick was groaning and

cursing healthy enough, so Siencyn told him to be quiet, it wasn't a
thing to blaspheme about. And he put Nick against a tree and Nick
said 'He's coming again,' only he didn't say it as polite as that. And
Siencyn saw the Jerry diving in from the sea again like second house
at the pictures and he saw the bren-gun the working party had
brought out with them ready loaded by a gorse bush just in front of
him in the open; so he said 'Look out, boys bach,' and made a dash
for the bren-gun and grabbed hold of it, kneeling, with the butt
against his hip. And the Jerry was coming straight for him with
spurts of flame coming from the wings and bullets like a little
shower of hail sweeping towards Siencyn. And a silvery bomb fell
out of the plane as it came to the bottom of its gradual dive and was
showing its nose to the climb, just at the sea edge of the minefield.
And Siencyn said 'Now!' and pressed the trigger as cool as you like.
And nothing happened. Oh Jawch, there's a pity for you, Siencyn
thought, what is the matter with the old thing? And the explosion
of the bomb knocked him over before he could see whether the
safety catch was on Automatic or Safe. And when they brought him
round with plenty of cold water and his arm in a sling, Spain was
kneeling by him and the captain fidgeting and muttering same as
usual, and he remembered he had something to tell Spain about,
but for the life of him he couldn't think what it was. And Spain said
'Well done, Siencyn boy. You're a chip off the old block, you are.'
And Siencyn said 'Is Nick Powell alright?' And Spain said 'Aye, it
was only a flesh wound; he's OK for the butchery business, don't
worry.' And Siencyn said, 'The gun wouldn't go.' And the captain
said 'No wonder, you bloody fool. It was on Safe. What the hell's the
good of wasting khaki and food and training on a cretin like you?'
And Siencyn, although he was on his back with his arm in a sling,
suddenly felt immensely stronger than the captain for the first time
in his life, and he looked at him and grinned and said 'You bastard!'

Well, the captain's face was a sight to behold. He pulled at his
sagging cheek and opened his mouth and stood on his toes and
didn't say a word. Then he said to Spain, 'You're a witness, Evans.'
And Spain said 'I didn't hear a thing, sir.' And he looked at the
captain with a funny look in his eyes; he'd killed a tidy few men in
Spain, Dan Evans had, and Siencyn got the wind up and he said,
'Don't do it, Dan bach. Leave him be now. We're all in the war
together so make friends, the two of you.' And the captain said
'Consider yourselves under arrest, both of you.' And off he went to

fetch the sergeant-major. So Dan sat on his heels like the colliers do in the back lanes and waited for somebody to come back, and kept on spitting and spitting and saying he'd give him what for if he dared to court-martial them. He knew very well the colonel would dismiss the case if he heard what the captain had said to Siencyn when he was knocked half daft by the bomb; and Dan said he'd get it brought up in Parliament if they did anything to them; and Siencyn lay against a tree as idle and as happy as ever he'd been in his life, because he'd called the captain a bastard and Dan had said 'Well done.'

Siencyn didn't take long to mend; his collar-bone wasn't broken, only bruised; and the colonel praised him in the court of enquiry that sat on Nick Powell's wound; and nothing was heard of the little difference they'd had with the captain, and everybody was buying him drinks in the Naffy for what he'd said. So he had a very placid fortnight on light duties because of his arm. And then, at the end of a fortnight, two things happened that demanded a good bit of thinking out.

First there came a letter for him, and it was a very short one, and it wasn't from Marged and it wasn't signed. Dan read it and said it was an anonymous letter. And it said that Marged was having a baby in case he was interested, and who was responsible, this person would like to know? Funny there'd been no baby in four years when he was living with her, and now as soon as he'd gone to serve his country she goes and gets in the family way. And then several names of likely men from the neighbouring farms and a hint that Marged had been seen coming out of the wood by Twm Gors's cottage late one night. And this person anonymous said it was a shameful sin if nobody could respect a soldier serving his country in her hour of need, and was pleased to sign at the bottom, Sincere Patriot.

Well, whether to ask for compassionate leave or not was the question, but Siencyn wouldn't go and tell the captain all these terrible stories about Marged fooling him, so Dan said why didn't he do a break and hitch-hike home. And he thought yes, he'd do that; but he had no idea at all where Penyrheol was from where they were then, and he'd never find it in a month of Sundays. So he made up a story with Dan that his mother was dead – which was true enough – and Dan wrote it out for him in case the captain asked to see the letter, which he would. And Siencyn was just off to see the sergeant-major to ask for an interview, when the runner came down and said they were both wanted in the company office. So up they went and the sergeant-major had a cunning look in his eyes as if he had them on toast at last, and he showed them into the office, quick march, right wheel, halt, left turn, salute, 'Privates 32 Evans and 51 Jones, Sir.' And the captain looked up after a minute as if he was busy, and said, 'You two are on draft for overseas service. Hand in your A.B.64 to the CQMS (Siencyn never knew what all the initials meant, but Dan would tell him afterwards), and take your blankets to the stores. Seven days' leave. Any questions?' 'No sir.' 'March them out, sergeant-major.' About turn, quick march, halt, dismiss.

'That's what comes of calling him a bastard, Siencyn,' Dan said, philosophically tracing the effect to its cause. 'You'll be able to see your missus, anyway, chum.'

They had their pay and ration cards and passes and off to the station, six miles of it, full kit, enjoying every inch of it. Dan said anonymous letters wasn't worth noticing, he'd had plenty in his time; and the best thing to do was to find the sod who wrote it, and not say a word to Marged. Siencyn said he wouldn't put it above Twm Gors, but he would put it above Marged, who was a good wife if trying at times. And so they parted at Paddington the best of friends, with Dan seeing Siencyn was on the right train and telling him to mind he came back and didn't shirk it, because Dan didn't want to go abroad by himself. So Siencyn told him not to worry, solong.

And nothing more to do except stand all the way to Cardiff, and then a seat the rest of the journey, change at Carmarthen and Pencader like Dan told him, and then safe and sound in Cardigan, having had sandwiches from an old lady before they got to Cardiff and cake and biscuits from another younger lady between Swansea and Carmarthen. He wasn't going to spend his pay himself. And he didn't tell anybody he was going overseas because it was information likely to aid the enemy, so he pretended he was nobody special. And so he started walking home along the old roads he knew inside out, singing *Jerusalem* and wondering if the chapel would be holding its Eisteddfod this week, and if so he'd sing *Jerusalem* in his battledress and walk away with the first prize over them in civvies.

And soon enough he was turning down the lane to the sea by the black wood and heard his employer's horses shuffling in the stalls; he stopped to listen to the good sound, and then went into the stable to take their heads in his arm and put his palm against their hot wet

nostrils. It was fine, that was, pushing old Deri aside to say good-
night and welcome-home to Nansi, and their hooves clashing on
the cobbles. It was only round the corner then to his own cottage
and he felt as if he'd never been away.

There was a black-out up in the back kitchen now, very posh, and
when he opened the door slowly Marged was sitting on a sack of
meal by the stick fire on the flagstone in the corner. But never such
a face did she have before he went away. No red in her cheeks at all,
but like a funeral in her black shawl and drooping shoulders. And
she looked at him like he was a ghost, never a word, but frightened
of him, and then again as if she was finished with him for good. It
gave him a bit of a turn; and before he could say 'Well, nghariad, it's
Siencyn turned up again,' she began to whimper to herself. Siencyn
knew there was a scene going to be, so he took his kit off and knelt
down by her with a sack under his knees not to spoil the trousers
he'd creased under his bed every night, and then he asked her what
was up with her. How they straightened it all out isn't anybody's
business except their own. Marged wasn't willing to believe he'd
forgotten about her letter owing to being knocked daft by a German
plane, but in the end believe it she did, and slowly she began to
think differently about him and not with despair and hatred the
way she had been since he hadn't replied. And then there was all the
old gossip, and a letter in the local paper about it too by somebody
signed Sincere Patriot; and she knew who it was, it was a certain
black-marketing grocer keeping a shop on the top road. And Siencyn said thank God it was a man, anyway, thinking what a pity if it
had been a woman he couldn't give a good lamping to. And, to cut a
long story short, Marged said she wanted it to be a boy and Siencyn
to be his name, and Siencyn showed her his new false teeth and she
wouldn't believe he took them out at night, so he said 'Wait and
see.' And she rubbed her cheek on his battledress and looked at the
shine on his boots and wouldn't believe they were his working
boots. And if everything wasn't as smooth as their words made it
sound, the rest was only a question of time, for a woman will mend
herself with time if so be the man means what he says when he
speaks kind to her. So she patched up alright with a bit of praise
from Siencyn which was as rare as Cadbury's chocolate to her and
every bit as sweet. And Siencyn felt worried and exhausted with
pulling her round to his way of seeing it all, and it was worse than
driving the old sow up the lane or helping to shoe a young colt, but

Jawch, it made all the difference. And next day he went without any malice to the certain grocer's just mentioned and after he'd pasted him good and proper he bore no ill feeling at all. And when they asked him how's the Army he said it was alright and nothing to worry about, although his mate Dan Evans said it wasn't much of a concern.

And then, the night before he went back, the chapel held its annual Eisteddfod, which was right in Siencyn's line having a rich tenor a bit loud for volume but very good for tone. And he went in his battledress as clean and straight as a new pin with vaseline on his hair the colour of swedes, and they all cheered when he came up to sing his version of *Jerusalem*. And he never let on to a soul that he was down as a C. of E. in the Army through no fault of his own, having told the clerk when asked his religion 'Christian, sir.' Not that there was any need to say sir to a clerk, but he was new to the game then. And it was fine to be standing there in the whitewashed old chapel with Marged sitting in the pew where he'd carved his initials fifteen years ago, and everybody quiet as the grave except old Twm Morris Cobbler at the harmonium, saying 'One Two Three Four – *Now.*' And off he went with old Twm creaking along just level with him and the faces of the congregation uplifted and swaying slowly as if there was a little breeze going across the pews. And he'd sung it so often in the back of a lorry on exercises in the Army, and in the latrines, and peeling potatoes on jankers, that it came now with all the intimacy and rejoicing of all that had happened to him and not harmed or beaten him. And when he'd finished there was a great silence on them all, and then the men wiped the sweat from under their celluloid collars, and the women sniffed at their hankies and wouldn't look up. And Siencyn walked down and sat by Marged. And then they began to clap, and Siencyn didn't think they were ever going to stop. And although the adjudicator was a conchy in the last war he didn't have any option about giving Siencyn the prize. No money in it, of course, not with singing sacred music; it was a different matter from money.

And Siencyn walked home with Marged arm in arm, and he said Dan Spain would write to her regular, but he didn't have the heart to tell her where he was going to, meaning abroad; not yet, because he could only just imagine himself going abroad, and as for coming back again, he couldn't see that at all. But there was nothing to be done about it, only go to bed early and poke his head out of the window to listen to the river and tell the cockerel mind to crow at five-thirty to catch the train. And that made Marged laugh for the first time, and Siencyn thought well, it's not so bad so far and no blame attached to me. And Marged promised she'd call the baby Dan as well as Siencyn. And they slept so sound that Jawch if he didn't miss the train. But never mind about that now.

A Piece of Cake

I DO not remember much of it; not beforehand anyway; not until it happened.

There was the landing at Fouka, where the Blenheim boys were helpful and gave us tea while we were being refuelled. I remember the quietness of the Blenheim boys, how they came into the mess-tent to get some tea and sat down to drink it without saying anything; how they got up and went out when they had finished drinking and still they did not say anything. And I knew that each one was holding himself together because the going was not very good right then. They were having to go out too often, and there were no replacements coming along.

We thanked them for the tea and went out to see if they had finished refuelling our Gladiators. I remember that there was a wind blowing which made the wind-sock stand out straight, like a signpost, and the sand was blowing up around our legs and making a rustling noise as it swished against the tents, and the tents flapped in the wind so that they were like canvas men clapping their hands.

'Bomber boys unhappy,' Peter said.

'Not unhappy,' I answered.

'Well, they're browned off.'

'No. They've had it, that's all. But they'll keep going. You can see they're trying to keep going.'

Our two old Gladiators were standing beside each other in the sand and the airmen in their khaki shirts and shorts seemed still to be busy with the refuelling. I was wearing a thin white cotton flying suit and Peter had on a blue one. It wasn't necessary to fly with anything warmer.

Peter said, 'How far away is it?'

'Twenty-one miles beyond Charing Cross,' I answered, 'on the right side of the road.' Charing Cross was where the desert road branched north to Mersah Matruh. The Italian army was outside Mersah, and they were doing pretty well. It was about the only time, so far as I know, that the Italians have done pretty well. Their morale goes up and down like a sensitive altimeter, and right then it was at forty thousand because the Axis was on top of the world. We hung around waiting for the refuelling to finish.

Peter said, 'It's a piece of cake.'

'Yes. It ought to be easy.'

We separated and I climbed into my cockpit. I have always remembered the face of the airman who helped me to strap in. He was oldish, about forty, and bald except for a neat patch of golden hair at the back of his head. His face was all wrinkles, his eyes were like my grandmother's eyes, and he looked as though he had spent his life helping to strap in pilots who never came back. He stood on the wing pulling my straps and said, 'Be careful. There isn't any sense not being careful.'

'Piece of cake,' I said.

'Like hell.'

'Really. It isn't anything at all. It's a piece of cake.'

I don't remember much about the next bit; I only remember about later on. I suppose we took off from Fouka and flew west towards Mersah, and I suppose we flew at about eight hundred feet. I suppose we saw the sea to starboard, and I suppose – no, I am certain – that it was blue and that it was beautiful, especially where it rolled up on to the sand and made a long thick white line east and west as far as you could see. I suppose we flew over Charing Cross and flew on for twenty-one miles to where they had said it would be, but I do not know. I know only that there was trouble, lots and lots of trouble, and I know that we had turned round and were coming back when the trouble got worse. The biggest trouble of all was that I was too low to bale out, and it is from that point on that my memory comes back to me. I remember the dipping of the nose of the aircraft and I remember looking down the nose of the machine at the ground and seeing a little clump of camel-thorn growing there all by itself. I remember seeing some rocks lying in the sand beside the camel-thorn, and the camel-thorn and the sand and the rocks leapt out of the ground and came to me. I remember that very clearly.

Then there was a small gap of not-remembering. It might have been one second or it might have been thirty; I do not know. I have an idea that it was very short, a second perhaps, and next I heard a *crumph* on the right as the starboard wing tank caught fire, then another *crumph* on the left as the port tank did the same. To me that was not significant, and for a while I sat still, feeling comfortable, but a little drowsy. I couldn't see with my eyes, but that was not significant either. There was nothing to worry about. Nothing at all. Not until I felt the hotness around my legs. At first it was only a warmness and that was all right too, but all at once it was a hotness, a very stinging scorching hotness up and down the sides of each leg.

I knew that the hotness was unpleasant, but that was all I knew. I disliked it, so I curled my legs up under the seat and waited. I think there was something wrong with the telegraph system between the body and the brain. It did not seem to be working very well. Somehow it was a bit slow in telling the brain all about it and in asking for instructions. But I believe a message eventually got through, saying, 'Down here there is a great hotness. What shall we do? (Signed) Left Leg and Right Leg.' For a long time there was no reply. The brain was figuring the matter out.

Then slowly, word by word, the answer was tapped over the wires. 'The – plane – is – burning. Get – out – repeat – get – out – get – out.' The order was relayed to the whole system, to all the muscles in the legs, arms and body, and the muscles went to work. They tried their best; they pushed a little and pulled a little, and they strained greatly, but it wasn't any good. Up went another telegram, 'Can't get out. Something holding us in.' The answer to this one took even longer in arriving, so I just sat there waiting for it to come, and all the time the hotness increased. Something was holding me down and it was up to the brain to find out what it was. Was it giants' hands pressing on my shoulders, or heavy stones or houses or steam rollers or filing cabinets or gravity or was it ropes? Wait a minute. Ropes – ropes. The message was beginning to come through. It came very slowly. 'Your – straps. Undo – your – straps.' My arms received the message and went to work. They tugged at the straps, but they wouldn't undo. They tugged again and again, a little feebly, but as hard as they could, and it wasn't any use. Back went the message, 'How do we undo the straps?'

This time I think that I sat there for three or four minutes waiting for the answer. It wasn't any use hurrying or getting impatient. That was the one thing of which I was sure. But what a long time it was all taking. I said aloud, 'Bugger it. I'm going to be burnt. I'm . . .' but I was interrupted. The answer was coming – no, it wasn't – yes, it was, it was slowly coming through. 'Pull – out – the – quick – release – pin – you – bloody – fool – and – hurry.'

Out came the pin and the straps were loosed. Now, let's get out. Let's get out, let's get out. But I couldn't do it. I simply lift myself out of the cockpit. Arms and legs tried their best but it wasn't any use. A last desperate message was flashed upwards and this time it was marked 'Urgent'.

'Something else is holding us down,' it said. 'Something else, something else, something heavy.'

Still the arms and legs did not fight. They seemed to know instinctively that there was no point in using up their strength. They stayed quiet and waited for the answer, and oh what a time it took. Twenty, thirty, forty hot seconds. None of them really white hot yet, no sizzling of flesh or smell of burning meat, but that would come any moment now, because those old Gladiators aren't made of stressed steel like a Hurricane or a Spit. They have taut canvas wings, covered with magnificently inflammable dope, and underneath there are hundreds of small thin sticks, the kind you put under the logs for kindling, only these are drier and thinner. If a clever man said, 'I am going to build a big thing that will burn better and quicker than anything else in the world,' and if he applied himself diligently to his task, he would probably finish up by building something very like a Gladiator. I sat still waiting.

Then suddenly the reply, beautiful in its briefness, but at the same time explaining everything. 'Your – parachute – turn – the – buckle.'

I turned the buckle, released the parachute harness and with some effort hoisted myself up and tumbled over the side of the cockpit. Something seemed to be burning, so I rolled about a bit in the sand, then crawled away from the fire on all fours and lay down.

I heard some of my machine-gun ammunition going off in the heat and I heard some of the bullets thumping into the sand near by. I did not worry about them; I merely heard them.

Things were beginning to hurt. My face hurt most. There was something wrong with my face. Something had happened to it. Slowly I put up a hand to feel it. It was sticky. My nose didn't seem to be there. I tried to feel my teeth, but I cannot remember whether I came to any conclusion about them. I think I dozed off.

All of a sudden there was Peter. I heard his voice and I heard him dancing around and yelling like a madman and shaking my hand

and saying, 'Jesus, I thought you were still inside. I came down half a mile away and ran like hell. Are you all right?'

I said, 'Peter, what has happened to my nose?'

I heard him striking a match in the dark. The night comes quickly in the desert. There was a pause.

'It actually doesn't seem to be there very much,' he said. 'Does it hurt?'

'Don't be a bloody fool, of course it hurts.'

He said he was going back to his machine to get some morphia out of his emergency pack, but he came back again soon, saying he couldn't find his aircraft in the dark.

'Peter,' I said, 'I can't see anything.'

'It's night,' he answered. 'I can't see either.'

It was cold now. It was bitter cold, and Peter lay down close alongside so that we could both keep a little warmer. Every now and then he would say, 'I've never seen a man without a nose before.' I kept spewing a lot of blood and every time I did it, Peter lit a match. Once he gave me a cigarette, but it got wet and I didn't want it anyway.

I do not know how long we stayed there and I remember only very little more. I remember that I kept telling Peter that there was a tin of sore-throat tablets in my pocket, and that he should take one, otherwise he would catch my sore throat. I remember asking him where we were and him saying, 'We're between the two armies,' and then I remember English voices from an English patrol asking if we were Italians. Peter said something to them; I cannot remember what he said.

Later I remember hot thick soup and one spoonful making me sick. And all the time the pleasant feeling that Peter was around, being wonderful, doing wonderful things and never going away. That is all that I can remember.

The men stood beside the airplane painting away and talking about the heat.

'Painting pictures on the aircraft,' I said.

'Yes,' said Peter. 'It's a great idea. It's subtle.'

'Why?' I said. 'Just you tell me.'

'They're funny pictures,' he said. 'The German pilots will all laugh when they see them; they'll shake so with their laughing that they won't be able to shoot straight.'

'Oh baloney baloney baloney.'

'No, it's a great idea. It's fine. Come and have a look.'

We ran towards the line of aircraft. 'Hop, skip, jump,' said Peter. 'Hop skip jump, keep in time.'

'Hop skip jump,' I said, 'Hop skip jump,' and we danced along.

The painter on the first aeroplane had a straw hat on his head and a sad face. He was copying the drawing out of a magazine, and when Peter saw it he said, 'Boy oh boy look at that picture,' and he began to laugh. His laugh began with a rumble and grew quickly into a belly-roar and he slapped his thighs with his hands both at the same time and went on laughing with his body doubled up and his mouth wide open and his eyes shut. His silk top hat fell off his head on to the sand.

'That's not funny,' I said.

'Not funny!' he cried. 'What d'you mean "not funny"? Look at me. Look at me laughing. Laughing like this I couldn't hit anything. I couldn't hit a hay wagon or a house or a louse.' And he capered about on the sand, gurgling and shaking with laughter. Then he seized me by the arm and we danced over to the next aeroplane. 'Hop skip jump,' he said. 'Hop skip jump.'

There was a small man with a crumpled face writing a long story on the fuselage with a red crayon. His straw hat was perched right on the back of his head and his face was shiny with sweat.

'Good morning,' he said. 'Good morning, good morning,' and he swept his hat off his head in a very elegant way.

Peter said, 'Shut up,' and bent down and began to read what the little man had been writing. All the time Peter was spluttering and rumbling with laughter, and as he read he began to laugh afresh. He rocked from one side to the other and danced around on the sand slapping his thighs with his hands and bending his body. 'Oh my, what a story, what a story, what a story. Look at me. Look at me laughing,' and he hopped about on his toes, shaking his head and chortling like a madman. Then suddenly I saw the joke and I began to laugh with him. I laughed so much that my stomach hurt and I fell down and rolled around on the sand and roared and roared because it was so funny that there was nothing else I could do.

'Peter, you're marvellous,' I shouted. 'But can all those German pilots read English?'

'Oh hell,' he said. 'Oh hell. Stop,' he shouted. 'Stop your work,' and the painters all stopped their painting and turned round slowly and looked at Peter. They did a little caper on their toes and began to chant in unison. 'Rubbishy things – on all the wings, on all the wings, on all the wings,' they chanted.

'Shut up,' said Peter. 'We're in a jam. We must keep calm. Where's my top hat?'

'What?' I said.

'You can speak German,' he said. 'You must translate for us. He will translate for you,' he shouted to the painters. 'He will translate.'

Then I saw his black top hat lying in the sand. I looked away, then I looked around and saw it again. It was a silk opera-hat and it was lying there on its side in the sand.

'You're mad,' I shouted. 'You're madder than hell. You don't know what you're doing. You'll get us all killed. You're absolutely plumb crazy, do you know that? You're crazier than hell. My God, you're crazy.'

'Goodness, what a noise you're making. You mustn't shout like that; it's not good for you.' This was a woman's voice. 'You've made yourself all hot,' she said, and I felt someone wiping my forehead with a handkerchief. 'You mustn't work yourself up like that.'

Then she was gone and I saw only the sky, which was pale blue. There were no clouds and all around were the German fighters. They were above, below and on every side and there was no way I could go; there was nothing I could do. They took it in turns to come in to attack and they flew their aircraft carelessly, banking and looping and dancing in the air. But I was not frightened, because of the funny pictures on my wings. I was confident and I thought, 'I am going to fight a hundred of them alone and I'll shoot them all down. I'll shoot them while they are laughing; that's what I'll do.'

Then they flew closer. The whole sky was full of them. There were so many that I did not know which ones to watch and which ones to attack. There were so many that they made a black curtain over the sky and only here and there could I see a little of the blue showing through. But there was enough to patch a Dutchman's trousers, which was all that mattered. So long as there was enough to do that, then everything was all right.

Still they flew closer. They came nearer and nearer, right up in front of my face so that I saw only the black crosses which stood out brightly against the colour of the Messerschmitts and against the blue of the sky; and as I turned my head quickly from one side to the other I saw more aircraft and more crosses and then I saw nothing but the arms of the crosses and the blue of the sky. The arms had hands and they joined together and made a circle and danced around my Gladiator, while the engines of the Messerschmitts sang joyfully in a deep voice. They were playing Oranges and Lemons and every now and then two would detach themselves and come out into the middle of the floor and make an attack and I knew then that it was Oranges and Lemons. They banked and swerved and danced upon their toes and they leant against the air first to one side, then to the other. 'Oranges and Lemons said the bells of St. Clements,' sang the engines.

But I was still confident. I could dance better than they and I had a better partner. She was the most beautiful girl in the world. I looked down and saw the curve of her neck and the gentle slope of her pale shoulders and I saw her slender arms, eager and outstretched.

Suddenly I saw some bullet holes in my starboard wing and I got angry and scared both at the same time; but mostly I got angry. Then I got confident and I said, 'The German who did that had no sense of humour. There's always one man in a party who has no sense of humour. But there's nothing to worry about; there's nothing at all to worry about.'

Then I saw more bullet holes and I got scared. I slid back the hood of the cockpit and stood up and shouted, 'You fools, look at the funny pictures. Look at the one on my tail; look at the story on my fuselage. Please look at the story on my fuselage.'

But they kept on coming. They tripped into the middle of the floor in twos, shooting at me as they came. And the engines of the Messerschmitts sang loudly. 'When will you pay me, said the bells of Old Bailey?' sang the engines, and as they sang the black crosses danced and swayed to the rhythm of the music. There were more holes in my wings, in the engine cowling and in the cockpit.

Then suddenly there were some in my body.

But there was no pain, even when I went into a spin, when the wings of my plane went flip, flip, flip, flip, faster and faster, when the blue sky and the black sea chased each other round and round until there was no longer any sky or sea but just the flashing of the sun as I turned. But the black crosses were following me down, still dancing and still holding hands and I could still hear the singing of their engines. 'Here comes a candle to light you to bed, here comes a chopper to chop off your head,' sang the engines.

Still the wings went flip flip, flip flip, and there was neither sky nor sea around me, but only the sun.

Then there was only the sea. I could see it below me and I could see the white horses, and I said to myself, 'Those are white horses riding a rough sea.' I knew then that my brain was going well because of the white horses and because of the sea. I knew that there was not much time because the sea and the white horses were nearer, the white horses were bigger and the sea was like a sea and like water, not like a smooth plate. Then there was only one white horse, rushing forward madly with his bit in his teeth, foaming at the mouth, scattering the spray with his hooves and arching his neck as he ran. He galloped on madly over the sea, riderless and uncontrollable, and I could tell that we were going to crash.

After that it was warmer, and there were no black crosses and there was no sky. But it was only warm because it was not hot and it was not cold. I was sitting in a great red chair made of velvet and it was evening. There was a wind blowing from behind.

'Where am I?' I said.

'You are missing. You are missing, believed killed.'

'Then I must tell my mother.'

'You can't. You can't use that phone.'

'Why not?'

'It goes only to God.'

'What did you say I was?'

'Missing, believed killed.'

'That's not true. It's a lie. It's a lousy lie because here I am and I'm not missing. You're just trying to frighten me and you won't succeed. You won't succeed, I tell you, because I know it's a lie and I'm going back to my squadron. You can't stop me because I'll just go. I'm going, you see, I'm going.'

I got up from the red chair and began to run.

'Let me see those X-rays again, nurse.'

'They're here, doctor.' This was the woman's voice again, and now it came closer. 'You have been making a noise tonight, haven't you? Let me straighten your pillow for you, you're pushing it on to the floor.' The voice was close and it was very soft and nice.

'Am I missing?'

'No, of course not. You're fine.'

'They said I was missing.'

'Don't be silly; you're fine.'

Oh everyone's silly, silly, silly, but it was a lovely day, and I did not want to run but I couldn't stop. I kept on running across the grass and I couldn't stop because my legs were carrying me and I had no control over them. It was as if they did not belong to me, although when I looked down I saw that they were mine, that the shoes on the feet were mine and that the legs were joined to my body. But they would not do what I wanted; they just went on running across the field and I had to go with them. I ran and ran and ran, and although in some places the field was rough and bumpy, I never stumbled. I ran past trees and hedges and in one field there were some sheep which stopped their eating and scampered off as I ran past them. Once I saw my mother in a pale grey dress bending down picking mushrooms, and as I ran past she looked up and said, 'My basket's nearly full; shall we go home soon?' but my legs wouldn't stop and I had to go on.

Then I saw the cliff ahead and I saw how dark it was beyond the cliff. There was this great cliff and beyond it there was nothing but darkness, although the sun was shining in the field where I was running. The light of the sun stopped dead at the edge of the cliff and there was only darkness beyond. 'That must be where the night begins,' I thought, and once more I tried to stop but it was not any good. My legs began to go faster towards the cliff and they began to take longer strides, and I reached down with my hand and tried to stop them by clutching the cloth of my trousers, but it did not work; then I tried to fall down. But my legs were nimble, and each time I threw myself I landed on my toes and went on running.

Now the cliff and the darkness were much nearer and I could see that unless I stopped quickly I should go over the edge. Once more I tried to throw myself to the ground and once more I landed on my toes and went on running.

I was going fast as I came to the edge and I went straight on over it into the darkness and began to fall.

At first it was not quite dark. I could see little trees growing out of the face of the cliff, and I grabbed at them with my hands as I went down. Several times I managed to catch hold of a branch, but it always broke off at once because I was so heavy and because I was falling so fast, and once I caught a thick branch with both hands and the tree leaned forward and I heard the snapping of the roots one by one until it came away from the cliff and I went on falling. Then it became darker because the sun and the day were in the fields far away at the top of the cliff, and as I fell I kept my eyes open and watched the darkness turn from grey-black to black, from black to jet black and from jet black to pure liquid blackness which I could touch with my hands but which I could not see. But I went on falling, and it was so black that there was nothing anywhere and it was not any use doing anything or caring or thinking because of the blackness and because of the falling. It was not any use.

'You're better this morning. You're much better.' It was the woman's voice again.

'Hallo.'

'Hallo; we thought you were never going to get conscious.'

'Where am I?'

'In Alexandria; in hospital.'

'How long have I been here?'

'Four days.'

'What time is it?'

'Seven o'clock in the morning.'

'Why can't I see?'

I heard her walking a little closer.

'Oh, we've just put a bandage around your eyes for a bit.'

'How long for?'

'Just for a while. Don't worry. You're fine. You were very lucky, you know.'

I was feeling my face with my fingers but I couldn't feel it; I could only feel something else.

'What's wrong with my face?'

I heard her coming up to the side of my bed and I felt her hand touching my shoulder.

'You mustn't talk any more. You're not allowed to talk. It's bad for you. Just lie still and don't worry. You're fine.'

I heard the sound of her footsteps as she walked across the floor and I heard her open the door and shut it again.

'Nurse,' I said. 'Nurse.'

But she was gone.

JACK LUSBY · 1913–1980

A Flying Fragment

It was hard on Mick Mooney that, near the end of his tether, he had to break in the rustiest bunch of pilots he'd encountered. Being the oldest, rustiest, and one of the slowest to get going, I was able to study him at uncomfortably close quarters.

It was said that his long and colourful Hurricane career included a Battle of Britain bullet in the head. This was hearsay.

Perhaps because planes and ships were scarce, or front-line losses temporarily few, odd times saw groups of aircrew mouldering in reserve or transit camps dotted round the world and, it seemed to them, forgotten. Via the back lanes of the East our small party moved slowly and spasmodically to Egypt.

There, after only three months to get acclimatized and say hello to old friends, who'd trekked round the globe the other way, we were told to fly.

'Hurricanes or Kitties – whichever they have when you get there. Be ready in half an hour.'

We reached our 'drome at midnight, packed like pigs in the back of a truck, dog-tired and stiff with cold.

'Out, bods!' cried a sing-song English voice.

It was a hard, white night. Scattered pagoda-like EPI tents squatted moon-hazed in the sand. The 'Out, bods' voice said 'Three to a tent, chums, wakey-wakey 0430 hours.'

I chucked two blankets on the ground and passed out.

Waking grunts and snarls revealed that the other numbed hip bones in the tent belonged to Steve and Hawkeye. The new boys comprised Australians, Englishmen, and Canadians, plus one, Rafe, who'd made his way to this RAF 'drome from Texas. Most were sergeant-pilots, and in age retired schoolboys.

The 'drome was a big claypan. Sustained by what passed for tea at an ME RAF station we gathered flying-gear and started walking to the Flight tent nearly a mile away. The ground was spread with thick white fog and its surface was treacherously greasy.

A prairie voice said 'After all, when you get right down to it, in what way is this any different from Miami?'

Someone said 'The things they don't tell you in books!'

We heard on either side the reluctant stuttering of cold Merlins. Occasionally, silhouetted against the fog, we saw the ghostly, humpbacked shapes of sleeping Hurricanes.

'Easy, easy,' said Rafe, 'or we trip on an erk in the dark.'

The English fitters and riggers *did* seem jockey sized. They could be heard rumbling batteries about, shocking their winged charges into a fury of wakefulness. Exhaust flames lit figures clinging limpet-like to cockpits in icy, fog-swirling prop-blasts. You felt the brittle pre-dawn tension of any wartime 'drome.

A blot ahead became the Flight tent. It was formed by three joined EPIs. Inside some Irving-jacketed fellows turned and looked us over. They were young, quiet, and looked tired. Operational men, instructing for a 'rest'.

There was a muttered 'Your turn, Kim.'

One of them hooked his elbows on the 'chute-bench and kept looking at our faces, harsh-lit by a hanging globe. He threw his cap back on the bench. Lank, bleached hair topped a healthy brown face; a horse-kick scar circled one of his amber eyes, which had the round, unblinking look seen in some 'old' fighter-pilots. Medium build, a policeman would have said. Outside it was still dark. A soft Canadian voice ruffled the silence.

'I'm Kimber. Here we teach you to fight and shoot; to use an airplane as a weapon, not an airborne automobile. I guess you all know by now if you hold it wrong it kills *you*. We've got about a week to teach you all we can. No time for horse-dung on your part or ours. Out there,' thumbing the west, 'it's really grim. The tougher we make it here the longer, maybe, you'll last. I hear most of you haven't flown in a long time. Here's where you catch up. You'll find it's like riding a bike; you just don't forget. In a week you'll be flying rings round *us*; and that's the way it should be.' But he seemed humbly aware of the gap he had to bridge between our knowledge and his.

From outside came the fog-muffled but sustained and unmistakable sound of an aircraft committed to flight. A glance ricocheted among the instructors. They straightened and strode out and we followed. The noise churned around in the distance and we heard a groaned 'Not again, Mick, not again!'

Cat's-eyes head-high in the fog grew to twin moons, and, when we uncrouched, the tent still breathed in the turbulence. Again the Hurricane's landing-lights spread at us rocking as wing-tips were lifted over ill-seen obstacles.

'Urrrr, Mick, ye don't have to do it,' burred a voice near by. Soon we heard him taxi-ing.

'Who was it?' asked Hawkeye.

Kimber sighed 'The Squadron Leader, seeing if the fog's cleared for flying.'

As the fog thinned, a couple of circuits in two-seater Harvards gave us a bit of the feel back. I heard a heart-warming Australian voice in the earphones: 'Give her a burst for luck on the home turn – go for a fast-wheeler – tell Flight next gent., please.'

After breakfast a languid, droopy-moustached and fashionably unkempt type was nursing a dachshund near a Hurricane. He beckoned and indicated the cockpit, assuring the animal that this would only take a minute. Sitting among the unfamiliar gadgets, I listened to the cockpit drill. It wasn't much trouble, eyes shut, to put a hand on this and that. Then the dachshund-fancier said 'Don't be more than an hour old boy. Oh, and the Squadron Leader's watching.' Then he went away.

Gear on and back in the aircraft, the situation still seemed unreal. A battery was trundled under the nose. A voice in the cockpit screeched the 'All clear, contact' routine and I saw gloved fingers press the maggie buttons. The thing started without the slightest hesitation, and off went the erks and battery. Looking around I saw other props spinning and ground-crews trotting on to wreak more havoc among the atrophied pilots. Hell, it *must* be fair dinkum. And 'the Squadron Leader's watching'.

Brakes off, my machine gambolled along to take-off point like a cocker promised a walk. Round the forty-four gallon marker drums and into wind. Nothing for it but to push the throttle and hope.

Taking over from the Hurricane a few minutes later I rediscovered the Suez Canal by some masterly pin-point navigation and sneaked furtively along it wondering if there were any way of landing invisibly. Unable to move the lever, I'd been beetling around the sky wheels-down. And since the same handle worked flaps, I could only look forward to a slightly spectacular, high-speed, flapless arrival. With no gatecrashing on my part, a meeting with the fog-dispersing Squadron Leader seemed imminent.

As the Hurri. slowed to about sixty, a utility overhauled it. The driver's face seemed mottled with rage; his mouth was opening and shutting. Unable to hear him, I waved in 'See you later' fashion and parked.

Carrying the 'chute over the sand to the Flight tent I could hear someone screaming as if in unbearable pain. It was Squadron Leader Mick Mooney. He was screaming at me.

I walked up to him and stood still, wincing.

He was slightly built, dark, and a thin Hollywood moustache writhed like a snake along the violent contortions of his upper lip. The nose was small, sharp and hooked; the eyes opal-black in wrinkled slits of skin. He was perhaps thirty. That's all I saw the first time. Suddenly his voice dropped to a comparatively soothing level.

'How long since *you* flew?'

'Getting on for a year, sir.'

'No excuse for assuming the Hurricane has a fixed undercart. Overheats the motor. Looks bloody awful . . . *Do you expect every —— in the RAF to fly wheels-down so* YOU *can stay in formation!*'

'No, sir.'

'What did you fly?'

'Wirraways, sir.'

'Wirraway? Wirraway? What is it? Some half-feathered marsupial?'

With that Mooney turned and walked into the tent.

Shortly my dog-nursing adviser came out looking somewhat unsettled. He made quite a speech.

'It's all right, you know. I've just lost a strip, too. "Careless instruction." Please don't do it again. At least you did bring the plane back; somebody's vanished with one. Probably hocked it in Cairo. The Squadron Leader is taking five of you up now; formation take-off. Do remember that release-tit on the undercart lever.'

He made for the nearest sandbag and sat on it.

It was nine o'clock.

In the tent Mooney said to us 'We fly Hurricanes hood open and goggles off. Better vision. We also like your *eyes open!* Wing-tip clear of the next man's, able to move forward or back and level with his roundel. Form up at take-off point in the order you get there. Now *get cracking!'*

When we faced up at the barrier Mooney was waiting with all the patience of a fire-engine at traffic-lights. I found myself next to him, and he stared at me with what could only have been recognition. Up went the thumbs and we were racing. Some gremlin got in front of the throttle lever and risked a hernia. I trailed lengths behind on take-off.

The rest of the flight was uneventful. Pansy, practice stuff; it steadied the flying a lot. Mooney swept the formation gracefully round to land like a matador spreading a cape.

I heard it as my feet hit the sand.

'Put that bloody parachute *back!'* Mooney was standing near his plane fifty yards away aiming the words like bullets.

Signing at the Flight he spat out, 'You can't overtake the leader on take-off; he's watching you and progressively opening the throttle. This time open *yours!* Aeroplanes *want* to fly, *but you've got to help a little bit!'*

At the last moment I had to switch to another machine, the heaviest, faster four-cannon job. It had a lot more power for take-off. There were just the two of us. Determined not to be left behind again, I shoved the throttle lever forward with commendable enthusiasm. The look on Mooney's face as I sailed past him and soared alone into the dust-haze will live with me for ever. Back there no doubt he was 'progressively opening the throttle' until it came out by the roots.

I waited in a gentle turn. He came sliding up on the inside like a wide-finned, sand-coloured fish and led. Just above a low, thin cloud-layer Mooney signalled 'Line astern'. In this position, behind and a shade below, you look as though the leader were pulling you on a short string. The still air caused not even the usual gentle lift and sway of one plane in relation to another. We were as if fixed in space for ever.

In a flash he was upside-down. He hung there for a moment studying my reaction, then plummeted from sight. As he screwed down, my heavier plane seemed to be catching up. The thin cloud-screen whipped away, the canal twirled up, streamed by my shoulder, flecked with felucca sails and went. Dust-haze, white flicker of cloud, blue sky and, thank God, Mooney. I came to heel like a guilty pup who'd almost lost its master.

Again he rolled, dived, pulled out and rocketed into the face of the sun. His black silhouette dissolved in the furnace. I found him right beneath me like a shark under a fishing-boat. We must have looked like a biplane. Then he skidded to one side and did a brace of beautiful rolls. Struth, I thought, the man must be happy! He'd damn near led me into the ground.

Mooney darted for home. As I was closing up for landing he shied violently sideways like a startled horse. I edged back alongside and we landed. On the ground he shouted 'Blast you! Out here *never* join up from astern – come in from the beam so we know what you are! You'd better get some lunch.'

Rafe was standing in the sun, hand-talking excitedly to Steve and some Canadians. The pilots' universal pantomime, infuriating when abused, can describe almost anything that happens in the air. Rafe's hands converged with a smack and separated, fluttering groundwards. The inevitable 'who was it?' brought 'Couple English fellers in a practice dogfight – man, you shoulder seen it. One baled out.'

The 'drome was now hot and dry. Walking to lunch Hawkeye said 'This time yesterday we were busy swatting flies at Almaza.'

Wacker said 'Yes, flat out trying to fill in time!'

Some of the lunch-time babble: 'They found the type who disappeared this morning, about thirty miles away.'

'OK?'

'Dead as a doornail – force-landed wheels down in soft sand.'

'Oh, bloody bad luck!'

'Bloody clueless!'

'Been up with friend Mooney?'

'Not yet and not anxious. Believe he put an Aussie through it this morning.'

'Don't worry. Puts everyone through it in turn.'

'Yes – if you don't stick in like a dart you're OK.'

About sundown a group of us, feeling justifiably weary, stood watching the last formations washing off speed before landing. Hurricanes came shoaling in shark-like over the sand; sank into the dusk and lost shape.

The beer tasted good. Even the food seemed palatable. The tension was off.

In the dark next morning Mooney performed his tent-high fog-churning chore and stepped into the Flight tent.

'Start with you again,' he said. 'Individual attacks with film. Come in from five hundred yards out and a thousand feet above. And for God's sake *fly!*'

We climbed, levelled, separated, and I turned to wait for him. The day exploded over Egypt in a kaleidoscopic broken-egg vastness of cloud and air. A black speck raced towards me along the rim of a mile-high blood-red cliff of cumulus. The world pitched on its side, streaked past the cowling, steadied, and there was Mooney far too small in the ringsight. I fired the camera-gun, broke away and climbed. Must be quicker next time.

After half an hour of this we dived to breakfast.

Armourers took the film, and I rather hoped they'd lose it. Mooney shouted 'Out of range and no deflection! *Get in close!* You don't hit 'em when you're pointing *at* 'em. Be here after breakfast and *bloody well get it right!*'

Rafe said 'Jeez, you must hate that guy.'

'No, strangely enough,' I said.

'Strangely enough, I *do!*' said an Englishman, with curious intensity. He was a tall bloke standing, bare-headed, in open battlejacket and shorts. His long, thin face was expressionless; and the reddish colour of his tight-kinked hair showed in the skin and flecked his eyes. He said no more.

Later Mooney was squatting, head bowed, on a sandbag. Faded cap, bulky fleece-lined jacket, spindly drab-clad legs. A white pup sat between his shoes and he was patting it. Suddenly, he twisted and shouted back into the Flight tent, 'Where's my bloody utility?' The pup scuttled away.

A sergeant came out and said 'Transport's fixin' it, sir.'

'Fixing it or mucking it?' He raced into the tent and grabbed the telephone. 'Transport? Bring back that bloody truck or I'll drive a Hurricane tail-up where I want to go! Get your bloody fingers out. *I've had you, Transport!*'

He crashed the phone to the table and ran to the nearest plane. The motor burst into life and the tail swung and lifted as he raced down the mile-long road to the administrative section. I sat and waited.

A plane had landed and taxied to a stop near by. I recognized the pilot as the red-haired Mooney-hater. He was said to be eccentric. Some fitters gathered expectantly. The pilot rose in the cockpit, stood rigid and announced at the top of his voice, 'Once again man has defied Nature.' The show was over.

Some of the erks were staring upward. A plane was spinning high in the sky. A sergeant growled 'Now then, lads, ain't y' seen 'em doin' that before?' They still looked up. Kimber, inside, sensed something and came out. 'Goddam it man, pull *out!*'

Mooney, who had returned unnoticed, said 'He can't, or he would,' and went into the tent.

Black smoke rose a couple of miles out in the sand and Mooney was saying on the phone 'I'll tell you, sir, when we know who it was,' when a Hurricane came in and landed very fast. When it taxied we saw a third of one wing was missing. It was Steve who climbed out. He was sweating and shivering.

He said 'Me and Wacker – did he get *out*, Freddie?'

I said 'No.'

Mooney said 'No; you seem to have won. See the MO, then see me.'

To me he said 'Up, Jackson – let's get some dung off our livers. *And this time come in close!*'

I found myself shouting 'I'm doing my best! I'll show you "coming in close!"'

Mooney's smile was like the Mona Lisa's.

A Canadian sergeant-instructor waiting near my plane said 'Take it easy; makin' guys mad's his technique.'

The first attack was far too close. The other plane suddenly overflowed ringsight, windscreen, and filled most of the view ahead. I wallowed in Mooney's wash before striking solid air and breaking away. My plane got the bit in its teeth and bored in each time as though bent on gnawing Mooney's tail off. When the cine-gun ran out of film we landed.

Mooney screamed 'You came to within *seven feet!* Are you trying to *mate 'em?*'

'Anything for variety,' I said.

No comment.

After lunch Mooney flew with the Eccentric; the post-mortem was a delight to hear.

'I propose to cite you as listless, slow, consistent only in unreliability, and without a vestige of natural ability.'

'But, sir, nothing detrimental, I hope!'

That night in the crowded film hut there was some beautiful demonstration stuff by Kimber – bead stuck like glue ahead of the target's spinning prop while the cloudy backdrop whirled and raced. My own film was frightening to watch. The target turned its tail into the camera and hurtled at us, filling the screen with belly and tail before it flicked from sight.

The film interpreter said 'God! You could count the rivets!'

There was another exclamation and someone said 'That was the Squadron Leader. He's gone.' Each pilot's films were run off to expert comment such as 'Deflection about right – slightly out of range – that's better – bad button-stabbing – longer squirts, please.'

The Eccentric's reel, after showing the usual whirling emptiness of sky with occasional views of aircraft, concluded with a screen-filling close-up of the stolid face of an armourer.

After a moment of stunned silence the interpreter said 'Surprise ending!'

Back in the sergeants' mess the senior WO answered a knock on the door and returned with the Squadron Leader, dapper and polished, black hair close-brushed and shining.

Tombstone asked 'Like a beer, sir?' Mooney dragged up a stick-and-canvas chair and sat down.

The Eccentric rose gracefully and carried his drink to the trestle bar. There, feet crossed, and comfortably hooked by his elbows, he stared back at us. A hanging bar-light glowed on the fiery hair, narrow forehead, high nose and cheekbones. The rest was shadow.

Mooney, sitting low in the chair, looked steadily at him, dead pan and rigid. I had a curious feeling that the Eccentric stood, remote, to better *concentrate* on Mooney. His attitude had a bone-pointing quality.

Tombstone came back and whacked beer on the table; and the honest sound was welcome.

Mooney said smoothly 'Ah! Quick work, Tomson – looks a nice drop. Luck!'

Turning my way, he said 'That was extremely dangerous today. Strike the happy medium. Smoke?'

More instructors came in and joined the growing circle. Flying reverted to its proper status – 'a piece of cake'; child's play.

An Englishman tossed in a suggestion for a list of fineable

offences to be posted in the Flight. From fifty-ackers for a landing- or taxi-ing-prang to ten for 'goddam' or 'son-of-a-bitch'.

Rafe said 'Yeah, and fifty for "a-a-actualleh!"'

'What price breaking a neck?' shot from the figure under the bar-light.

There was a noticeable sprinkling of DFCs and a couple of DFMs on the instructors' khaki tunics. Affecting eye-trouble, Rafe jumped in with 'so many goddam gongs here a guy could hammer out the Anvil Chorus!'

Steve's laugh startled me – he'd been unnaturally quiet for a kid who laughed easily.

Mooney turned on him. 'Hear you've some damned good songs, Hampton. What about it?'

The usual all-in sing-song developed from tentative 'da-de-das' among the more cautious to full-throated competition, ending in husky good-nights and sleep.

One morning was cloudless and perfect for shadow-shooting. We did this in pairs using the four-cannon machines. You dived at the other man's shadow, and the spurts of sand showed where your shells were hitting. Burton, an English pupil, went with Hawkeye. Hawkeye returned alone and reported Burton crashed while shooting.

Mooney, writing at a trestle-table, grunted, 'Probably selected his own shadow and pressed home the attack.'

Thwaites, of the dachshund, picked up a piece of cloth, walked to the roster-board and looked inquiringly at Hawkeye, who nodded. Thwaites erased Burton's name and went to the telephone.

About an hour later, Lofty, who did everything with a flourish, turned an ordinary run-of-the-mill forced landing into an arrival to write home about. When the engine cut he dropped the wheels and tried to reach the 'drome. Skimming a distant sandhill, he hit a nearer one and bounced two hundred yards on to the runway. No damage. Lofty had already established a formidable reputation for luck at poker, crap, and the Gezira races; so, naturally, Mooney was flying and not available for immediate comment.

He was giving the Eccentric a last-chance test in individual combat. On the joystick were two buttons, one camera and the other guns; and it was important not to confuse exercises. After this one Mooney treated his languid opponent to a brilliant, if vitriolic, discourse on deflection.

He was saying 'Well, what the bloody hell *were* you aiming at? Certainly couldn't have been me!' when he noticed a rigger at attention beside him. 'Well, what do you want?'

'Sergeant Smithers, sir; he just found a bullet hole in your tail-plane, sir.'

Mooney swung back to face the Eccentric, who didn't miss the trick. 'Certainly couldn't have been me,' he said.

Mooney knew when to be silent.

In the mess afterwards I heard a whisper that the Eccentric a-a-actually was really rather hot. Just didn't want to be in it. Someone had seen him doing things when he thought no one was looking. And that a few days ago he'd forgotten himself and pulled off a wizard bit of flying, then deliberately mucked it up. Rafe voiced a wish that in his own case this process could be occasionally reversed. The man from Texas provided the following morning's chai-time entertainment:

'Ambitioning' to ultimately join a Yank unit, he'd 'organized' a Kittyhawk. Landing the first time, he was travelling so fast that when he tried to put the flaps down nothing happened. He touched down at some extravagant speed, hurtled across the 'drome with fire-tender in pursuit, saw a sandbank and date-palms coming at him, took off again and barely cleared them. He went round again and this time got in nicely.

As we picked up our tea-mugs again Kimber said 'God send me back to the war where I'm safe.'

'Touching on that,' said Thwaites, 'Mick intends to give the hundred-and-nine a whizz round after lunch.'

The captured Messerschmitt 109 was a neat little job; and half the fuselage seemed engine. It heated quickly on the ground and was started up at take-off point. Mooney got in and went. The cooling system blew up and an oil-pipe burst. With cockpit full of fumes and oil, the ME came over at about a hundred and fifty feet, leaving a snowy trail of glycol.

Mooney, half-blinded, and with little control, was a trier. He skidded round and reached the runaway via a gap between some tents and a parked Tomahawk. The Messerschmitt crouched steaming with fury; and Lofty said 'Must be a one-man dog'.

Mooney drove to the mess.

Before breakfast on our second-last day the Eccentric stood facing Mooney on the sand between their planes. We could hear Mooney's voice, pitched high.

'That was a bloody stinking gutless imitation of an attack! Your breakaway perfect example of straight and level flying! Aren't you *game to do it!*'

What the Eccentric said we don't know. Mooney seemed about to spring; then turned and came toward the tent. The Eccentric just stood out there staring after him.

During that afternoon vapour trails marked the high, blue ceiling of the sky; and, looking up, we saw a pin-point star of fire.

Mooney burst out '*Burn, you bastard, burn!*' and watched it down the long air-lane to the horizon. Some Arab workmen also watched; and one asked 'Inglezi?'

Mooney blasted them. 'How the bloody hell should *we* know? *Escut! Yallahimshi!*'

He strode off, his small black shoes jabbing the sand.

Thwaites said to Kimber 'Saw him cannon-firing at a camel today, all directions. Wog chappie scuttling around seeking safe side of the beast.'

An Australian instructor laughed. 'Believe he'd spend his last leave with a saucer of milk and a waddy – killing cats.'

I said 'Oh, I dunno – saw him one day patting a pup.'

'Probably interrupted him,' said the Eccentric. 'Anyway, he shan't kill *me!*'

There were curious glances at the speaker; the chatter had ended on a wrong note.

Trudging over a sandhill in the dark next morning, pilots saw a plane, wing-lights ablaze, rolling along the surface of the low fog.

'Aha! The act's improving!' exclaimed someone unseen.

This was the day of the ultimate demonstration.

The crew of the Nazi JU88, briefed to scan the port, had no thought of meeting Mooney in the final frenzy. The 88's four-Messerschmitt escort, too, must have been surprised. Mooney had attained the suicidal recklessness which sometimes accompanies the limit of fatigue.

In a bloodshot mackerel sky the four school Hurricanes weaved in loose patrol formation at 15,000 feet, Mooney and his three charges – Lofty, the Eccentric, and myself. It was the hour when

'Lo! The hunter in the East has caught the sultan's turret in a noose of light.'

At the sight of a simple, stupid minor accident Mooney had led us off downward in silent fury. In the bracing upper air the camouflaged, light-bellied planes performed a wobbegong quadrille. I was singing with the engine 'First lady forward; second lady back.'

Our leader, just ahead, rolled violently, and, wings vertical, skidded high above. Beneath him streaked a three-pronged, black-crossed shape and a Hurricane shrank in vertical pursuit. They faded chameleon-like into the emptiness below.

My head almost whanged the cockpit edge; it surprised me that the plane was diving and dodging.

A Hurri. was plunging abreast of me, barrelling. Beyond it another was simply standing on its nose. And hurtling past us dived the four Messerschmitts. Sleek darts with a flash of sun on them.

Intent on removing the threat that was Mooney, they'd left their run too late. As my controls glued stiff with speed I saw an orange-coloured shooting-star below.

The radio crackled in my ears, and this time I got some words '– get 'em on the way up.'

The Eccentric turned away; he was pulling out. With the anticipation of a veteran he cut the corner of the Germans' dive and zoom. I followed, with a momentary impression that he'd done this thing before; and sand, sea, and sky all misted into blackness.

With vision clearing and face back in position, I saw one of the gnats, rocketing after Mooney, trailing smoke. As the Hurricane behind it pulled away an ME followed with the inevitability of a shadow. I heard myself screech something on the radio.

We all winged over in a curve of flight that seemed as pre-ordained as the path of planets.

A Hurricane like a humpbacked projectile came firing on a tangent, and I hastily took thumb off cannon-button. The Eccentric's German shadow staggered, flipped over, shedding pieces from a wing-root and vanished. Something struck my plane with a terrifying 'Crack!'

Desperate shove on rudder-pedal, stick in corner, and I spiralled in a maelstrom of confusion. I lifted hard against the safety-harness and slammed back with a spine-buckling jar. The goggles dropped down over my eyes and I snatched left hand from throttle and pushed them off.

There was a taste of bile, smell of petrol, black-out, sight again. Going straight up.

Comparative calm, and an even keel restored, with no apparent damage, I did some overdue looking around.

To my left an ME nosed shell-like from the depths, turned, levelled. Above, a Hurricane poised, falcon-like, careening, whirled, and with split-second fury struck.

A black-crossed wing spun feather-light in a dust of smaller fragments. Flame blossomed in the air below; then the sky was empty.

I flew home feeling that I'd sat out an exhausting film.

On the 'drome:

'Freddie! Were you in that do? Here, have a smoke!'

'Light it for me. I was there – and that's about all.'

'Lofty's back – boy, you should see his kite!'

'They reckon Mooney got an eighty-eight, and an ME went off smoking.'

'On a training flight!'

'Probably arranged the whole thing.'

'Oh, fair go!'

Kimber came into the circle with Lofty. He said 'OK? Well, what did *you* see of it?'

'A bloody awful collision – Hurricane rammed an ME.'

'So the ack-ack says on the phone. See who it was?'

'No.'

'The long red guy – pounds to ackers,' said Rafe.

I said 'Well, he shot one down, I think.'

With the phone filling in the gaps, the picture fell together: the JU88 skimming the desert, burning like a torch; the doomed reargunner still firing point-blank back at Mooney. In the vengeful skyward chase two ME's hit, and the collision.

Someone suggested that whoever rammed the German had been hit mortally; nothing to lose. A German had baled out OK.

My plane seemed to have been struck by a bit off another aircraft.

A Hurricane screamed low across the 'drome, flashed over us, zoomed, and circled to land.

A dozen voices: *'Mooney!'*

The prop stopped spinning and the pilot shed his headgear. We saw the red thatch of the Eccentric. It was the first time we'd seen him laughing.

JULIAN MACLAREN-ROSS · 1912–1964

I had to go sick

I HADN'T been in the Army long at the time. About a week, not more. We were marching round the square one afternoon and I couldn't keep in step. The corporal kept calling out 'Left, left,' but it didn't do any good. In the end the corporal told me to fall out. The platoon sergeant came rushing up and said 'What the hell's wrong with you, man? Why can't you hold the step?'

I didn't know, I couldn't tell him. There was an officer on the square, and the sergeant-major and they were both watching us.

'Got anything wrong with your leg?' the sergeant said. 'Your left leg?'

'I've got a scar on it Sergeant,' I told him.

'Dekko,' the sergeant said.

So I rolled up my trouser leg and showed him the scar on my knee. The sergeant looked at it and shook his head. 'That don't look too good, lad,' he said. 'How'd you come to get it?'

'I was knocked down by a bike. Years ago.'

By this time the sergeant-major had come up and he looked at the scar too. 'What's your category, lad?' he asked me. 'A1?'

'Yes sir.'

'Well you go sick tomorrow morning and let the MO have a look at that leg. Meantime sit in that shed over there till it's time to fall out.'

There was a Bren Gun lesson going on in the shed when I got there. My arrival interrupted it. 'Who the hell are you?' the NCO taking the lesson asked me. 'What d'you want?'

'I've been sent over here to sit down Corporal.'

'To sit down?'

'Sergeant-major sent me.'

'Oh well if he sent you that's all right. But don't go opening your trap, see? Keep mum and don't say nothing.'

'Very good Corporal.'

'Not so much of it,' the corporal said.

The lesson went on. I listened but couldn't understand what it was all about. I'd never seen a Bren Gun before. And then the corporal's pronunciation didn't help matters. I sat there in the shed until everyone else had fallen out. Then the sergeant-major came over to me.

'Fall out,' he said. 'What're you waiting for. Parade's over for the day, you're dismissed. And don't forget – you go sick tomorrow morning,' he shouted after me.

'How do I go sick?' I asked the other fellows, back in the barrack-room.

They didn't know, none of them had ever been sick. 'Ask the Sarnt' they said.

But I couldn't find the sergeant, or the corporal either. They'd gone off to a dance in the town. So I went down to the cookhouse and there was an old sweat sitting on a bucket outside, peeling spuds. You could see he was an old sweat because he was in shirt sleeves and his arms were tattooed all over. So I asked him how to go sick and he said 'Ah, swinging the lead, eh? MO'll mark you down in red ink, likely.'

'What happens if he does that?'

'CB for a cert. Scrubbing, or mebbe a spot of spud bashing. You won't get less than seven days, anyhow.'

'What, seven days CB for going sick?'

'Sure, if you're swinging the lead. Stands to reason. There ain't nothing wrong with you now is there? A1, aintcher?'

'Yes.'

'There you are then. You'll get seven all right,' said the sweat. 'What d'you expect. All you lads are alike. Bleeding lead swingers the lot of you.'

He spat on the ground and went on peeling spuds. I could see he wasn't going to say any more so I walked on. Further along I stopped by another old sweat. This second sweat was even older and more tattooed than the first one. And he hadn't any teeth.

'Excuse me,' I said, 'Can you tell me how to go sick?'

'Go sick?' said this second, toothless sweat. 'You don't want to do that.'

'Why not?' I said.

'Well look at me. Went sick I did with a pain in the guts, and what's the MO do? Silly bleeder sent me down the Dental Centre and had them take all me teeth out. I ask you, do it make sense? Course it don't. You got the guts-ache and they pull out all your teeth. Bleeding silly. And they ain't given me no new teeth neither and here I been waiting six munce. No,' said the sweat, 'You don't want to go sick. Take my tip, lad: keep away from that there MO long as you can.'

'But I've got to go sick. I've been ordered to.'

'Who by?'

'Sergeant-major.'

'What's wrong with you?'

'My leg, so they say.'

'Your leg? Then mebbe they'll take your teeth out too. Ain't no knowing what they'll do once they start on you. I'm bleeding browned-off with the bleeding sick I am.'

'Well how do I go about it?'

'See your Orderly Sarnt. Down Company Office. He's the bloke you want.'

On the door of the orderly sergeant's bunk it said KNOCK AND WAIT. I did both and a voice shouted 'Come in, come in. Don't need to bash the bleeding door down.'

There was a corporal sitting at a table covered with a blanket writing laboriously on a sheet of paper.

'Yeh?' he said, looking up. 'What d'you want?'

'I was looking for the Orderly Sergeant,' I said.

'I'm the Orderly Sergeant,' said the corporal. 'State your business and be quick about it. I ain't got all night.'

'I want to go sick Sergeant. I mean Corporal.'

'Don't you go making no smart cracks here,' said the corporal. 'And stand properly to attention when you speak to an NCO.'

'Sorry Corporal.'

'Ain't no such word in the British Army,' the corporal told me. 'Now what's your name? Age? Service? Religion? Medical Category? Okay, you parade outside here 8.30 tomorrow morning. On the dot.'

I went to go out, but the corporal called me back. 'Here, half a mo. How d'you spell Picquet. One K or two?'

'No K's at all Corporal,' I told him.

'Listen didn't I tell you not to be funny? I'll stick you on a chitty so help me if you ain't careful. How d'you mean, no K's. How can you spell Picquet without no K's?'

I explained. The corporal looked suspicious. 'Sure? You ain't trying to be funny?'

'No Corporal. P-i-c-q-u-e-t.'

'Okay.' He wrote it down. 'Need a bleeding dictionary to write this bastard out,' he muttered, and then looking up: 'All right, what're you waiting for. Scram. Gillo! And don't forget: 0830 tomorrow. Bring your small kit in case.'

I didn't like to ask him in case of what. I got out quick before he gave me scrubbing or spud-bashing or tried to take my teeth out maybe.

I didn't sleep too well that night, I can tell you. Next morning at 0830 there I was outside the orderly sergeant's bunk with my small kit: I'd found out from our sergeant what that was. There were quite a lot of other fellows there as well. It's funny how they pass you A1 into the army and then find out you're nothing of the sort. One of these fellows had flat feet, another weak lungs, and a third reckoned he was ruptured.

After a while the corporal came out. 'All right,' he said. 'Get fell in, the sick.'

We fell in and were marched down to the MI Room.

'Keep in step, you!' the corporal shouted at me. 'Christ, can't you keep step?'

Down at the MI Room it said on the walls NO SMOKING, NO SPITTING, and we sat around waiting for our names to be called out. At last mine was called and I went in. The MO looked up. 'Yes, what's wrong with you?'

I looked round. There were two fellows standing behind me waiting their turn. A third was putting on his trousers in a corner. More crowded in the doorway behind. I felt silly with all these fellows listening in. I didn't know what to say.

'Come on, out with it,' said the MO. 'Or perhaps it's something you'd rather say in private?'

'Well sir, I would prefer it.'

'Right. Come back at five tonight.'

I went out again.

'What'd you get?' the orderly sergeant asked me.

'He said to come back at five Corporal.'

'What's wrong? Got the clap?'

'No Corporal.'

'Crabs, maybe?'

'No, not crabs.'

'Well what the hell you want to see him in private for, then? Only blokes with VD see him in private as a rule. Unless they've crabs.'

At five I reported back to the MI Room.

'Right,' said the medical corporal. 'This way. Cap off. Don't salute.'

The MO said, 'Ah yes. Sit down and tell me about it.'

I did. He seemed a bit disappointed that I hadn't VD but in the end he examined my leg.

'Does it hurt? No? What about if you kneel on it? H'm, yes, there's something wrong there. You'd better see the specialist. Report here tomorrow at ten.'

The specialist was at a hospital some miles away from the camp. He said 'Try and straighten the leg. What, you can't? All right. Put your trousers on and wait outside.'

Pretty soon an orderly came out with a chitty. 'You're to have treatment twice a week,' he told me. 'Electrical massage. This way.'

I followed him down a lot of corridors and finally out into the grounds and up some steps into a hut with MASSAGE on a board outside it. There I lay down on a table and a nurse strapped some sort of pad on my thigh. After that they gave me a series of shocks from an electric battery. It lasted about half an hour.

'Feeling better?' the nurse asked me when it was over.

'No,' I said.

I could hardly walk.

'That'll wear off by and by,' said the nurse.

I drove in by an ambulance to the MI Room.

'Had your treatment?'

'Yes sir.'

The MO started to write something on a piece of paper. I was a bit nervous in case he used the red ink. But he didn't after all. He used blue ink instead. 'Give this to your orderly sergeant,' he said.

On the piece of paper it said. 'Att. C.'

'Attend C!' said the orderly sergeant. 'Cor you got it cushy ain't you?'

'What's it mean Corporal?' I asked.

'Attend C? Excused all duties. Bleeding march coming off tomorrow and all.'

Two days later I went to the hospital again. After a week or two of treatment I'd developed quite a limp. The fellows all said I was swinging the lead. I limped about the camp doing nothing, in the intervals of having more electric shock. Then, after about three weeks, the MO sent for me again.

'Is your leg any better now?'

'No sir,' I said.

'Treatment not doing you any good?'

'No sir.'

'H'm. Well I'd better put you down for a medical board in that case.'

So I didn't even go to the hospital any more. I used to lie on my bed all day long reading a book. But I got tired of that because I only had one book and I wasn't allowed out owing to being on sick. There weren't any other books in the camp. Meanwhile the fellows were marching and drilling and firing on the range, and the man in the next bed to me suddenly developed a stripe. This shook me, so I thought I'd go and see the sergeant-major.

I was a bit nervous when I got to his office. The sergeant-major had an alarming appearance. He looked almost exactly like an ape. Only he'd less hair on him, of course. But he was quite a decent fellow really.

When I came in he was telling two clerks and an ATS girl how he'd nailed a native's hand to his desk during his service in India. He broke off this recital when he saw me standing there. 'Yes, lad, what d'you want?'

I explained that I was waiting for a medical board and meantime had nothing to do, as I was excused parades.

'But d'you WANT something to do?' the sergeant-major asked. He seemed stupefied.

'Yes sir,' I said. 'I didn't join the Army to do nothing all day.'

The two clerks looked up when I said that, and the ATS stared at me with her mouth open. The sergeant-major breathed heavily through his nose. Then he said, 'Can you use a typewriter, lad?'

'Yes sir,' I said.

'Ah!' He jumped up from his table. 'Then sit you down here and show us how to use this ruddy thing. It's only just been sent us, see, and none of us know how to make the bleeder go.'

It was a very old typewriter, an Oliver. I'd used one before, so I didn't find it too difficult. Soon I was typing out long lists of names and other stuff full of initials and abbreviations that I didn't know the meaning of. Sometimes I couldn't read the handwriting, especially if one of the officers had written it, but the ATS used to translate for me.

Then one day the company commander walked in.

'Who's this man?' he said, pointing at me with his stick.

'Sick man, sir,' the sergeant-major said. 'Waiting a medical board.'

'Well he can't wait for it here. We're not allowed any more clerks. You've enough clerks already,' and he walked out again, after hitting my table a whack with his stick.

'All right, fall out,' the sergeant-major said to me. 'Back to your bunk.'

'Now we've no one to work the typewriter,' he said. 'Have to do it all by hand. Hell.'

Next day the orderly sergeant told me to go sick again. I'd got used to it by now. The other fellows called me the MO's right marker.

This time it was a new MO: the other one had been posted elsewhere.

'Well what's wrong with you?' he said.

I explained my case all over again.

'Let's see your leg.' He looked at it for a moment and then said, 'Well there's nothing wrong with that, is there?'

'Isn't there, sir?'

'No.' He poked at the scar, seized hold of my leg, bent it, straightened it a few times and then looked puzzled. 'H'm. There is something wrong after all. You'd better have a medical board.'

'I'm down for one already, sir.'

'What? Well why the devil didn't you say so then? Wasting my time. All right. You can go now.'

In the morning the orderly sergeant came into our hut. 'Get your small kit together,' he said, 'and be down the MI Room in ten minutes. You're for a medical board. It come through just now.'

At the hospital I sat for some time in a waiting room and nobody came near me. It was another hospital, not the one I used to go to for treatment. Then at last an officer came in. I stood up. He was a colonel.

'Carry on, carry on,' he said, and smiled very kindly. 'What's *your* trouble eh?'

'I'm waiting for a medical board, sir.'

'A medical board? What for?'

'I have trouble with my knee, sir.'

'Oh? What happens? Does it swell up?'

'No sir.'

'What, no swelling? H'm. Well come with me, we'll soon have you fixed up.' I followed this kindly colonel to the reception desk. 'Take this man along to Ward 9,' he told an orderly.

So I went along to Ward 9 and all the beds in it were empty except for one man sitting up in bed doing a jigsaw puzzle.

'Watcher, mate,' this man said. 'What you got? Ulcers, maybe?'

'Ulcers? No,' I said.

Then a nurse came in. 'Ah, you're the new patient. This way to the bathroom. Here are the pyjamas you change into afterwards.'

'Pyjamas?' I said

'Yes,' said the nurse. 'And directly you've bathed and got your pyjamas on you hop into this bed here,' and she pointed to one next the man with ulcers.

'But I don't want to go to bed,' I said. 'I'm not a bed patient. There's nothing wrong with me.'

'Then why are you here?'

'Nothing wrong with me like that, I mean. I'm waiting for a medical board.'

'Oh. Wait here a moment, please.' She fetched the orderly. The orderly said, 'SMO's orders he was to be brought here. Said it hisself. The SMO Ward 9, he said.'

'But this ward is for gastric cases,' the nurse said. 'This man isn't a gastric case.'

'I don't know nothing about that,' the orderly told her, and he went off.

The nurse said, 'There's some mistake. I'll see about it while you have your bath.'

So I had a bath and when I came out she gave me some blue clothes and a shirt and a red tie to put on and said I needn't go to bed.

'You'll have to stay here until we get this straightened out,' she said. 'Would you like anything to eat?'

'I would, thank you Nurse.'

'Well there's only milk pudding. This ward's for gastrics you see.'

'You won't get very fat on that, mate,' the man with ulcers said.

He was right. I ate two lots of milk pudding but still felt hungry afterwards. Then later on the MO came round. A lieutenant, he was. Quite young. He looked at my leg and said, 'This man's a surgical case, Nurse. What's he doing in here?'

'SMO's orders, doctor.'

'Oh. Well he'll have to stay here then.'

'How long will it be before I get this medical board, sir?' I said.

'Medical board? Might be months. Meantime you stay here. Yes, you can have chicken. Give him some chicken, Nurse.'

So he went away and I ate the chicken.

'Wish I was you, mate,' said the man with ulcers.

It wasn't so bad being in the hospital except that you only got eight-and-six on pay day. Every morning I used to go down to the massage department. 'Electrical massage's no good for your trouble,' said the MO. 'We'll try ordinary massage.' So I had ordinary massage and then sat on a table with a weight tied to my leg swinging it to-and-fro.

'Now I know what swinging the lead means,' I said.

I used to have to lie down for two hours a day to recover from the treatment. I was limping quite heavily by the time the MO put his head in one morning and said 'You're for a Board today. Twelve o'clock down in my office.'

I waited outside the office nervously. I thought they might order me to have my teeth out. But they didn't. I was called in and there were three medical officers, one a lieutenant-colonel, who asked me a lot of questions and examined my leg, and then I went back to the ward.

'How'd you get on, mate?' asked the ulcers-man. 'What'd they do?'

'I don't know,' I said. 'They didn't tell me.'

But that evening the MO came in and said, 'You've been graded B2.'

'What does that mean, sir?'

'Garrison duties at home and abroad.'

'Can I go back to the camp then, sir?'

'Not until the papers come through.'

A few days later he sent for me. In his office. 'Something's gone wrong,' he said. 'We've slipped up. It seems you should have seen the surgical specialist before having the Board. But you didn't, so these papers aren't valid. You'll have to have another Board now.'

'When'll that be, sir?'

'I don't know. Don't ask me.'

So that afternoon I saw the surgical specialist. He was a major, although he seemed quite young. He was very nice and cheerful and laughed a lot.

'Lie down on the table,' he said. 'That's right. Relax. Now bend the knee. Now straighten it. Hold it. Hold it. Try to hold it steady. Ha ha! You can't, can you? Ha ha! Of course you can't. You've got no tendon in it, that's why. The patella tendon. It's bust. How long ago did you say the accident . . .? Sixteen years? Good lord, nothing we can do about it now. You'll have to be awfully careful, though. No running, no jumping. If you were to jump down into a trench your leg'd snap like a twig. Can't understand how they ever passed you A1. Ha ha! Well I'll make my report on you right away. Oughtn't to be in the infantry with a leg like that at all.'

I went back to Ward 9. It was supper time. Junket.

'Can't keep it down,' said the man with ulcers, and he proved this by bringing it up again.

Well then the MO went on leave.

'Now you stay here,' he told me, 'until the next Board comes off. Don't suppose it'll be till I'm back from my seven days. Meantime you stay put.'

'Yes sir,' I said.

But in the morning a new MO came round. He was a captain. With him was the Matron. 'Stand by your beds!' he called out as he came in.

The ward had filled up in the last week or two, but most of the patients were in bed, so they couldn't obey. The five of us who were up came belatedly to attention.

'Bad discipline in this ward Matron,' the captain said. 'Very slack. Who's the senior NCO here?'

There was only one NCO among the lot of us: a lance-corporal. He was up, as it happened, so he came in for an awful chewing-off.

'You've got to keep better order than this, Corporal,' said the captain. 'See that the men pay proper respect to an Officer when he enters the ward. If I've any further cause for complaint I shall hold you responsible. Also the beds aren't properly in line. I'm not satisfied with this ward, not satisfied at *all*. I hope to see some improvement when I come round tomorrow. Otherwise . . .'

He walked on round the beds examining the patients in turn. The ward was electrified. He ordered most of the bed patients to get up and those who were up to go to bed. Except the lance-corporal, who had to keep order, and me. As for the man with ulcers, he was ordered out of the ward altogether. I was last on the list, standing by the end bed, when he came up.

'This man is fit to return to his unit Matron,' he said when he'd looked at me.

'But he's awaiting a medical board Doctor,' the matron said.

'Well he can wait for it at his unit. We're not running a home for soldiers awaiting medical boards. I never heard of such a thing.'

'Lieutenant Jackson said . . .'

'Never mind what he said. I'm in charge here now, and I've just given an order. This man will return to his unit forthwith.'

Then he walked out and the matron went too. Two nurses came in and helped the man with ulcers into a wheelchair. 'So long, mates,' he said, then they wheeled him away. I don't know what became of him: he just disappeared. After that we straightened the beds and got them all in line.

'Keep order,' said the lance-corporal. 'Why the hell should I keep order. I'm not an NCO no more, they'll revert me soon's I get back. I'm Y listed, see? A bloody private, so why should I bother? Bleeding sauce.'

I wondered when they were going to chuck me out. Forthwith, he'd said, and forthwith turned out to be the next day.

I left about two o'clock. In a lorry. It dropped me at the station and I'd two hours to wait for a train. At last I got back to the camp and it looked all changed somehow, with no one about. Everything seemed shut up. I reported to the orderly sergeant's bunk. Sitting in it was a corporal I'd never seen before.

'Who're you?' he said. 'What d'you want?'

I told him.

'No one told us you was coming,' said this new corporal, scratching his head. 'All the others have cleared off. Jerry been bombing the camp, see? We've been evacuated. Last draft leaves tomorrow.'

'Am I on it?'

'You'll be on it all right.'

'Well where do I sleep? And what about my kit.'

'That'll be in the stores, I suppose. Buggered if I know. I'm from another company, I don't know nothing about you. Wait here, I'll see the storeman.'

But the storeman was out, and the stores were locked up. The corporal came back scratching his head.

'Buggered if I know when he'll be back. Gone on the piss I

shouldn't wonder. You better find a place to kip down. Here's a coupla blankets, if that's any use to you.'

Eventually I found a barrack room that wasn't locked: all the other huts were closed up. There were two other blokes in this room, both out of hospital. 'Where're we going to, mate?' they asked me.

'Damned if I know.'

'Nobody bloody well does know, that's the rub.'

At last, after a lot of conjecture, we dossed down for the night. It was autumn by now and turning cold and my two blankets didn't keep me very warm. I slept in all my clothes. Jerry came over during the night but didn't drop any bombs, or if he did we didn't hear them.

Then in the morning the corporal appeared. 'I've found some of your kit left.' Most of it had been pinched. My overcoat was gone and another one, much too small, left in its place.

'I don't know nothing about it,' said the storeman.

'You better get some breakfast,' the corporal said. 'I'll sort this lot out for you.'

Breakfast was a bacon sandwich, all the cookhouse fires had been let out.

'Bloody lark this is, ain't it?' said the cooks.

'You're telling us,' we said.

Then we paraded on the square, about forty of us. Don't know where all the others came from. Other companies I suppose. A lieutenant was in charge of us.

'Where's your equipment?' he asked me.

'I've never been issued with it, sir,' I said.

'Never been issued with equipment!'

'No sir. I was excused parades. And then I've just got out of hospital. I have the papers here, sir, that they gave me.'

'Oh all right. I'll take charge of them.' He took the long envelope from me. Then a sergeant turned up and shouted 'Shun! By the left, quick – MARCH!'

We started off.

'Keep in step, there!' the sergeant shouted at me. 'Can't you keep in step? What the hell's the matter with yer!'

'I'm excused marching, Sergeant,' I said. 'I've just come from hospital.'

'Oh. All right lad. Fall out. Wait here.' He went up to the officer and saluted. ''Scuse me, sir, there's a man here excused marching, sir.'

'What's that? Excused marching? Well he'll have to bloody well march. This isn't a convalescent home.'

'It's five miles to the station, sir.'

'Oh well, damn it, what d'you want done? Shove him on a truck or something. *Can't march*, indeed. He'd march soon enough if Jerry was after him.'

So the sergeant told a truck to stop and helped me to board it. It was full of kits and very uncomfortable, I nearly fell off twice. I felt a mass of bruises when we got to the station, and my leg had begun to ache. I sat down on a trolley and waited for the train to come in. It didn't come in for an hour, and the men who'd marched up meantime stood around and argued about where we were going. Some said Egypt, but others said no because we weren't in tropical kit. So then they said Scotland and THEN Egypt. I personally didn't care where we were going. I was fed up with the whole business, and my leg ached badly: I'd hit my bad knee getting down from the truck.

Then the truck came in and it turned out to be full of recruits from another regiment going to wherever we were going, a new camp somewhere or other, and so we'd nowhere to sit. We stood for a long time in the corridor and then I tried sitting on my kit but that wasn't a success because fellows kept falling over me and one of them kicked my bad leg. I was pretty browned off by this time, so I got up and was going to sock him, but another chap got in front of me and said, 'You can't hit a sick man.'

'Who's a sick man?' I said. 'I'm a sick man.'

'So am I,' said the man I wanted to sock. 'I'm sick too. Hell I got a hernia so bad they daren't operate. I'm waiting my ticket.'

'Sorry, mate,' I said, 'I didn't know.'

'That's okay,' he said so we shook hands and he gave me some chocolate out of his haversack: we'd got bloody hungry by now.

'What about some grub?' everyone was saying. 'Where's the grub?'

By and by it came round in tins. A sergeant brought it.

'What's this?' we said.

'Beans. Take one.'

'Where's the meat?'

'You've had it,' said the sergeant. Everyone cursed. Then an officer came round, a captain. 'Any complaints?'

'What about some more food, sir,' we said.

'There isn't any. I've had none myself,' he said. 'Mistake some-where.'

'You're telling us,' we said, but not to him.

It was dark when we got to this other town and the searchlights were up overhead. We formed up outside the station. Our sergeant appeared and recognized me. 'I'll see to you in a minute,' he said. But he couldn't, because all the transport had already gone. So I had to march after all. It was three miles, and after all that standing about I felt done in when we got to the new camp. We had a hot meal and I'd have slept like the dead if Jerry hadn't dropped a bomb somewhere near the barracks and woken me up.

'Bugger it,' I said. 'Now we'll have to go to the trenches.'

But they didn't blow the alarm after all, so we went off to sleep again.

In the morning I was down for sick, but the MO at this camp proved to be a much tougher proposition than any I'd yet encoun-tered.

He said, 'What d'you mean, you've had a medical board? How can you have had a medical board? Where're your papers?'

'I gave them to the officer in charge of the draft, sir.' I said.

'Well *I* haven't got them. What was the officer's name?'

'I don't know, sir.'

'You don't know. My God you give your papers to an officer and you don't even know his name.' The MO held his head in his hands. 'God deliver me,' he said, 'from such idiocy.'

'I don't think I'm especially idiotic, sir,' I said.

'Your opinion of yourself is entirely irrelevant,' said the MO. 'And you must remember who you're talking to.'

'Yes sir,' I said.

'Silence!' said the medical corporal, who'd come up at this.

The MO said, 'Now what's all this nonsense about a medical board? What happened? Were you regraded?'

'Yes sir. B2.'

'Let's see your pay-book. Corporal, get his AB64 Part I.'

I produced my pay-book.

'Not in it, sir,' said the corporal. 'A1 it says here.'

'I know,' I said, 'but . . .'

'Silence!' said the corporal. 'Speak only when you're spoken to.'

The MO had his head in his hands again. 'All this shouting,' he said. 'If that man gives any more trouble you'll have to charge him, Corporal.'

'Yes sir,' said the corporal.

'Now listen,' the MO said to me, speaking very quietly. 'You say you've had a medical board. You say you've been regraded. Well you haven't. It's not in your pay-book. Therefore you've not been re-graded at all. You're lucky not to be charged with stating a false-hood, understand? Now don't come here again with any more nonsensical stories or you'll find yourself in trouble. Corporal, march this man out.'

'But sir . . .' I said.

'Come on, you!' the corporal said. So I went. Two days later we started training, and the new sergeant found out I couldn't march and sent me sick again. It was another MO this time and he had my papers, they'd turned up again, and he said I've got to have another medical board.

That was a month ago, and I'm still waiting. I've not done much training so far, and I've had to pay for all the kit I had pinched at the other camp, and all I hope is this: that when they give me the Board, I don't have to go sick any more afterwards. I don't care if they grade me Z2 or keep me A1, so long as I don't have to go sick. I've had enough of it. I'm fed up.

There's Something in the Air

ALL that spring and summer we lived in a big, old cream house surrounded by trees that lay under the downs within sight of the sea. The walls of the mess were bright green, but it was never a green like the green of the fresh mown lawns of the house, or the new leaves of the limes, or the green of the summer meadows under the hills. On hot clear days the sea-light over the sea made the high clouds like ripples of snow and the barrage balloons of passing ships melted into the sky like big bubbles of shining cloud.

Neither Anderson nor Auerbach got up till twelve. Because they were night-fighters their night was day, and part of their day was night, and in this and a few other simple facts they were alike, doing the same things. The few simple facts were that they flew Hurricanes, belonged to the same squadron, were very volatile and had shot down many aircraft by night. But in everything else it seemed to me they had nothing in common at all.

Anderson was English; Auerbach was Czech. Anderson was about six-foot two, but Auerbach was a little man about five feet and a half. Anderson had gone practically straight from school to fly, but Auerbach had first to escape from Czechoslovakia down into the Mediterranean and through North Africa and so to France before he was able to reach England. Anderson, fair and fresh-faced, with a small corn-brown moustache, looked rather aristocratic in a manner that could not have been anything else but British. His moustache alone was an emblem, plain as the Union Jack.

But Auerbach did not look particularly Czech or, though his ancestors had been notable military people, particularly aristocratic. He did not look particularly anything. He had in him something of the element of the anonymous peasant. In his tender, crafty, smiling blue eyes there was a profound watchfulness. It was the sort of look that might have been inherited from generations of people perpetually wondering how long the things they possess are going to remain their own. They are watching to see that they are not cheated. That look sometimes made Auerbach, in spite of a sort of a cunning vivacity, look quite old.

In many other things Anderson and Auerbach were not the same. Anderson was very much the young blood whose life was split fairly evenly between flying and girls, and his leaves were beautiful and wild. Auerbach had married an English girl, and was now a settled man. He sometimes looked rather shy and there was a record of how once, before he was married, he had taken a girl out for the evening and how, in the darkness, coming home, he had kissed her good-night on the forehead.

All that late spring and early summer Anderson and Auerbach flew together. It was one of those periods in a station when the unity and life of a good squadron becomes too strong to become a local thing, compressed within itself, meaning something only to a few people. It breaks out, and spreading, warm and energetic and fluid, becomes a large thing, meaning something to many people.

It was one of those periods when everything was good. The weather was good and calm and sunny, the sea-light lofty and pure over the sea by day. The nights were good and starry, with no ground mist and just the right cover of cloud. The squadron was good and proud and knew itself. The things it did were good and the news of its doings were in the papers. Whenever you came into the mess or the billiard-room or the dining-room and heard laughter boiling over too richly you knew it was that squadron laughing. You knew by their laughter that they wanted nothing else than to be kept as they were, flying by night together, shooting up trains on the flat lands of northern France, shooting down careless Dorniers over their own aerodromes. They had found each other. The positive and exuberant feeling of their discovery spread over the station, from Erks to WAAFs and from WAAFs to officers, until all of us felt it there.

But the best of all that feeling came from Anderson and Auerbach. Every night Anderson and Auerbach flew out over northern France, separately, to wait for enemy bombers coming home from raids on Britain. And every morning, when we came down to breakfast, long before Anderson and Auerbach were up, we heard only one question. It was not 'What is there for breakfast?' or 'What is in the papers?' as if we had any fond ideas that either would be any different from the morning before, but only 'How many did Anderson and Auerbach shoot down?'

When that spring began Anderson and Auerbach had each shot down nine aircraft, all by day. The weather in the winter had been very bad. The long period of inaction began to be broken in the month of April. It had then been a long time since either Anderson or Auerbach had shot anything down. Now they began to shoot something down almost every night. It struck me that what they were doing was very like poaching: something of the same instinct took them alone, across Channel, to roam craftily above the 'dromes of northern France, waiting for stray victims. It was only in the way they did this that they seemed, as always and in almost everything else, very different. Anderson's way was to choose an aerodrome and fly to it and impatiently round it, waiting for the 'drome lights to be switched on and watching for the navigation light of returning bombers. If the light did not come on very soon he lost eagerness and flew away to another 'drome, always impatient and volatile and eager until something happened, always furious and blasphemous when nothing did.

But all that Auerbach did was to wait. Auerbach had patience. It was the patience of craftiness: of the man who sits above a rabbit hole, waiting to strike. Auerbach had come from Czechoslovakia and the Mediterranean and North Africa and France for the purpose of striking and now, as I looked at it, a few moments more waiting would not matter. So it was Anderson, they said, who had the brilliance and Auerbach, they said, who had the luck: whereas it was really only the difference between a man who had infinite patience and one who had none at all.

So almost every morning, by one or two and sometimes three aircraft, we heard that Anderson and Auerbach had raised the score; and almost every noon I used to see Anderson and Auerbach themselves, getting up after their late sleep. What they told me and the way they told it was, as always, very different.

About noon Auerbach was always in the billiard-room. He was not particularly good but he played like a clown in a circus and there was always a crowd watching him. He had a droll and magnetic way of laughing and the laughter in the billiard-room used to bubble over when Auerbach was there.

'Nice going,' I would say. 'What were they?'

'I think all Dornier 217's. I'm not sure. Perhaps one Heinkel 111.'

'Very nice.'

'Peez of cake.'

Every noon, while Auerbach was playing billiards, Anderson was on the terrace of the house, sun-bathing, alone. Auerbach used to say very little. He used to give a wink and a nod and a flick of his thumb and it was an understanding between us: the common language that needed no elaboration. But Anderson, lying back on the cream stone terrace, eyes shaded against the sun, his moustache looking more corn-brown and more British than ever against his naked body, liked to talk about what happened. 'Yes, and Auerbach got three! Two Dorniers and a Heinkel and a probable, the sod. God, he has the luck. There I stayed over the same 'drome for twenty minutes and not a sausage. Five minutes after I leave it Auerbach comes and they light up the whole bloody Christmas tree.'

'Luck,' I said.

'Luck, hell,' he said. 'He's got some sixth sense or something. He knows which bloody 'drome they'll use and when they'll use it.'

'Just crafty,' I said. 'You can see it in his eyes.'

'Crafty as hell,' he said.

'And you?' I said. 'I hear you got one?'

'One solitary 217. They switched all the bloody 'drome lights on and there they were, as big as hell, about a dozen of them. Then as soon as I hit him they put everything out and I was finished.'

'You must be equal with Auerbach now,' I said.

'No, he's one up on me. The lucky sod, he's always one up on me.'

'Tomorrow you'll probably get six,' I said.

'Me?' he said. 'The only time I ever see six is when the bloody ammo runs out.'

What he said turned out to be true. The next night he saw twenty; the lights of the 'drome and the lights of the bombers were like the lights of a party round a Christmas tree. Anderson went in with great excitement and began to line them up. He hit the first Dornier at only a hundred feet, and she blew up underneath him almost before he had time to pull out of the dive. There is something about being hit at a hundred feet which does not seem to be in the rules and the confusion must have been very great.

The lights of the 'drome continued to burn as brilliantly as ever and the lights of the incoming bombers were not switched off. All Anderson had to do was to turn and come in again and hit a Heinkel. He saw it crash in wreaths of orange fire in the black space beyond the circle of light. Then he hit another and he saw it too burning among the lights, as if something in the Christmas tree had fallen and caught fire. Even then the lights of the 'drome still kept burning and the bombers circled round like coloured fireflies. It was all so fantastic, with the red and white light shining in the darkness and the coloured lights moving in the sky and the orange fires breaking the darkness, that Anderson could not believe it to be true. It was only when he had the fourth bomber lined up and pressed the tit and nothing happened except a fraction of a second burst that he knew the ammo was spent and it was real after all.

I do not know how many Auerbach got that night; but by the end of May he and Anderson were still almost equal, and by the beginning of June what they did was in the papers every day. The papers had their photographs too and I suppose the photographs were something like them. But what the papers printed was really a comic story. It was the story of two men with eagle eyes, though sometimes it was cat's eyes and sometimes it was hawk's eyes, who stalked over France every night in the darkness.

We liked especially the word stalk, since it is the one thing an aeroplane does not do, and thinking of the clear, youthful, exuberant eyes of Anderson and of the crafty, friendly blue eyes of Auerbach, we liked the nonsense about the eyes. From the newspapers you got the impression that Anderson and Auerbach were a pair of heroic bandits who behaved with copybook courage and were in some way supernatural. This attitude was perhaps excusable, since the newspapers never saw Anderson lying naked in the sun, blaspheming about the luck of Auerbach, or Auerbach playing snooker, with a laughing audience who got more fun out of Auerbach potting the black than they got out of his putting a Heinkel down.

It was excusable because, after all, the newspapers could not know the feeling that comes from a squadron which is at the crest of things: the warm and positive excitement that we felt all that spring and which went on expanding and flowing outward all that summer. They did not know about Auerbach playing billiards and comic games of snooker, or about his kissing a girl on the forehead in the dark. They did not know about Anderson lying on his back in the sun and looking at the green summer leaves and the green grass spreading to the foot of the dark hills and saying, a little solemnly, because this was his first year in England since the war began: 'You can't believe how bloody wizard it is. You can't know what it is to see the leaves so green on the trees.'

There seemed no reason why this feeling and this squadron, and above all why Anderson and Auerbach, should not have gone on for ever. There seemed no reason why Anderson and Auerbach should ever stop those simple and disastrous journeys over France. But there comes a time when every squadron is held to have earned its rest; when some obscure department somewhere, by something written in a paper, breaks a tension and a feeling that can never be put on paper at all.

And finally it was time to say goodbye on an evening in July. The weather had broken suddenly and the wind blew cold and gusty between the dispersal huts on the 'drome, raising dry clouds of sand. The Hurricanes were lined along the perimeter. The pilots were not very happy but they pretended to be very happy and the sergeant pilots fondled the busts of each other's Mae Wests and said heavy farewells.

There were many people there to say goodbye. We shook hands with everybody once and wished them luck, and then the take-off was delayed and we shook hands with everyone again. We all promised to write and knew that we should never keep the promises. Anderson addressed the pilots in language as if they were going to play football, and we all said goodbye once more. Then for the second time the take-off was delayed and the little WAAFs who had at last begun to dry their tears began to cry all over again.

It was only when the take-off had begun at last that I realized that Auerbach was not there. Auerbach was going one way; the squadron another. Auerbach had not come to say goodbye. The Hurricanes flew once round the 'drome, in two flights of six, black against the grey evening sky, gradually formating. The little WAAFs cried a little harder and the wind blew a little harder in a grey wave over the leaves of the potato patch beside the hut. I lifted my hand at last and drove away.

At the mess I found Auerbach alone. The ante-room was almost empty and there was no one laughing in the billiard-room.

'You didn't come,' I said to Auerbach.

'No.'

'You don't like goodbyes,' I said.

'No.' He looked at me with tender and now serious blue eyes that the newspapers had been vainly trying for weeks to describe. 'No, I do not like fuss,' he said. 'No fuss.'

I did not say anything. I walked away and into the garden. The grass and the leaves and the meadows under the hills were still green, but it was no longer the wonderful green of early summer. I walked across the grass and looked up at the empty sky and realized suddenly that something had gone.

All summer there had been something in the air. It was there no longer now.

The Disinherited

On that station we had pilots from all over the world, so that the sound of the mess, as someone said, was like a Russian bazaar. They came from Holland and Poland, Belgium and Czechoslovakia, France and Norway. We had many French and they had with them brown and yellow men from the Colonial Empire who at dispersal on warm spring afternoons played strange games with pennies in the dry, white dust on the edge of the perimeter. We had many Canadians and New Zealanders, Australians and Africans. There was a West Indian boy, the colour of milky coffee, who was a barrister, and a Lithuanian who played international football. There was a man from Indo-China and another from Tahiti. There was an American and a Swiss and there were negroes, very black and curly, among the ground crews. We had men who had done everything and been everywhere, who had had everything and had lost it all. They had escaped across frontiers and over mountains and down the river valleys of Central Europe; they had come through Libya and Iran and Turkey and round the Cape; they had come through Spain and Portugal or nailed under the planks of little ships wherever a little ship could put safely to sea. They had things in common with themselves that men had nowhere else on earth, and you saw on their faces sometimes a look of sombre silence that could only have been the expression of recollected hatred. But among them all there was only one who had something which no one else had, and he was Capek the Czech. Capek had white hair.

Capek was a night-fighter pilot, so that mostly in the daytime you would find him in the hut at dispersal. The hut was very pleasant and there was a walnut piano and a radio and a miniature billiard-table and easy chairs that had been presented by the mayor of the local town. No one ever played the piano but it was charming all the same. On the walls there were pictures, some in colour, of girls in their underwear and without underwear at all, and rude remarks about pilots who forgot to check their guns. Pilots who had been flying at night lay on the camp beds, sleeping a little, their eyes puffed, using their flying jackets as pillows; or they played cards and groused and talked shop among themselves. They were bored because they were flying too much. They argued about the merits of a four-cannon job as opposed to those of a single gun that fired through the air-screw. They argued about the climate of New Zealand, if it could be compared with the climate of England. They were restless and temperamental, as fighter pilots are apt to be, and it seemed always as if they would have been happier doing anything but the things they were.

Capek alone did not do these things. He did not seem bored or irritable, or tired or temperamental. He did not play billiards and he did not seem interested in the bodies of the girls on the walls. He was never asleep on the beds. He never played cards or argued about the merits of this or that. It seemed sometimes as if he did not belong to us. He sat apart from us, and with his white hair, cultured brown face, clean fine lips and the dark spectacles he wore sometimes against the bright spring sunlight he looked something like a middle-aged provincial professor who had come to take a cure at a health resort in the sun. Seeing him in the street, the bus, the train or the tram, you would never have guessed that he could fly. You would never have guessed that in order to be one of us, to fly with us and fight with us, Capek had come half across the world.

There was a time when a very distinguished personage came to the station and, seeing Capek, asked how long he had been in the Air Force and Capek replied 'Please, seventeen years.' This took his flying life far back beyond the beginning of the war we were fighting; back to the years when some of us were hardly born and when Czechoslovakia had become born again as a nation. Capek had remained in the Air Force all those years, flying heaven knows what types of plane, and becoming finally part of the forces that crumbled away and disintegrated and disappeared under the progress of the tanks that entered Prague in the summer of 1939. Against this progress Capek was one of those who disappeared. He disappeared in a lorry with many others and they rode eastward towards Poland, always retreating and not knowing where they were going. With Capek was a man named Machakek, and as the retreat went on Capek and Machakek became friends.

Capek and Machakek stayed in Poland all that summer, until

the chaos of September. It is not easy to know what Capek and Machakek did; if they were interned, or how, or where, because Capek's English is composed of small difficult words and long difficult silences, often broken only by smiles. 'All time is retreat. Then war start. Poland is in war. Then Germany is coming one way and Russia is coming another.' In this way Capek and Machakek had no escape. They could go neither east nor west. It was too late to go south, and in the north Gdynia had gone. And in time, as Germany moved eastward and Russia westward, Capek and Machakek were taken by the Russians. Capek went to a concentration camp, and Machakek worked in the mines. As prisoners they had a status not easy to define. Russia was not then in the war and Czechoslovakia, politically, did not exist. It seemed in these days as if Russia might come into the war against us. It was very confused and during the period of clarification, if you could call it that, Capek and Machakek went on working in the concentration camp and the mine. 'We remain,' Capek said, 'one year and three quarter.'

Then the war clarified and finally Capek was out of the concentration camp and Machakek was out of the mine. They were together again, still friends, and they moved south, to the Black Sea. Standing on the perimeter track, in the bright spring sun, wearing his dark spectacles, Capek had so little to say about this that he looked exactly like a blind man who has arrived somewhere, after a long time, but for whom the journey is darkness. 'From Black Sea I go to Turkey. Turkey then to Syria. Then Cairo. Then Aden.'

'And Machakek with you?'

'Machakek with me, yes. But only to Aden. After Aden Machakek is going to Bombay on one boat. I am going to Cape Town on other.'

'So Machakek went to India?'

'To India, yes. Is very long way. Is very long time.'

'And you – Cape Town?'

'Yes, me, Cape Town. Then Gibraltar. Then here, England.'

'And Machakek?'

'Machakek is here too. We are both post here. To this squadron.'

The silence that followed this had nothing to do with the past; it had much to do with the present; more to do with Machakek. Through the retreat and the mine and the concentration camp, through the journey to Turkey and Cairo and Aden, through the long sea journey to India and Africa and finally England, Capek and

Machakek had been friends. When a man speaks only the small words of a language that is not his own he finds it hard to express the half-tones of friendship and relief and suffering and most of what Capek and Machakek had suffered together was in Capek's white hair. But now something had happened which was not expressed there but which lay in the dark, wild eyes behind the glasses and the long silences of Capek as he sat staring at the Hurricanes in the sun. His friend Machakek was dead.

The handling of night-fighters is not easy. It was perhaps hard for Capek and Machakek that they should come out of the darkness of Czechoslovakia, through the darkness of the concentration camp and the mine, in order to fight in darkness. It was hard for Machakek who, overshooting the 'drome, hit a telegraph post and died before Capek could get there. It was harder still for Capek, who was now alone.

But the hardest part of it all, perhaps, is that Capek cannot talk to us. He does not know words that will express what he feels about the end of Machakek's journey. He does not know words like endurance and determination, imperishable and undefeated, sacrifice and honour. They are the words, anyway, that are never mentioned at dispersals. He does not know the words for grief and friendship, homesickness and loss. They are never mentioned either. Above all he does not know the words for himself and what he has done.

I do not know the words for Capek either. Looking at his white hair, his dark eyes and his long hands, I am silent now.

FLYING OFFICER 'X' (H. E. BATES) · 1905–1974

No Trouble at All

THE day was to be great in the history of the Station; it was just my luck that I didn't come back from leave until late afternoon. All day the sunlight had been a soft orange colour and the sky a clear wintry blue, without mist or cloud. There was no one in the mess ante-room except a few of the night-staff dozing before the fire, and no one I could talk to except the little WAAF who sits by the telephone.

So I asked her about the show. 'Do you know how many have gone?' I said.

'Ten, sir,' she said.

'Any back yet?'

'Seven were back a little while ago,' she said. 'They should all be back very soon.'

'When did they go? This morning?'

'Yes, sir. About ten o'clock.' She was not young; but her face was pleasant and eager and, as at the moment, could become alight. 'They looked marvellous as they went, sir,' she said. 'You should have seen them, sir. Shining in the sun.'

'Who isn't back? You don't know?'

But she did know.

'K for Kitty and L for London aren't back,' she said. 'But I don't know the other.'

'It must be Brest again?' I said.

'Yes, sir,' she said. 'I think it's Brest.'

I didn't say anything, and she said, 'They are putting you in Room 20 this time, sir.'

'Thank you. I'll go up,' I said.

As I went upstairs and as I bathed and changed I made calculations. It was half-past three in the afternoon and the winter sun was already growing crimson above the blue edges of flat ploughed land beyond the Station buildings. I reckoned up how far it was to Brest. If you allowed half an hour over the target and a little trouble getting away, even the stragglers should be back by four. It seemed, too, as if fog might come down very suddenly; the sun was too red and the rim of the earth too blue. I realized that if they were not back soon they wouldn't be back at all. They always looked very beautiful in the sun, as the little WAAF said, but they looked still more beautiful on the ground. I didn't know who the pilot of L for London was; but I knew, and was remembering, that K for Kitty was my friend.

By the time I went downstairs again the lights were burning in the ante-room but the curtains were not drawn and the evening, sunless now, was a vivid electric blue beyond the windows. The little WAAF still sat by the telephone and as I went past she looked up and said:

'L for London is back, sir.'

I went into the ante-room. The fire was bright and the first crews, back from interrogation, were warming their hands. Their faces looked raw and cold. They still wore sweaters and flying-boots and their eyes were glassy.

'Hallo,' they said. 'You're back. Good leave?' They spoke as if it was I, not they, who had been 300 miles away.

'Hallo, Max,' I said. 'Hallo, Ed. Hallo, J.B.'

I had been away for five days. For a minute I felt remote; I couldn't touch them.

I was glad when someone else came in.

'Hallo. Good trip?'

'Quite a picnic.'

'Good. See anything?'

'Everything.'

'Good show, good show. Prang them?'

'Think so. Fires burning when we got there.'

'Good show.'

I looked at their faces. They were tired and hollow. In their eyes neither relief nor exhilaration had begun to filter through the glassiness of long strain. They talked laconically, reluctantly, as if their lips were frozen.

'Many fighters?'

'Hordes.'

'Any trouble?'

'The whole bloody crew was yelling fighters. Came up from everywhere.'

'Any Spits?'

'Plenty. Had five Me.'s on my tail. Then suddenly wham! Three Spits came up from nowhere. Never saw anything like those Me.'s going home to tea.'

'Good show. Good show.'

The evening was darkening rapidly and the mess-steward came in to draw the curtains. I remembered K for Kitty and suddenly I went out of the ante-room and stood for a moment in the blue damp twilight, listening and looking at the sky. The first few evening stars were shining and I could feel that later the night would be frosty. But there was no sound of a plane.

I went back into the ante-room at last and for a moment, in the bright and now crowded room, I could not believe my eyes. Rubbing his cold hands together, his eyes remote and chilled, his sweater hanging loose below his battledress, the pilot of K for Kitty was standing by the fireplace. There was a cross of flesh-pink elastic bandage on his forehead and I knew that something had happened.

'Hallo,' I said.

'Hallo,' he said. 'You're back.'

For a minute I didn't say anything else. I wanted to shake his hand and tell him I was glad he was back. I knew that if he had been in a train wreck or a car crash I should have shaken his hand and told him I was glad. Now somebody had shot him up and all I said was:

'When did you get in?'

'About an hour ago.'

'Everything OK?'

'Wrapped her up.'

'Well,' I said. 'Just like that?'

'Just like that,' he said.

I looked at his eyes. They were bleared and wet and excited. He had made a crash landing; he was safe; he was almost the best pilot in the outfit.

'Anyone see me come in?' he said.

'Saw you from Control,' someone said.

'How did it look?'

'Perfect until the bloody airscrew fell off.'

Everyone laughed: as if airscrews falling off were a great joke. Nobody said anything about anybody being lucky to be back, but only:

'Have an argument?'

'Flak blew bloody great bit out of the wing. The intercom went and then both turrets.'

'Many fighters?'

'Ten at a time.'

'Get one?'

'One certain. Just dissolved. One probable.'

'Good show. What about the ships?'

'I think we pranged them.'

'Good show,' we said. 'Good show.'

We went on talking for a little longer about the trip: beautiful weather, sea very blue, landscape very green in the sun. And then he came back to the old subject.

'How did I land? What did it look like?'

'Beautiful.'

'I couldn't get the tail down. Both tyres were punctured.'

'Perfect all the same.'

He looked quite happy. It was his point of pride, the good landing; all he cared about now. With turrets gone, fuselage like a colander, wings holed, and one airscrew fallen off, he had nevertheless brought her down. And though we all knew it must have been hell no one said a word.

Presently his second dicky came into the ante-room. He was very young, about nineteen, with a smooth aristocratic face and smooth aristocratic hair. He looked too young to be part of a war and he was very excited.

'Went through my sleeve.'

He held up a cannon shell. Then he held up his arm. There was a neat tear in the sleeve of his battledress. He was very proud.

'And look at this.'

Across the knuckles of his right hand there was a thread line of dried blood, neat, fine, barely visible. He wetted his other forefinger and rubbed across it, as if to be sure it wouldn't wash away.

'Came in on the starboard side and out the other.'

'Good show,' said somebody quite automatically. 'Good show.'

'Anybody hurt?' I asked.

'Engineer.'

'Very bad?'

'Very bad. I bandaged him and gave him a shot coming home.'

As he went on talking I looked down at his knees. There were dark patches on them, where blood had soaked through his flying-suit. But all that anyone said was:

'Think you pranged them?'

'Oh! sure enough. They've had it this time.'

'Good show,' we said. 'Good show.'

Now and then, as we talked, the little WAAF would come in from the telephone to tell someone he was wanted. With her quiet voice she would break for a moment the rhythm of excitement that was now rising through outbursts of laughter to exhilaration. She would hear for a second or two a snatch of the now boisterous but still laconic jargon of flight, 'Think we may have pranged in, old boy. Good show. Piece of cake. No trouble at all,' but there would be no sign on her calm and rather ordinary face that it conveyed anything to her at all. Nor did the crews, excited by the afternoon, the warmth and the relief of return, take any notice of her. She was an automaton, negative, outside of them, coming and going and doing her duty.

Outside of them, too, I listened and gathered together and finally pieced together the picture of the raid; and then soon afterwards the first real pictures of operations were brought in for the Wing Commander to see, and for a moment there was a flare of excitement. We could see bomb-bursts across the battleships and the quays and then smoke over the area of town and docks. 'You think we pranged them, sir?' we said.

'Pranged them? Like hell we did.'

'Good show. Bloody good show.'

'Slap across the Gluckstein.'

'No doubt this time?'

'No doubt.'

'Good show,' we said. 'Good show.'

At last, when the photographs had been taken away again, I went out of the ante-room into the hall. As I walked across it the little WAAF, sitting by the telephone, looked up at me.

'A wonderful show, sir,' she said.

I paused and looked at her in astonishment. I wondered for a moment how she could possibly know. There had been no time for her to hear the stories of the crews; she had not seen the photographs; she did not know that K for Kitty had been wrapped up and that it must have been hell to land on two dud tyres and with a broken airscrew; she did not know that the ships had been hit or that over Brest, on that bright calm afternoon, it had been partly magnificent and partly hell.

'How did you know?' I said.

She smiled a little and lifted her face and looked through the glass door of the ante-room.

'You can tell by their faces, sir,' she said.

I turned and looked too. In the morning we should read about it in the papers; we should hear the flat bulletins; we should see the pictures. But now we were looking at something that could be read nowhere except in their eyes and expressed in no language but their own.

'Pretty good show,' I said.

'Yes, sir,' she said. 'No trouble at all.'

The Crew of the Jackdaw

I WAS awake before Sticks put his hand on my shoulder. I knew before he told me. 'Old man's going in,' he said, 'get your bloody self up.' But I didn't need any telling. I knew by the feel of her. She was jumping now. I could hear the water falling on the deck above my head and then running aft. I thought she was dragging; her head seemed to be paying off all the time and I could feel her chunk, bite and then slip again.

'Did Skips radio in?' I said.

'Aye. It's OK.'

'Christ! she's dragging.'

'Aye. Some bloody game.'

'Anyone else put in a call?'

'Beer 3, and Beer 7.'

'Suppose the others are tight up against the north shore, riding it out?'

'Yer, suppose.' Sticks wanted to get going on deck.

'Who's Beer 7 tonight,' I said, 'She's near us.' I was pulling on my sea-boots.

'That flat whore Sandy on the *Jackdaw*, I think.'

'Christ man! He'll be way in ahead of us. He can do 9 to our 6½ knots.'

'That's right. You ready yet?'

I put a body and soul lashing on a toggle hitch around over my oilskin coat – I wish those Navy boys 'ud give us oil-frocks, they're the things to keep you dry, unless you're pooped and it comes up over your sea-boots.

'Come on,' I said; I was ready; 'I'll kick the winch in.'

The chief had the engine going but it was still very hot from having the lamps on. I felt the sweat come out on me going through the engine-room, then I lifted the box lid and kicked her in; she clanged and juddered then the shaft started. That deisel oil smelt like hell – I wouldn't be in the black watch for much.

On deck there was some noise and it was hell of a dark too after the light in the cabin. The wind took you by the ears and laid everything flat. I waited in the lee of the wheelhouse till I could see, then went up forward. The dawn wasn't far off when your eyes got used to it, but I didn't like to look at the seas – Christ man, they were too big – and breaking. Better to keep your eyes inside. The wind took the tops clean off the seas and blew them straight out to leeward in a line. Some wind – moving solid now. You could hear it go past you like a train.

The old man flashed his torch to tell us he'd given her a turn ahead slow and we pulled the bar over, but even with four turns on the barrel she surged and we couldn't get much. We tried again and then Sticks kicked me as I pulled and we clewed up and had a look. There was something quite near, riding on the sea and sliding past us. A buoy with a light on it. The light was out but we knew it was one of the Channel buoys. We'd dragged alright. I went aft, but the skipper had already seen it. 'Better clear out quick,' he said, 'slip the lot, it's buoyed,' and I was thankful. I was afraid for Sticks' hands in the winch with her surging like that. Sticks looked at me and grinned. 'We're right in the middle of the bastard channel,' he shouted, 'better slip, eh?' I waved my hand. Our lights weren't much good and if a ship should come through they wouldn't see us at all in this. We must have dragged a mile. 'Slip 'er,' I shouted at him, but he understood my hand signal.

As the end of the warp went over the side, her head came off, before she had way enough and she took three big bastards. They came white and creaming over the rail. I took the first, then I slid down the waterways. I felt my nails in the wood of the deck and that water was cold – cold right to the back of your throat. Something hit me and it was Sticks' boot. We both finished up together abeam of the mizzen.

It was cold.

'– between the mizzen and the wheelhouse,' Sticks said. I could hear him when he put his mouth to my ear. I got my arms hooked through the rails and then banged on the wheelhouse to tell the skipper we were alright. The *Queen* was marching now and you could feel her shudder.

Sticks grinned and undid his hands for a moment to make like he was swimming; I laughed.

'All ready for off?' I said.

'Aye – it won't be long now by the looks.'

'It's a bastard.'

'Too bloody true – the gaffer left it too long.'

'Uh uh, they never ought to send us out in these herrin' boxes this weather.'

'That's it.'

'– they've got the weather forecasts – we ain't.'

'That's it.'

'They'll be ashore now snug in the lee of bum island.'

'That's it, townie, you said it.' It was blowing so Sticks couldn't spit up to windward like he wanted to when I said that. It got him angry.

I wanted to smoke and I nudged Sticks and pointed to my mouth and shouted 'tabs', but his were all wet too. It was the hell of a thing.

Well, they turned the lights for us and we came on in through the Gates. Waiting for the lights out there, dodging head to wind, the old *Queen* rose to the seas and passed 'em all under her, clean and dry. Once far off I thought I saw the navigation lights of the *Jackdaw*; she was coming in from the NE – if Sandy was pushing her she'd be plenty wet I knew. They turned the lights and I banged on the wheelhouse and the skipper brought her round nice in a slick. She rolled twice – hard, dipped one up into the lee scuppers – I could hear it boiling and spilling there, and then came round stern on to the seas. With the weather on the quarter Sticks and I went around forward of the wheelhouse. The gaffer had the windows all down because of the spray and I saw the engineer and the cook and the stoker there behind him. They wore their life-belts and the cook was green. With the following sea the *Queen* surged and yawed, and the waves marched past. I saw the old man spin the wheel and I knew she was difficult on the helm. I knew she wanted to broach to all the time. I wouldn't have liked his job. We all grinned at each other; it was too far to shout and there was nothing to say.

When next I looked aft, I saw the *Jackdaw* coming up fast in the grey dawn light. She'd dip down behind a big one, but when she rode high I could see the broken water at her stem and her crew clinging to the lee side of the wheelhouse. Her lights were still on and she looked grey and white there, with the small water round her and the points of red and green light. She was coming up on us fast. Sandy must be using all of his nine knots.

'The old bastard,' I said. 'Aye, he knows these parts,' said Sticks, 'and so he ought; he's a native – fished out of the Firth all his life. He'll be all snugged down before we're up to the Lady' – and he was right. Sandy'd got the knives in for sure.

We passed through the shoal water half-way between the booms and the seas were all haycock. At the second gate vessel the *Jack-daw* was almost abeam. Sandy was driving her fast and we could see all the green foul on her bottom as she rolled like a wild thing along the seas; they were short and deep and when she straddled too she looked like she was hung from her stem-posts. Sandy came quite close up to windward and I could smell his exhaust smoke trailing over the water. He was at the wheel and I could see the pipe in his mouth. He had a scarf round his neck and his cap pulled well down – he was bald. Behind him was that short-arsed engineer – Snuffy they cry him; all the rest of the crew were taking it outside in the lee. There was that big Aberdonian, Lofty, and that Newfoundland kiddie I always felt sorry for being so far from home, and Snowy that was really too old for this and owed me five bob and a packet of duty free's, and Doddie from Buckie, and that dark-faced manny they cry the Bamboo Kid and coming from somewhere in the south. I never did see their officer; he must have been below for something – or maybe he was sick; and it's bad luck to all the RNVRs I'd say, even if he is gone now. They was all there right enough, and Sandy had the windows down and leans out and waves his pipe, and Lofty and Dod give us a good spit in our direction, while Snowy held up a rope end. They was all grinning. Sticks and I signed back. We knew they'd be in and out of this long before us. Our boys just looked. When you're being passed you don't do much beyond try not to notice.

Sticks pointed. '— cutting across,' he shouted in my ear.

To the west of the second gate boat is a green wreck buoy. It marks a tug that was blown up in the beginning. Once you could see her funnel tip and the brass of her whistle, but someone took the whistle and then the funnel went – even at low water; but for a long time you could see the mast with a golden cockerel at the truck. Now even that is gone; she must have broken up or rolled over; but we always gave her a wide berth and kept the green buoy well on our port-hand coming in.

Sandy was cutting in, putting the *Jackdaw* on her SW by S. course right inside the boom, and going round behind the wreck off the swept channel.

'Silly bugger,' I said.

Sticks put his hand up with the thumb down. The skipper leaned out and touched my arm to tell me about it, and I nodded to say I'd seen it. I could tell by his mouth what he thought of Sandy too.

We steamed on west as the *Jackdaw* was drawing away from us fast into the south. Sometimes we could only see her mast and wheelhouse, then she'd ride up out of it, wild and sheering and we'd see all along her decks as she slipped over the top of a sea; she was making plenty of flurry. The crew were still there, clinging on, and I saw Dod wave again and give the old 'V' sign like Churchill.

I never did really see it happen, only out of the corner of my eye – and Sticks was the same. The sound didn't seem to reach us at all, only in torn tags like a headsail when it bursts out of the bolt ropes. It all happens out of order; so that afterwards when you put it together it never does fit. So now I saw the *Jackdaw*, her bows just rising to a big sea; there was spray across her and her decks wet and shining in the dawn. Snuffy must have been below in the engine-room, because she was shooting black smoke out of her false funnel; it eddied up and then cut off sharp with the wind and came down flat, fitting itself over the seas. I know I saw that, but afterwards I didn't know. I know I heard a sound, and afterwards I was sure of that. It was a big sound. It seemed to come from very far off and from close up too. It was like when you fired the Hotchkiss, and the bullets went feathering through the air; then it hit us and it was like your head was in a bucket and someone hitting it with a hammer. I felt it in my feet and legs and in my ears, and it was a big sound. When I looked for the *Jackdaw* she wasn't there; there was a great slab of water, white, like a fountain and big waves ringing away from it. It was raining heavily and all blowing off to leeward and in the air were men – men with flying arms and legs, and there were pieces of wood and the wheelhouse floating all by itself, with the lifebuoy off its hooks quite close, and all flying out. Then men floated flat out, or with arms and legs flying; they were bent backwards and although I knew it was the crew, they didn't look like men – just shapes, held together by clothes. They hung there and then started to come down with the rain. They looked funny. They looked very funny. I turned to Sticks, and he was laughing there, they looked so funny and I had to laugh too. We both laughed and I felt the tears in my eyes; but although it felt like laughing it wasn't really, only a twist in the side.

Whenever the skipper had seen her hit he put the helm hard aport and she came round in a jump. The wreck buoy was just under our lee and I saw its sides ropy with weed, plunging in the seas, and I hoped we wouldn't foul it. The *Queen* held up off it, but if we'd been towing a small boat we would have lost it. She was rolling badly in the pit of the seas and I heard the gaffer shout for Sticks and me to get the boat-hooks and stretchers and stand by. It was difficult to keep your footing the way he was handling her. He took her right in over the small water of the wreck, and I surely thought we'd touch and take the bottom clean out of her and join the old tug down below there; but he kept her straight at it and now we met three breaking rings of sea coming out and away from where the *Jackdaw* had been. I was down under the winch and I felt the seas go green over my back. I hoped we wouldn't founder – there'd be no one to pick up Sandy and his boys. She had her decks full of water, but she came up alright.

When we came up to where they'd been the oil made a coloured slick on the water and we came through it solid, and everything in the world floating in it. I saw the stem with jagged wood, red and blue, from the blast; big pieces of solid deck-planking cut like with a knife; the mizzen mast; a mop and fender; a mat and then a cap.

It was quite light now but I couldn't see any of the crew yet. I saw something black and it was a lambie coat; you could tell by the hood and the toggles. It was blown up with the air in it and felt soft to the boat-hook point. I held up my hand to stop; I was afraid we'd cut him in two with the prop. The skipper gave her just one turn full astern and she came up nice and easy with the way just off her and laying in among the jobble of oil and wreckage. That was a proper bunch of buggers.

Well we found most of the crew – enough to match up, and they were difficult to get aboard because only their clothes held them together and the weight of the water in them made the stuff tear. Sticks found a cod-end from the trawl gear and we sank that under them and then hove taut. It wasn't easy. We never did find anything of the young officer, he must have gone down with the mid-ship section that wouldn't float because of the engine in her. We fished up Sandy and old Snuffy and Dod, but he wasn't worth the keeping, and then we found two of the others and they were gone too. Sandy was alive; I could feel his heart, but his head was cut, and with the blood and oil and scum on him I didn't know him till he opened his

mouth and spat out his teeth and said 'a bluidy mine be-christ'.
Then I knew who it was. His legs and ankles were smashed, the
bone coming out white through his trousers. He was in a bad shape.
I didn't know what to do for him. Dod I didn't want to look at. He
was gone anyway; and Snuffy was all broken up. I knew we couldn't
get them below, so Sticks fetched my blankets and his own, and
that's where we went wrong. But there it is, and we did it. We
couldn't know then and we were doing the best we could for the
boys. Sticks went away down and when he brought up those blankets it was a bad thing he was doing; but then it seemed the best,
and we didn't know. The skipper shouted for us to get his too, and
Sticks went away below again and brought them up. We wrapped
those lads up on the deck there the best we could; it wasn't much.

Well, we cruised around and we didn't find nothing else worth
salving, only a dan and another fender or two – nothing. The tide
and weather were starting to break up the scum and we'd drifted
two miles to the west. The skipper radioed in and they said to
proceed to the harbour and they'd have an ambulance waiting.

'An ambulance and a butcher's cart is what they need,' said
Sticks, and he was right.

Crouching there I lit a cigarette and put it between Sandy's lips; it
wasn't much good – waste of a tab – he couldn't hold it, and the end
got sodden with the oil.

Snuffy hadn't caught the oil much; his face was only streaked.
White skin and black oil it was – like a clown at the circus; but he
was in the hell of a shape down below, and we didn't know what to
do with either of 'em, so we just sat there and kept the spray off, and
hoped it was going to be alright for them both. You can't do much.
It's too big a thing. I crouched over Sandy, his head in my lap; and
Snuff that owed me five bob and a packet of duty free Woods, lay
beside him and I looked up and all the boys were just holding on to
the rail and looking at us – not laughing any more but just looking
solemn like at a funeral where there are flowers and clay and brass
handles, and slow moving feet. I could see the skipper at the wheel
and he was the lucky one – he was busy with his course, and getting
her in as soon as he could now that we couldn't do any more out
there. I didn't know which of the rest of the *Jackdaw* crew we had
there, except Dod; you couldn't see, they was all mixed up, they lay
up against the rail with the old cod-end over them and a lashing
round all to keep 'em from rolling. I saw the boys' faces, standing

there by the wheelhouse looking and I said 'You bastards 'ud better sing' and I began to sing 'Rose of Tralee' that I always like and Sticks came in with me, then the little cook that we cry the Duke because his name is Wellington – he joined in. After that we had 'Roll out the Barrel' and then the stoker pipes up with 'I'm the man that makes the Smoke come out o' the lum – choo! choo!' and we followed that with 'They all get on to the fireman when the ship is very slow' – and we were singing fine, with never a hymn to make us sad, when we came in between the pierheads. The berthing master was there and a crowd 'round him, watching, and he said for us to go to the north side.

The skipper brought her in nice and easy – wouldn't crack an egg – and the doctor came aboard and the sick-bay lads sent down those bamboo and canvas stretchers. They got Sandy and Snuffy all snugged up and away first, wrapped up in our blankets and looking as pretty as you like, and everyone lending a hand to bring 'em up gentle, but they had a hell of a job to fit the other boys into the stretchers, and in the end they just put 'em in a canvas sling. The doctor said Sandy was OK – might get over it – you know how these doctors are – wanting to be wise – and that Snuffy had a chance too – so I might get my five shillings back. I'd looked in his pockets and it wasn't there, only the packet of duty free's he owed me, and they were useless with the sea water and the oil, so I left them.

When they'd all gone and the ambulance had driven off ringing its bell they posted a sentry over us. We lay quiet there under the wall and heard the wind go marching over our heads, and us as snug as you like; and I remembered what it had been like out there, and I was glad we were in. It was quiet where we were, but a big swell was coming in over on the south side and I stood on the deck with Sticks and we both said how glad we were to be in. The cook called 'tea up', but we still stood there, and then he shouted 'come and get yer tea man', and we went on down below. The warmth of the cabin hit you and the table looked good there under the skylight and the stove burning mellow there, and everything warm and snug. We had our sheggie – and that was well laced with rum – yes, they must have drained the bloody jar to make it that way. I slept good after it. I turned in all standing. I slept good, but I slept cold – my blankets was ashore wrapped round Sandy and old Snuffy. Perhaps they needed 'em more than I did.

Mysterious Kôr

FULL moonlight drenched the city and searched it; there was not a
niche left to stand in. The effect was remorseless: London looked
like the moon's capital – shallow, cratered, extinct. It was late, but
not yet midnight; now the buses had stopped the polished roads and
streets in this region sent for minutes together a ghostly unbroken
reflection up. The soaring new flats and the crouching old shops
and houses looked equally brittle under the moon, which blazed in
windows that looked its way. The futility of the black-out became
laughable: from the sky, presumably, you could see every slate in
the roofs, every whited kerb, every contour of the naked winter
flowerbeds in the park; and the lake, with its shining twists and
tree-darkened islands would be a landmark for miles, yes, miles,
overhead.

However, the sky, in whose glassiness floated no clouds but only
opaque balloons, remained glassy-silent. The Germans no longer
came by the full moon. Something more immaterial seemed to
threaten, and to be keeping people at home. This day between days,
this extra tax, was perhaps more than senses and nerves could bear.
People stayed indoors with a fervour that could be felt: the buildings strained with battened-down human life, but not a beam, not a
voice, not a note from a radio escaped. Now and then under streets
and buildings the earth rumbled: the Underground sounded loudest
at this time.

Outside the now gateless gates of the park, the road coming
downhill from the north-west turned south and became a street,
down whose perspective the traffic lights went through their un-
meaning performance of changing colour. From the promontory of
pavement outside the gates you saw at once up the road and down
the street: from behind where you stood, between the gateposts,
appeared the lesser strangements of grass and water and trees. At
this point, at this moment, three French soldiers, directed to a
hostel they could not find, stopped singing to listen derisively to

the water-birds wakened up by the moon. Next, two wardens coming off duty emerged from their post and crossed the road diagonally, each with an elbow cupped inside a slung-on tin hat. The wardens turned their faces, mauve in the moonlight, towards the Frenchmen with no expression at all. The two sets of steps died in opposite directions, and, the birds subsiding, nothing was heard or seen until, a little way down the street, a trickle of people came out of the Underground, around the anti-panic brick wall. These all disappeared quickly, in an abashed way, or as though dissolved in the street by some white acid, but for a girl and a soldier who, by their way of walking, seemed to have no destination but each other and to be not quite certain even of that. Blotted into one shadow, he tall, she little, these two proceeded towards the park. They looked in, but did not go in; they stood there debating without speaking. Then, as though a command from the street behind them had been received by their synchronized bodies, they faced round to look back the way they had come.

His look up the height of a building made his head drop back, and she saw his eyeballs glitter. She slid her hand from his sleeve, stepped to the edge of the pavement and said: 'Mysterious Kôr.'

'What is?' he said, not quite collecting himself.

'This is –

> Mysterious Kôr thy walls forsaken stand,
> Thy lonely towers beneath a lonely moon –

– this is Kôr.'

'Why,' he said, 'it's years since I've thought of that.'

She said: 'I think of it all the time –

> Not in the waste beyond the swamps and sand,
> The fever-haunted forest and lagoon,
> Mysterious Kôr thy walls –

– a completely forsaken city, as high as cliffs and as white as bones, with no history——'

'But something must once have happened: why had it been forsaken?'

'How could anyone tell you when there's nobody there?'

'Nobody there since how long?'

'Thousands of years.'

'In that case, it would have fallen down.'

'No, not Kôr,' she said with immediate authority. 'Kôr's altogether different; it's very strong; there is not a crack in it anywhere for a weed to grow in; the corners of stones and the monuments might have been cut yesterday, and the stairs and arches are built to support themselves.'

'You know all about it,' he said, looking at her.

'I know, I know all about it.'

'What, since you read that book?'

'Oh, I didn't get much from that; I just got the name. I knew that must be the right name; it's like a cry.'

'Most like the cry of a crow to me.' He reflected, then said: 'But the poem begins with "Not" – "Not in the waste beyond the swamps and sand——" And it goes on, as I remember, to prove Kôr's not really anywhere. When a poem says there's no such place——'

'What it tries to say doesn't matter: I see what it makes me see. Anyhow, that was written some time ago, at that time when they thought they had got everything taped, because the whole world had been explored, even the middle of Africa. Every thing and place had been found and marked on some map; so what wasn't marked on any map couldn't be there at all. So *they* thought: that was why he wrote the poem. "The world is disenchanted," it goes on. That was what set me off hating civilization.'

'Well, cheer up,' he said; 'there isn't much of it left.'

'Oh, yes, I cheered up some time ago. This war shows we've by no means come to the end. If you can blow whole places out of existence, you can blow whole places into it. I don't see why not. They say we can't say what's come out since the bombing started. By the time we've come to the end, Kôr may be the one city left: the abiding city. I should laugh.'

'No, you wouldn't,' he said sharply. '*You* wouldn't – at least, I hope not. I hope you don't know what you're saying – does the moon make you funny?'

'Don't be cross about Kôr; please don't, Arthur,' she said.

'I thought girls thought about people.'

'What, these days?' she said. 'Think about people? How can anyone think about people? How can anyone think about people if they've got any heart? I don't know how other girls manage: I always think about Kôr.'

'Not about me?' he said. When she did not at once answer, he turned her hand over, in anguish, inside his grasp. 'Because I'm not there when you want me – is that my fault?'

'But to think about Kôr *is* to think about you and me.'

'In that dead place?'

'No, ours – we'd be alone there.'

Tightening his thumb on her palm while he thought this over, he looked behind them, around them, above them – even up at the sky. He said finally: 'But we're alone here.'

'That was why I said "Mysterious Kôr".'

'What, you mean we're there now, that here's there, that now's then? . . . *I* don't mind,' he added, letting out as a laugh the sigh he had been holding in for some time. 'You ought to know the place, and for all I could tell you we might be anywhere: I often do have it, this funny feeling, the first minute or two when I've come up out of the Underground. Well, well: join the Army and see the world.' He nodded towards the perspective of traffic lights and said, a shade craftily: 'What are those, then?'

Having caught the quickest possible breath, she replied: 'Inexhaustible gases; they bored through to them and lit them as they came up; by changing colour they show the changing of minutes; in Kôr there is no sort of other time.'

'You've got the moon, though: that can't help making months.'

'Oh, and the sun, of course; but those two could do what they liked; we should not have to calculate when they'd come or go.'

'We might not have to,' he said, 'but I bet I should.'

'I should not mind what you did, so long as you never said, "What next?"'

'I don't know about "next", but I do know what we'd do first.'

'What, Arthur?'

'Populate Kôr.'

She said: 'I suppose it would be all right if our children were to marry each other?'

But her voice faded out; she had been reminded that they were homeless on this his first night of leave. They were, that was to say, in London without any hope of any place of their own. Pepita shared a two-roomed flatlet with a girl-friend, in a bystreet off the Regent's Park Road, and towards this they must make their half-hearted way. Arthur was to have the sitting-room divan, usually occupied by Pepita, while she herself had half of her girl-friend's bed. There was really no room for a third, and least of all for a man, in those small rooms packed with furniture and the two girls' belongings: Pepita tried to be grateful for her friend Callie's forbearance – but how could she be, when it had not occurred to Callie that she would do better to be away tonight? She was more slow-witted than narrow-minded – but Pepita felt she owed a kind of ruin to her. Callie, not yet known to be home later than ten, would be now waiting up, in her housecoat, to welcome Arthur. That would mean three-sided chat, drinking cocoa, then turning in: that would be that, and that would be all. That was London, this war – they were lucky to have a roof – London, full enough before the Americans came. Not a place: they would even grudge you sharing a grave – that was what even married couples complained. Whereas in Kôr. . .

In Kôr. . . . Like glass, the illusion shattered: a car hummed like a hornet towards them, veered, showed its scarlet tail-light, streaked away up the road. A woman edged round a front door and along the area railings timidly called her cat; meanwhile a clock near, then another set further back in the dazzling distance, set about striking midnight. Pepita, feeling Arthur release her arm with an abruptness that was the inverse of passion, shivered; whereat he asked brusquely: 'Cold? Well, which way? – we'd better be getting on.'

Callie was no longer waiting up. Hours ago she had set out the three cups and saucers, the tins of cocoa and household milk and, on the gas-ring, brought the kettle to just short of the boil. She had turned open Arthur's bed, the living-room divan, in the neat inviting way she had learnt at home – then, with a modest impulse, replaced the cover. She had, as Pepita foresaw, been wearing her cretonne house-coat, the nearest thing to a hostess gown that she had; she had already brushed her hair for the night, rebraided it, bound the braids in a coronet round her head. Both lights and the wireless had been on, to make the room both look and sound gay: all alone, she had come to that peak moment at which company should arrive – but so seldom does. From then on she felt welcome beginning to wither in her, a flower of the heart that had bloomed too early. There she had sat like an image, facing the three cold cups, on the edge of the bed to be occupied by an unknown man.

Callie's innocence and her still unsought-out state had brought her to take a proprietary pride in Arthur; this was all the stronger, perhaps, because they had not yet met. Sharing the flat with Pepita, this last year, she had been content with reflecting heat of love. It was not, surprisingly, that Pepita seemed very happy – there were times when she was palpably on the rack, and this was not what Callie could understand. 'Surely you owe it to Arthur,' she would then say, 'to keep cheerful? So long as you love each other——'. Callie's calm brow glowed – one might say that it glowed in place of her friend's; she became the guardian of that ideality which for Pepita was constantly lost to view. It was true, with the sudden prospect of Arthur's leave, things had come nearer to earth: he became a proposition, and she would have been as glad if he could have slept somewhere else. Physically shy, a brotherless virgin, Callie shrank from sharing this flat with a young man. In this flat you could hear everything: what was once a three-windowed Victorian drawing-room had been partitioned, by very thin walls, into kitchenette, living-room, Callie's bedroom. The living-room was in the centre; the two others open off it. What was once the conservatory, half a flight down, was now converted into a draughty bathroom, shared with somebody else on the girls' floor. The flat, for these days, was cheap – even so, it was Callie, earning more than Pepita, who paid the greater part of the rent: it thus became up to her, more or less, to express goodwill as to Arthur's making a third. 'Why, it will be lovely to have him here,' Callie said. Pepita accepted the good will without much grace – but then, had she ever much grace to spare? – she was as restlessly secretive, as self-centred, as a little half-grown black cat. Next came a puzzling moment: Pepita seemed to be hinting that Callie should fix herself up somewhere else. 'But where would I go?' Callie marvelled when this was at last borne in on her. 'You know what London's like now. And, anyway' – here she laughed, but hers was a forehead that coloured as easily as it glowed – 'it wouldn't be proper, would it, me going off and leaving just you and Arthur; I don't know what your mother would say to me. No, we may be a little squashed, but we'll make things ever so homey. I shall not mind playing gooseberry, really, dear.'

But the hominess by now was evaporating, as Pepita and Arthur still and still did not come. At half-past ten, in obedience to the rule of the house, Callie was obliged to turn off the wireless, whereupon silence out of the stepless street began seeping into the slighted room. Callie recollected the fuel target and turned off her dear little table lamp, gaily painted with spots to make it look like a toadstool, thereby leaving only the hanging light. She laid her hand on the kettle, to find it gone cold again and sigh for the wasted gas if not for her wasted thought. Where are they? Cold crept up her out of the kettle; she went to bed.

Callie's bed lay along the wall under the window: she did not like sleeping so close up under glass, but the clearance that must be left for the opening of door and cupboards made this the only possible place. Now she got in and lay rigidly on the bed's inner side, under the hanging hems of the window curtains, training her limbs not to stray to what would be Pepita's half. This sharing of her bed with another body would not be the least of her sacrifice to the lovers' love; tonight would be the first night – or at least, since she was an infant – that Callie had slept with anyone. Child of a sheltered middle-class household, she had kept physical distances all her life. Already repugnance and shyness ran through her limbs; she was preyed upon by some more obscure trouble than the expectation that she might not sleep. As to *that*, Pepita was restless; her tossings on the divan, her broken-off exclamations and blurred pleas had been to be heard, most nights, through the dividing wall.

Callie knew, as though from a vision, that Arthur would sleep soundly, with assurance and majesty. Did they not all say, too, that a soldier sleeps like a log? With awe she pictured, asleep, the face that she had not yet, awake, seen – Arthur's man's eyelids, cheekbones and set mouth turned up to the darkened ceiling. Wanting to savour darkness herself, Callie reached out and put off her bedside lamp.

At once she knew that something was happening – outdoors, in the street, the whole of London, the world. An advance, an extraordinary movement was silently taking place; blue-white beams overflowed from it, silting, dropping round the edges of the muffling black-out curtains. When, starting up, she knocked a fold of the curtain, a beam like a mouse ran across her bed. A searchlight, the most powerful of all time, might have been turned full and steady upon her defended window; finding flaws in the black-out stuff, it made veins and stars. Once gained by this idea of pressure she could not lie down again; she sat tautly, drawn-up knees touching her breasts, and asked herself if there were anything she should do. She parted the curtains, opened them slowly wider, looked out – and was face to face with the moon.

Below the moon, the houses opposite her window blazed black in transparent shadow; and something – was it a coin or a ring –

glittered half-way across the chalk-white street. Light marched in past her face, and she turned to see where it went: out stood the curves and garlands of the great white marble Victorian mantel-piece of that lost drawing-room; out stood, in the photographs turned her way, the thoughts with which her parents had faced the camera, and the humble puzzlement of her two dogs at home. Of silver brocade, just faintly purpled with roses, became her house-coat hanging over the chair. And the moon did more: it exonerated and beautified the lateness of the lovers' return. No wonder, she said to herself, no wonder – if this was the world they walked in, if this was whom they were with. Having drunk in the white explana-tion, Callie lay down again. Her half of the bed was in shadow, but she allowed one hand to lie, blanched, in what would be Pepita's place. She lay and looked at the hand until it was no longer her own.

Callie woke to the sound of Pepita's key in the latch. But no voices? What had happened? Then she heard Arthur's step. She heard his unslung equipment dropped with a weary, dull sound, and the plonk of his tin hat on a wooden chair. 'Sssh-sssh!' Pepita exclaimed, 'she *might* be asleep!'

Then at last Arthur's voice: 'But I thought you said——'

'I'm not asleep; I'm just coming!' Callie called out with rapture, leaping out from her form in shadow into the moonlight, zipping on her enchanted housecoat over her nightdress, kicking her shoes on, and pinning in place, with a trembling firmness, her plaits in their coronet round her head. Between these movements of hers she heard not another sound. Had she only dreamed they were there? Her heart beat: she stepped through the living-room, shutting her door behind her.

Pepita and Arthur stood the other side of the table; they gave the impression of being lined up. Their faces, at different levels – for Pepita's rough, dark head came only an inch above Arthur's khaki shoulder – were alike in abstention from any kind of expression; as though, spiritually, they both still refused to be here. Their features looked faint, weathered – was this the work of the moon? Pepita said at once: 'I suppose we are very late?'

'I don't wonder,' Callie said, 'on this lovely night.'

Arthur had not raised his eyes; he was looking at the three cups. Pepita now suddenly jogged his elbow, saying, 'Arthur, wake up; say something; this is Callie – well, Callie, this is Arthur, of course.'

'Why, yes, of course this is Arthur,' returned Callie, whose can-

did eyes since she entered had not left Arthur's face. Perceiving that
Arthur did not know what to do, she advanced round the table to
shake hands with him. He looked up, she looked down, for the first
time: she rather beheld than felt his red-brown grip on what still
seemed her glove of moonlight. 'Welcome, Arthur', she said. 'I'm so
glad to meet you at last. I hope you will be comfortable in the flat.'

'It's been kind of you,' he said after consideration.

'Please do not feel that,' said Callie. 'This is Pepita's home, too,
and we both hope – don't we, Pepita? – that you'll regard it as yours.
Please feel free to do just as you like. I am sorry it is so small.'

'Oh, I don't know,' Arthur said, as though hypnotized; 'it seems a
nice little place.'

Pepita, meanwhile, glowered and turned away.

Arthur continued to wonder, though he had once been told, how
these two unalike girls had come to set up together – Pepita so
small, except for her too-big head, compact of childish brusqueness
and of unchildish passion, and Callie, so sedate, waxy and tall – an
unlit candle. Yes, she was like one of those candles on sale outside a
church; there could be something votive even in her demeanour.
She was unconscious that her good manners, those of an old-
fashioned country doctor's daughter, were putting the other two at
a disadvantage. He found himself touched by the grave good faith
with which Callie was wearing that tartish housecoat, above which
her face kept the glaze of sleep; and, as she knelt to relight the gas
ring under the kettle, he marked the strong, delicate arch of one
bare foot, disappearing into the arty green shoe. Pepita was now too
near him ever again to be seen as he now saw Callie – in a sense, he
never *had* seen Pepita for the first time: she had not been, and still
sometimes was not, his type. No, he had not thought of her twice;
he had not remembered her until he began to remember her with
passion. You might say he had not seen Pepita coming: their love
had been a collision in the dark.

Callie, determined to get this over, knelt back and said: 'Would
Arthur like to wash his hands?' When they had heard him stumble
down the half-flight of stairs, she said to Pepita: 'Yes, I was so glad
you had the moon.'

'Why?' said Pepita. She added: 'There was too much of it.'

'You're tired. Arthur looks tired, too.'

'How would you know? He's used to marching about. But it's all
this having no place to go.'

'But, Pepita, you——'

But at this point Arthur came back: from the door he noticed the wireless, and went direct to it. 'Nothing much on now, I suppose?' he doubtfully said.

'No; you see it's past midnight; we're off the air. And, anyway, in this house they don't like the wireless late. By the same token,' went on Callie, friendlily smiling, 'I'm afraid I must ask you, Arthur, to take your boots off, unless, of course, you mean to stay sitting down. The people below us——'

Pepita flung off, saying something under her breath, but Arthur, remarking, 'No, I don't mind,' both sat down and began to take off his boots. Pausing, glancing to left and right at the divan's fresh cotton spread, he said: 'It's all right is it, for me to sit on this?'

'That's my bed,' said Pepita. 'You are to sleep in it.'

Callie then made the cocoa, after which they turned in. Preliminary trips to the bathroom having been worked out, Callie was first to retire, shutting the door behind her so that Pepita and Arthur might kiss each other good-night. When Pepita joined her, it was without knocking: Pepita stood still in the moon and began to tug off her clothes. Glancing with hate at the bed, she asked: 'Which side?'

'I expected you'd like the outside.'

'What are you standing about for?'

'I don't really know: as I'm inside I'd better get in first.'

'Then why not get in?'

When they had settled rigidly, side by side, Callie asked: 'Do you think Arthur's got all he wants?'

Pepita jerked her head up. 'We can't sleep in all this moon.'

'Why, you don't believe the moon does things, actually?'

'Well, it couldn't hope to make some of us *much* more screwy.'

Callie closed the curtains, then said: 'What do you mean? And – didn't you hear? – I asked if Arthur's got all he wants.'

'That's what I meant – have you got a screw loose, really?'

'Pepita, I won't stay here if you're going to be like this.'

'In that case, you had better go in with Arthur.'

'What about me?' Arthur loudly said through the wall, 'I can hear practically all you girls are saying.'

They were both startled – rather that than abashed. Arthur, alone in there, had thrown off the ligatures of his social manner: his voice held the whole authority of his sex – he was impatient, sleepy, and he belonged to no one.

'Sorry,' the girls said in unison. Then Pepita laughed soundlessly, making their bed shake, till to stop herself she bit the back of her hand, and this movement made her elbow strike Callie's cheek. 'Sorry,' she had to whisper. No answer: Pepita fingered her elbow and found, yes, it was quite true, it was wet. 'Look, shut up crying, Callie: what have I done?'

Callie rolled right round, in order to press her forehead closely under the window, into the curtains, against the wall. Her weeping continued to be soundless: now and then, unable to reach her handkerchief, she staunched her eyes with a curtain, disturbing slivers of moon. Pepita gave up marvelling, and soon slept: at least there is something in being dog-tired.

A clock struck four as Callie woke up again – but something else had made her open her swollen eyelids. Arthur, stumbling about on his padded feet, could be heard next door attempting to make no noise. Inevitably, he bumped the edge of the table. Callie sat up: by her side Pepita lay like a mummy rolled half over, in forbidding, tenacious sleep. Arthur groaned, Callie caught a breath, climbed lightly over Pepita, felt for her torch on the mantelpiece, stopped to listen again. Arthur groaned again: Callie, with movements soundless as they were certain, opened the door and slipped through to the living-room. 'What's the matter?' she whispered. 'Are you ill?'

'No; I just got a cigarette. Did I wake you up?'

'But you groaned.'

'I'm sorry; I'd no idea.'

'But do you often?'

'I've no idea, really, I tell you,' Arthur repeated. The air of the room was dense with his presence, overhung by tobacco. He must be sitting on the edge of his bed, wrapped up in his overcoat – she could smell the coat, and each time he pulled on the cigarette his features appeared down there, in the fleeting, dull reddish glow. 'Where are you?' he said. 'Show a light.'

Her nervous touch on her torch, like a reflex to what he said, made it flicker up for a second. 'I am just by the door; Pepita's asleep; I'd better go back to bed.'

'Listen. Do you two get on each other's nerves?'

'Not till tonight,' said Callie, watching the uncertain swoops of the cigarette as he reached across to the ashtray on the edge of the table. Shifting her bare feet patiently, she added: 'You don't see us as we usually are.'

'She's a girl who shows things in funny ways – I expect she feels bad at our putting you out like this – I know I do. But then we'd got no choice, had we?'

'It is really I who am putting you out,' said Callie.

'Well, that can't be helped either, can it? You had the right to stay in your own place. If there'd been more time, we might have gone to the country, though I still don't see where we'd have gone there. It's one harder when you're not married, unless you've got the money. Smoke?'

'No, thank you. Well, if you're all right, I'll go back to bed.'

'I'm glad she's asleep – funny the way she sleeps, isn't it? You can't help wondering where she is. You haven't got a boy, have you, just at present?'

'No. I've never had one.'

'I'm not sure in one way that you're not better off. I can see there's not so much in it for a girl these days. It makes me feel cruel the way I unsettle her: I don't know how much it's me myself or how much it's something the matter that I can't help. How are any of us to know how things could have been? They forget war's not just only war; it's years out of people's lives that they've never had before and won't have again. Do you think she's fanciful?'

'Who, Pepita?'

'It's enough to make her – tonight was the pay-off. We couldn't get near any movie or any place for sitting; you had to fight into the bars, and she hates the staring in bars, and with all that milling about, every street we went, they kept on knocking her even off my arm. So then we took the tube to that park down there, but the place was as bad as daylight, let alone it was cold. We hadn't the nerve – well, that's nothing to do with you.'

'I don't mind.'

'Or else you don't understand. So we began to play – we were off in Kôr.'

'Core of what?'

'Mysterious Kôr – ghost city.'

'Where?'

'You may ask. But I could have sworn she saw it, and from the way she saw it I saw it, too. A game's a game, but what's a hallucination? You begin by laughing, then it gets in you and you can't laugh it off. I tell you, I woke up just now not knowing where I'd been; and I had to get up and feel round this table before I even knew where I was. It wasn't till then that I thought of a cigarette. Now I see why she sleeps like that, if that's where she goes.'

'But she is just as often restless; I often hear her.'

'Then she doesn't always make it. Perhaps it takes me, in some way—— Well, I can't see any harm: when two people have got no place, why not want Kôr, as a start? There are no restrictions on wanting, at any rate.'

'But, oh, Arthur, can't wanting want what's human?'

He yawned. 'To be human's to be at a dead loss.' Stopping yawning, he ground out his cigarette: the china tray skidded at the edge of the table. 'Bring that light here a moment – that is, will you? I think I've messed ash all over these sheets of hers.'

Callie advanced with the torch alight, but at arm's length: now and then her thumb made the beam wobble. She watched the lit-up inside of Arthur's hand as he brushed the sheet; and once he looked up to see her white-nightgowned figure curving above and away from him, behind the arc of light. 'What's that swinging?'

'One of my plaits of hair. Shall I open the window wider?'

'What, to let the smoke out? Go on. And how's your moon?'

'Mine?' Marvelling over this, as the first sign that Arthur remembered that she was Callie, she uncovered the window, pushed up the sash, then after a minute said: 'Not so strong.'

Indeed, the moon's power over London and the imagination had now declined. The siege of light had relaxed; the search was over; the street had a look of survival and no more. Whatever had glittered there, coin or ring, was now invisible or had gone. To Callie it seemed likely that there would never be such a moon again; and on the whole she felt this was for the best. Feeling air reach in like a tired arm round her body, she dropped the curtains against it and returned to her own room.

Back by her bed, she listened: Pepita's breathing still had the regular sound of sleep. At the other side of the wall the divan creaked as Arthur stretched himself out again. Having felt ahead of her lightly, to make sure her half was empty, Callie climbed over Pepita and got in. A certain amount of warmth had travelled between the sheets from Pepita's flank, and in this Callie extended her sword-cold body: she tried to compose her limbs; even they quivered after Arthur's words in the dark, words *to* the dark. The loss of her own mysterious expectation, of her love for love, was a small thing beside the war's total of unlived lives. Suddenly Pepita flung out one hand: its back knocked Callie lightly across the face.

Pepita had now turned over and lay with her face up. The hand that had struck Callie must have lain over the other, which grasped the pyjama collar. Her eyes, in the dark, might have been either shut or open, but nothing made her frown more or less steadily: it became certain, after another moment, that Pepita's act of justice had been unconscious. She still lay, as she had lain, in an avid dream, of which Arthur had been the source, of which Arthur was not the end. With him she looked this way, that way, down the wide void pure streets, between statues, pillars and shadows, through archways and colonnades. With him she went up the stairs down which nothing but moon came; with him trod the ermine dust of the endless halls, stood on terraces, mounted the extreme tower, looked down on the statued squares, the wide, void, pure streets. He was the password, but not the answer: it was to Kôr's finality that she turned.

Fear of Death

WHY did I want to join the Navy and fight? Mostly I wished to test the unknown in myself. As a child I was once accidentally pushed into a park lake on Boxing Day. I must have been terrified, but I cannot recall my fear. All that remains is a memory, bright after thirty years, of lying on my back under the water, looking up as if into a frosted mirror and seeing a white shadow cross the rippling grey when a swan paddled over me, in hopes that the disturbance meant bread crusts. I was too young to realize death. Later, a youth, I was trapped by the tide on a cliff-bound Devon shore. But I had time to seek ways of escape, and I did not believe I should die. So although I was alone, I was not afraid.

But when I was in the Mediterranean last summer . . . Rommel had crossed the Egyptian border. Alexandria was preparing to defend itself. No British ship expected, in those waters, to escape attack by aircraft, warship or submarine – or any two of these and sometimes all three.

The first day I tasted action was sunny, but a sharp wind blew, making stays and wires hiss. Coming off duty I paused on the gun deck to watch the ship swing through the creamy sea, to count the attending destroyers and the stolid merchantmen smoking along in line ahead like chaperoned dowagers.

Then I went down to my mess deck and began to darn a sock. Three of the relieved watch took their soap and towels to the bathroom. Others dragged the leather seats off the long stools, laid them on the deck and went to sleep. One wrote a letter. Some chatted, an odd mixture of Cockney, Liverpool, Glasgow, Yorkshire, Canadian and other accents.

I had finished the warp of my darn and started on the weft when the alarm sounded: a series of urgent longs on the buzzer. It was also the first time most of my messmates had gone into action – indeed the first time some of them had been to sea. I don't know what I expected our first reactions to be; but not something so entirely unheroic as bad temper. I was annoyed at having to put my sock away half-darned. The sleepers resented being wakened up. The letter-writer flung his pen down with an exclamation of anger. A formerly active service AB, recalled after serving his time, said: '—— it! Just like them bastards to wait till we're off watch.' There he spoke for all. He stood on the stool and made a short speech to the canary he had bought ashore and hung in its cage above the mess table. 'Yer've got yer seed,' he said, gravely, 'an' yer've got yer water. Fill yer belly till I comes back. So long, cock.' The bird hopped sharply on its perch.

Then the unanimous rush for gas masks, tin hats, anti-flash gear, oilskins and sea-boots, the clank of feet up the iron ladder, the crash of the hatch cover shutting off the empty deck, the milling of dozens of men in the narrow alleyways as they sought their stations, petty officers shouting 'Double away there!' in the detached, irritated tones of men already looking inward to their own fate, the steady shuffle-shuffle of rubber and leather on linoleum.

I remembered, as I pushed my way to my magazine, aft, how in war films of infantry advancing their pace seemed as slow as a dream. So with us, until the press thinned out and we could run. Ahead of me, in the engine room flat, I heard a sudden yell of laughter. Two stokers, taking a shower when the buzzer went, had been caught naked. As they shoved frantically against the human stream their towels were snatched from around their waists and the alleyway resounded with the echo of flat hands against bare buttocks. The stokers were grinning. One hadn't had time to dry his body.

The hatchway to my magazine lay just aft the wardroom. I glanced in as I passed. It was empty. Periodicals sprawled on the padded benches and the carpeted deck. On the arm of a chair a book had been placed, covers up, so that the owner need not search for his place when he returned.

Down the vertical ladder to the flooding cabinet, down again to the magazine. The face of one of the damage control party peered at us from above. 'All down?' he shouted. 'All down', replied the corporal of marines in charge, and the rating, like a dandyish racing motorist in his white anti-flash helmet and long white gloves, descended to the cabinet and closed the armoured, counter-weighted hatch, so heavy that it took his full strength to move. Then, as the weight balanced and started in his favour, it fell with a jar. A pause, as he climbed up again, and then the dropping of the top cover and snick of its clips.

So there we were, a dozen blue-overalled men in this chilly cavern stacked from deck to deckhead with cordite and shells – safe so long as no bomb struck or, if the magazine had to be flooded, we could get out before the water rose; and with some prospect of escape if the ship, supposing her torpedoed, did not sink too quickly. Either the armoured hatch might be raised by the pressure of shoulders, or we might follow each other up the ladder inside the turret. There was just enough room to squeeze in there and haul oneself up the iron rungs, wet with warm oil dripping down from the pump that moved the guns. The pump was pounding now like an excited heart, and the turret slowly swung to meet the bombers, German or Italian, that we knew were coming in. Shut off below in a clamour of sound – the pump, the rattle of steel shell and brass cartridges in the racks, the communicated vibration of the propeller shafts on either side – we should have to guess its progress from the way the turret swung, from the abrupt lift of the deck as the ship heeled in a quick evasive turn to dodge a stick of bombs, from the commander's voice through the loud speaker should a lull allow him to broadcast a commentary. But we could not hear his voice unless we climbed the ladder and held our faces to the speaker.

The telephone rang from above. The corporal pressed his answering buzzer and jammed his ear against the instrument, listened, yelled back a jest I could not catch and told us to stand by. I had unclipped a number of charges and the bar of the first shell rack had been taken down. The shell hoist was loaded and men stood by the cordite lifts, waiting for the automatic doors to open. I held a charge in my arms. We were all ready. There was time to think and I was unsure whether I liked my thought, which was not that I might die but that I wanted to live lest my death should bring sorrow to those who loved me. The idea fascinated. I was filled with a sorrow in which lay no regret for the stopping of my own breath; I felt what I imagined would be the ache and emptiness in *their* hearts.

Masochism or vanity, or both, the notion drew me further. How would A and B adjust their lives, when they could no longer share mine? Would C mind very much, or D and E remember me for long? From the desolation of this self-torture I was glad to be freed by what sounded, in the general din, like a couple of polite coughs. Our guns had opened fire. The hoists began to work.

The next hour gave us no time for thought. We were all too busy, lifting the 80lb shells out of the racks, shovelling in the cordite whenever the doors opened, sliding on the greasy grating as the ship rolled, chipping flesh off knuckles and elbows, swearing, sweating and laughing when somebody lurched or fell. And all the time, the remote, irregular cough of the guns, and every now and then a curious thud against the ship's side that shook the magazine – the near misses of the unseen bombs, whistling down in the sunlight.

Then we had our first lull and I the glad relief of not having been too much afraid. The corporal rang up his friend the sergeant in the turret to find out what had happened. A boy of twenty, a clerk in civil life, who had told me once that his ambition was to find a cure for cancer, took out of his overalls a pamphlet on biochemistry. A stout, fat-cheeked youth, who had come into the Navy from a Thames barge, squatted down and began to read an oily, battered copy of *No Orchids for Miss Blandish*. Two others resumed an earlier, giggly wrestling bout. The rest I could not see; the charge cases hid them. I could hear their voices, casual to the point of anti-climax.

Was this all, then? Did the prospect of death mean no more than a check to a clerk's dream, the interruption of a book and the post-ponement of childish horseplay? I look round at my companions, to divine if I could, behind this extrovert behaviour, some secret speculation. It was then that I noticed the man in the corner. I didn't know his name (it turned out later that none of us did) or anything about him. He might have been thirty; he could have been forty. He never chatted to anyone and seemed to have no friends or interests in the ship, but lived his own withdrawn life. He was sitting now on a sand-filled fire bucket, his hands laid inertly on his knees, his colourless face a stare of strain, as if death had spoken to him already and he knew he was lost. (Which might have been so, for the next day he was removed from the magazine and, at his own request, made an anti-aircraft lookout, and at his post a bullet from a Junkers killed him.)

I wanted to ask him what thoughts he had, to be thus paralysed. Or was his fear without form? Or was he afraid of fear, as most men are until they have tried themselves out. But these questions are not to be asked – and the telephone had rung again, the turret was turning. Again the discreet cough, the choking, the stumbling and the oaths. But this time the atmosphere was new. The constraints were gone. The question mark poised in every brain had vanished. For good or ill, we each had our answer. One man sang as he staggered from the racks with his shells; and I, who suddenly felt happy and free, knew why. He had passed his test; he was on good terms with his spirit.

We all, in more or less degree, shared this strange intoxication – except the corporal of marines, to whom action was ordinary, and the pale man in the corner, who sat on, not watching, seeing nothing. The corporal stumbled over the deck to him. 'Well strike me pink!' he exclaimed. 'What the hell do you think this is, mate? A make-and-mend? Come on then, stand easy's over.' Whereupon the man rose from his bucket, walked over to the turret and began to climb up the escape ladder – not with panic speed but deliberately, as if in obedience to an order. The corporal watched him with dropped jaw, charged after him and pulled him down again by his heels. 'You can't do that there 'ere,' he said, patiently.

The man stood where the corporal had pushed him, against an empty shell rack, his hands by his side, still silent, like a martyr with eyes of pain. And the corporal could find nothing more to say. He put his arms akimbo, then scratched the back of his head with his right hand. But it was beyond him to deal with a man in a trance. He could only point to the fire bucket, and the man returned there and stood like a statue. Thus he was when the second and final action of that day ended, the 'All clear' was broadcast, the armoured hatch was opened from above, and we were free. Nobody spoke to the man whose nerve was gone and nobody looked at him, except that the corporal, who always left the magazine last, said to him with a rough, puzzled gentleness: 'Up you go, mate.'

I found my mess-deck half-wrecked by a heavy bomb which had crashed through without exploding, fractured a water pipe, smashed table and hurled jags of metal through lockers, hammocks and fittings. Most of the lights were out. At the forward end, which was undamaged, grimy men clustered around the tables smoking, talking of the action and of friends who were wounded or dead, and of how they had died. At the end of the table a youngster sat crying openly like the child he had so recently been. He had seen his 'winger', his best friend, decapitated. Grief and shock joined in the tears that drew two pink lanes down his grease-stained cheeks. The old AB was searching among debris for the corpse of his canary. The place had the air of a cemetery chapel.

No consolation, no comfort, was offered. They were inarticulate men, unable to frame the smooth sympathies of a politer life. I think they were more instinctive then men of education, and out of their instinct knew that grief cannot be soothed by those it does not touch. So they talked and argued and boasted around the weeping boy as though he wasn't there.

The AB found his crushed and muddied bird and showed it to us. He leaned across the table, his mouth tight with anger. He had placed the bird in a dirty handkerchief. Somebody spoke the epitaph: 'Poor little bastard! 'E never done nobody no 'arm.' The AB laid a chunk of fractured piping beside the corpse, wrapped it up carefully and tied a reef knot in the handkerchief. Then he left the mess. We knew what he was going to do. Dead men over the side in weighted canvas, a canary in a knotted handkerchief – it seemed no parody. All were victims.

Nobody knew what to say next. We became embarrassed by our own silence. At last the leading hand of that mess stood up. 'Well, what about some eats?' he asked, nervously, uncertain whether the idea was fitting. We consented by moving away so that the table could be laid, with the boy still sobbing at the end of it, and none telling him he was in the way of the cooks as they lifted plates and mugs down from the rack above him.

The food was brought from the galley, the bread dumped on the white American cloth. I was astonished at my hunger. The old AB, the sobbing boy, whose tears had now become hiccups at which even he himself laughed, everybody ate an enormous meal.

The Sea and the Sky

. . . SHE watches me intently as I talk, and every line of her body flatters my wit. The restaurant is crowded, but not too much, and the band plays my favourite tunes, but not too many, and the pianist is as good as I'd like to be.

Supper has taken us some time but we have not eaten much. Our wine glasses wink across the table for they are laughing at us because we are mortal and they can only be broken.

Where did she get that expression in her eyes? She is not as old as her eyes nor as young as her hands. We dance and there is divine sympathy in the touch of her thighs against mine. The lights are dimmed and the pianist syncopates a Chopin nocturne. The dresses of the women tell more lies than I can count. As we dance she presses closer in my arms and then we do not need to talk any more. . . .

'Bogey!'

What is it about her scent?

'Bogey!'

The lights are nearly out—

'Hey! Come on then.'

Somebody has broken a glass—

'Bogey? It's a quarter to four.'

A hand on my shoulder, sleep falling from my spirit like a dust sheet from a marble statue. Scent, music, girl in my arms; fug, weariness, hammock swinging. . . .

'For Christ's sake, Bogey, its bloody near four o'clock.'

I have the morning watch. The sea and the sky are grey and cold.

The wind sighs and scurries about the corners of the wheelhouse. The officer of the watch stamps cold feet on the bridge above our heads. The gyro compass chatters incessantly. It is very sensitive and protests metallically if the ship's head moves half a degree. I am bo'sun's mate of the watch so I sit in the wheelhouse beside the quartermaster. I must call out the reliefs for the lookouts and pipe my orders from the bridge all round the ship.

'What's the time, Bogey?' Most of the QMs like me to keep the clock out of sight, for time on watch is like watching a pot boil.

'Quarter to five.'

'What about a jug of tea?'

'I'll make one when I go below to shake Taff.'

'What time's that?'

'Now. I'd almost forgotten.'

'You're not with us, are you, Bogey?'

'Not at this bloody hour of the morning.'

I go below to shake Taff. I do not like to wake a sleeping man. I have done it too many times, seen too many sleep-drawn faces, heard too many weary shudders from half-conscious lips. . . . I feel sad when I put my hand on the relaxed shoulder, when it is warm and snug, when I can tell by the breathing how tired the man is. The face asleep is never the face awake.

As I balance beside Taff's hammock I hesitate, I wonder what are his dreams and where his spirit wanders. I believe that the spirit leaves the body when it sleeps, and who am I to drag it back to the limitations of consciousness and time?

What can you tell about a man from his face when his mind is dreaming? Only the devil would ask that question and wait for an answer. Those who are tough and vicious sleep with innocent smiles on their lips. Those who are quiet, soft-voiced, sleep with the mouths contracted, the eyebrows down-drawn and the cheeks twisted. You cannot comment, you must not deduce.

Taff is very hard to wake up. He is a short, stocky Welshman, a natural wit, an instinctive fighter. He is moody and when he has had too much rum it is best to keep out of his way. He cannot be pacified or consoled; whatever you say will be wrong. Then he is chokker. He will throw sea-boots or mess traps about and he will not care whether he hits anything or not.

His face is expressionless now. His breathing is deep and erratic.

I put my hand on his shoulder. Gradually I increase the pressure and call his name. This is the best way to wake a man, without making him start in his hammock, for all of us sleep expecting either action stations or torpedoes. There are quite enough 'panics' without some fool shaking you in your hammock as if the ship were going down.

'Taff? It's a quarter to five.'

'Ugh!' He is not conscious yet.

'Come on, Taff. You're on watch in fifteen minutes.'

'Wha'sser time?'

'I told you. Getting on for ten to five. Daisy had a ping about an hour ago.'

'Where's the convoy?'

'Right astern. We're doing an ASDIC sweep.'

'All right, Bogey. Got a fag?'

Taff is an Asdic rating. They work with headphones and they pick up echoes underwater and can get the bearing and distance of the echo and often they can tell if it's a sub or not. Sometimes they mistake the echo of a shoal of fish for a sub. Sometimes we laugh at the 'panic' and sometimes we curse. A 'ping' is the slang term for an echo.

I go up to the wheelhouse.

'Tramp's just caught it up.'

'Where?'

'Right astern of the convoy.'

'Tin fish?'

'Yes. Too many bloody subs about.'

'Did Daisy ping it?'

'No. Destroyer did, she dropped some charges. I expect the sub dived as soon as she'd fired her fish. Did you make the tea?'

I go below again. Taff gives me a wicked look. He thinks I have come down to see if he is turning out. He is rather sensitive on that point.

It is dark on the mess-deck. The ship is rolling and I have forgotten to bring my torch. I stagger about lighting matches, ducking beneath the swinging hammocks. I find the jug in the big fanny. The tea is kept in a tin chest with the sugar. I can never find it during the night watches. The caterer is a thrifty Yorkshireman. He always stows it away in some inaccessible corner of the mess shelf so that the night watchmen won't dig out on the sugar. I've got a fair idea where he put it. Somebody's hammock is slung there. I crawl, insinuate, balance, twist myself between the lockers, the hammock, the mess shelf and an inert form flaked out on the table. I find the chest. I take a handful of tea and sugar and must now extricate myself with one hand.

My matches fall out of the top pocket of my overalls. It is too dark to find them. Condensed milk is on the table. Why the man asleep has not kicked it off with his foot I do not know.

I pour milk into the jug and throw in my handful of tea and sugar. I am too mad to make a trip to the galley with just the jug and the tea and then return to the mess to add the precise amount of milk. I get two cups. Precariously I struggle along the deck shielding the top of the jug with my arm. Experience has taught me how much tea can be lost out of a jug by one of those sudden gusts of wind.

Wearily I enter the wheelhouse. How pleased the QM will be.

'Where the hell have you been, Bogey? Growing the bloody tea?'

Taff comes through the wheelhouse on his way to the bridge to relieve Daisy. The Asdic rating who will be off watch as soon as Taff relieves him is called Bell. That is why he is nicknamed Daisy. They call me Bogey because my name is Knight.

'What time do the pubs open around here?' Taff looks anxiously at the QM. We are north of Spitzbergen and wherever the tired eyes look the sea and the sky are grey and cold.

The QM tells Taff to go and get stuffed. Taff grins maliciously.

'You don't drink, do you, Cecil?' He jumps up the bridge ladder before the insulted QM can catch him. Even QMs leave the wheel, even in the Navy, when a messmate becomes too humorous. We are a minesweeper. One of the little ships and discipline is not so strict. I hear one of the lookouts shout. Another ship has caught it up. She is an oiler and when she was hit a sheet of orange-black flame mocked the grey sky.

The QM sucks his teeth.

'That's the second. Where was she, Bogey?'

'Right astern of the convoy.'

'Bloody hell! We're right ahead.'

I don't say anything.

I come down from the wheelhouse to take the sea temperature. The black shining deck rises beneath my feet. I look outboard. I have begun to hate the horizon; void, vapid, insipid, cloud-cluttered sky. I have begun to hate the monotonous blustering waves. Always they must caress the sides of the ship. She moves sullenly and blowsily; her sensuality like a sodden barmaid tolerant with boredom.

I hate the pure air for it never smells of anything. My nostrils are *bored*. The galley always smells the same. The mess-deck always stinks of fetid sweat, of stubbornly dying fag-ends. I think of

Sackville Street, Charlotte Street, Leicester Square, Soho. Onions, petrol fumes, hot tar, cow dung. I think of the land. Paper boys, song of the subway, flash of slim silk-clad legs jumping a bus. I think of women. I think of one girl. I always thought her stockings too short until I found out how long her legs were. That was a great moment because she said:

'Where did you learn to make love?'

I didn't answer and even when she'd got her breath back she didn't repeat the question. She was an unusual girl.

I fall out of my dream and find myself on the quarterdeck. I must sling a canvas bag over the side to get a sample of the sea water and then dip the thermometer into it.

The kitten plays with the end of the bag. She crouches, haunches quivering with controlled excitement. She leaps suddenly, high into the air with her white tummy flashing and lands viciously on the wriggling cord. Her brother watches big-eyed from behind a bollard. He is unaccountably electrified. He charges his sister, bucking grotesquely. They roll on the deck, caught in mimic battle terrible to watch.

Half an hour ago two of the merchant ships were torpedoed. Against the great circle of the horizon they had seemed static models on a paper sea whose rollers could roll no higher. Now there is motion. Steam from the exploded engine-room hangs against the side of the tramp. Cotton wool that has a brutal realism.

The two kittens spit with intensity; back legs kicking viciously; baby-blue eyes tight closed; tails hysterical with wrath. The cat cries. The tom stops for an instant, blinks and looks nonchalantly in the opposite direction. Then the cat jumps high into the air and disappears behind the bollard. She is watching. She is waiting. . . .

Now there is movement. The tramp is sinking. A wisp of smoke from her stack wavers in the air. I look at that smoke and think how it reminds me of a house in a valley. Then it was a blue June day. Now it is a grey arctic day. But the smoke is just the same. The smoke from the tramp looks quiet and peaceful but I know that there on the sinking ship some seaman flashes a picture in his mind of his house in a valley, and that the wavering smoke for him has no garish similitude. I know the feeling that the deck can no longer keep the cold water from your limbs. She is going down. The little black figures that I can see on her foc'sle will have to swim. Some will drown. Some need not care.

The cat streaks across the deck and lands on the tom's back. She has him by the neck. Is life war, is war life?

The sea temperature is twenty. The little black figures won't swim for long. Soon I shall pipe 'Blue Watch to cruising stations'. When my relief comes up, hating the cold air, I can go below. I hating the thick air he hates to leave.

I am hungry and there are air pockets in my stomach. For a long time I stand thinking about it all and then the PO of the watch on deck sings out:

'Pipe Blue Watch to cruising stations, Bogey.'

As I go below I glance back over my shoulder. The sea and the sky are grey and cold.

The Soldier Looks for his Family

THE first bomb fell as the soldier got off the train. It fell just outside the station and the blast picked up the soldier and flung him against the wall. From the roof, a semicircle of glass and steel, long splinters spun through the air. There was shouting outside, and people were running. Then the sirens began to sound all over the city.

The soldier was in a hurry to get home to his family. He knew his wife would be frightened by the guns, and they might be starting at any moment now. He walked past the deserted ticket gate and into the street. There was no moon and the city was black and quiet. Even the noise of the explosion and the frantic haste of hurrying feet had gone. It was on the wide pavement, where his feet crunched splintered glass, that the military policeman stopped him.

'Where are you going?'

The soldier looked up at the sky. He had hardly heard the question. It was still very quiet, and as yet there was no sound of the planes above.

'Where are you going?'

'Home,' said the soldier. He was listening for the plane, quite intently. It seemed that nothing was so important as the syncopated noise of the engines at that moment. The policeman was listening too, and there was a pause before he spoke again.

'Have you got a pass?'

The questions were asked and answered automatically. Indifferent actors hurrying through their lines with an eye on the vast darkness of the auditorium. The policeman held out his hand and the soldier put his inside his blouse, and then the guns began. They had not found the plane but were feeling in the sky for it. First, the rippling flash beyond the silhouettes of dark houses, and then the heaving belching noise of the discharge. It went on intermittently, flash, thunder, darkness, the leaping shadows of the houses with their chimneys darting up like derisive fingers. And policeman and soldier watched it, heads turned toward it, one with a hand thrust out and the other with a hand inside his blouse. The soldier felt suddenly a great sadness as he thought of his wife and what the noise of these guns must be doing to her.

The policeman said, 'Let me see the pass. Hurry up, soldier, it's getting hot!' And as he said it the guns roared again in agreement.

The soldier looked at the man who had stopped him. Red light from the gun flashes caught the chiaroscuro of his features. He was very tall, the visor of his cap down over his nose, and the deep eye-holes behind it. The cap-badge shone from the sullen glow of his scarlet cap. He did not look human, thought the soldier. His belt shone on the bend of his chest, and the flap of his pistol-holster had been loosened. His hand was still held out and the soldier gave it the pass.

The policeman could not read it. He turned it to the gun flashes and held it up to his face. His lips parted with tense concentration and seemed to snarl, but his voice was friendly.

'I can't see the blasted thing. It's all right.'

The soldier looked up. Craned his neck. In a short silence he had heard the enemy plane.

The second bomb fell and exploded on the station.

It was all noise, suffocation and an irresistible weakness. The soldier was forced back against the station wall. He did not know whether the policeman had quickly thrust him there or the bomb had tossed him against it. It was like a strong, a very strong hand on his chest, pressing hard, convexing his ribs, and behind him the stones heaved. His knees gave way and he didn't know that he rolled over and over into the gutter because he was unconscious when that happened . . .

The liquid spurting violently into his face was hot. It hit him regularly and he struggled away from it for it had a disgusting taste. He tried to stand up but he was too weak. The air was thick and dusty, and behind him the rolling angry rustle of falling debris. His mouth fell open and he tried to breathe. He did not think he had been hurt, but as the station behind him burst into fire he saw that his hands and clothes, white with dust, were patched here and there with red. And his face was wet. He wiped it with his hand and saw that it was blood. He struggled to his knees and was sick in the gutter because he thought that he was seriously hurt and it frightened him.

Other bombs were falling. They hit the city regularly and it recoiled beneath them and answered from the flame-lips of its guns. The soldier held his head between his hands and felt that he wanted to cry because he had come home and been bombed. If he could get to his feet he would be able to walk home and find his wife; and she would have a cup of tea for him, and perhaps they could shut out the noise of the bombs and the waterfall of falling rubble. But then more bombs fell, *one . . . two . . . three . . .* and the soldier was sick again.

'Soldier!'

The cry was faint, but he recognized the military policeman's voice, and he looked about him until he saw the man lying on his back about ten yards away. The red cap had rolled from his head and what hair he had was close-cropped and insignificant. His eyes were frightened and he was clutching at his groin.

He had only one leg now. The other had gone it seemed and the blood pounded regularly from what was left of the thigh. A man can't last more than seven minutes when the femoral artery has been severed. Life jets away as regularly as from a pump, and the military policeman knew that. He was trying to force a fist down on the pressure-point. But it wasn't enough. The blood spurted its liberation through his fingers. He must have been holding his hand there for over two minutes to judge by his face.

'Soldier!'

There were many fires in the city now. The noise they made, and of people's voices, was clamorous, but in this courtyard of the station there were only two soldiers, and the one who was sick looked at the one who was dying very rapidly.

The policeman was too weak to call again, but he opened his mouth and looked at the soldier. The soldier got up and stumbled across. He did not like looking at the blood but he fumbled along the mangled thigh and tried to put pressure on the critical point with both his thumbs. He could feel the blood knocking steadily, gently, and he pressed harder. The policeman groaned. The blood would not stop its flow, and the soldier raised himself on his toes until his body was arched, and he leant on the man's groin. His respirator slipped round from his back and hung beneath him. His cap fell over the other man's face. And he tried to press harder. The concentration left him quite weak and he trembled.

He must have leant on the groin for more than five minutes after the man died. There was a lot of blood and the bombs were still falling.

And then the soldier got up and went to find his family. He walked down the main street to a turning beyond the cupola which surrounded the obese equanimity of the old queen. She sat there in bronze silence, only the flames lighting up her indifference and the Bible on her knees. Beneath the stone fountain at her feet three Medical Corps men were sheltering, and they shouted to the soldier to come under there with them, but he did not answer and went on down the turning. He had put on his steel helmet and he was anxious to get home to his family.

It was a short turning, and should have led to the street in which he lived. But the street was not there, or rather its skeleton watched him eyeless. The bombs had matched its length precisely and the soldier did not recognize it now. He stood and looked at it. Flames lit one end where there were people and the quarrelling tangle of fire hoses. The wind brought moisture to his face, and it clung there like tears. Now and then a bomb fell within a half a mile or so and it stirred up the dust until it was mud that the hoses flung on his cheeks. Everything had happened so quickly, so violently, in the midst of so much noise, that it made little impression upon him. An invisible hand, as if flung in front of his face to ward off a blow, shut out of sight what was happening.

His house was to the right, should have been to the right. On the other side of the road, down by the flames. He walked in the gutter toward it, for the pavement was crowded with masonry and the gesticulating caricatures of iron railings. Water from the playing hoses caracoled toward the drains over his boots. He was looking among the shells of houses for his own.

He recognized the doorsteps. They were all that was to be recognized. Five of them, undamaged, that went up into nothingness and hung over the gap where his house had been. He recognized them because he had painted them green, dark green with white black-out lines. And there they were still. But the white black-out lines weren't necessary tonight for the public house, burning at the end of the road, gave a brilliant light. There was plenty of dust and people were coughing. The soldier could hear them coughing, even above the noise of the fire and the bombs still falling.

He took off his respirator and steel helmet and sat down on his doorstep. It bent beneath his weight and mortar fell from it to the pit below. He felt as if nothing could touch him. He did not want to look behind him to the house in case there was something to be seen there that might make this tragedy real. So he sat hoping that he might be sick again.

Firemen were running out fresh hose. They passed and repassed him but none of them looked at him. They were trying hard to put out the fire and they were not noticing the bombs. They were very busy, and the soldier, forgetting that something terrible had happened to him, something so terrible that it had as yet made no impression on him, envied these firemen.

He sat there a long time alone. It was a warden who spoke to him first and advised him to take shelter, because anyway the rescue party would be along shortly to get out the bodies below him. It had been a direct hit, he said, and the soldier realized what had happened. He looked at the warden quite calmly and began to cry. At first it didn't hurt as badly as being told that his leave, this precious leave, had been cancelled, and then he looked at the warden calmly and began to cry. His big face became stupid with the tears tracing dusty lines down it, and the long hands dropping between his knees. And the warden, thinking that perhaps he had shock, ordered him away roughly. But the soldier went on crying quietly because this was his second leave and he had made a lot of plans. He told the warden about them, but the warden hurried away to the fire, and, in his place, the wind brought the dust and smoke, the water and smell of beer from the burning public house. The soldier went on talking and he talked to the darkness between the doorsteps at his feet.

Even as he talked he remembered that the military policeman had been holding his leave pass when the second bomb fell. He wondered where it was, whether he ought to go back and look for it. It would be a pity if he were picked up without a pass. It would spoil his leave.

It was silly to sit there, and he stopped crying because that was silly too. He ought to try and find Lil. Perhaps she hadn't been in, although she was expecting him, perhaps she hadn't been in, just the same. Or the children.

The raid was getting worse – even worse. If he sat there long enough perhaps another bomb would hit him. Third time lucky. It might be best. There wasn't much sense in anything else. Camp,

war, being away from home, and not being able to say in letters
what you were feeling.

Dear darling Lil, I hope I will be home on leave soon. It will be nice to see
you and the kids again for us older men don't get so used to the army
quickly like the young ones do. And when I come home I can get that bit of
yard dug up and perhaps you can keep some hens there so that the kids will
have an egg now and then. We are having route marches and we get lectures,
but I'm always thinking about you . . .

'Dear darling Lil' and 'Your ever-loving husband, Sid.' He'd try to
write something better next time, so that Lil could know how
much he liked being her husband, and what he had in mind for the
children's future. He'd write more next time to take her mind off
the war. She was a good girl, was Lil, and she was pretty too. People
didn't seem to see things like that. The films were wrong there. In
films only the officers had pretty girls, and the soldiers had fat
wives who nagged. He'd tell Lil that in his next letter.

But, it's funny, you can't write letters to corpses. Though, if they
delivered the letters here, and the postman pushed them down
through the bricks and the plaster and the window glass, maybe Lil
would reach up a hand sometime and get the letters and read them
out to the children, if she could see down there in the dark.

The third bomb shouldn't be long now. Maybe it would come
before the warden returned to move him on. But although the
bombs fell and fires blossomed out into poppy flowers all over the
city, the raiders had exhausted themselves as far as this street was
concerned, and the soldier sat untouched on his doorstep while the
firemen tried to put out the fire in the public house.

Down to his left, away from the fire, there was a mobile canteen.
It had been driven on to a pile of rubble and left there, tilted
drunkenly, with its mudguards bent and its headlamps on. It wasn't
far from the soldier, a matter of a few yards, and he could see the red
triangle on its side. One of the windows in the offside door was
broken, all the glass gone but for a spear-headed piece that stuck up
and reflected the ruddy fire-glow.

There was someone in the cab. A white face. It might have been a
woman there was so much hair. But the face seemed shapeless.
There were no eyes, no nose, nothing familiar like that, and he
looked at it for some time before he realized that the woman had
covered her face with her hands, and was sitting there quite still.

The clefts between her fingers were dark shadows and her finger-nails were scarlet almost. She didn't move, although he watched her closely for some time.

Curiously he got up and walked over to the car. She was a young girl. He could tell that by the softness of her hands, the lustre of her hair, dusty though it was beneath the grey steel of the civilian helmet. He could smell perfume, and he thought of how Lil had looked when he married her. He reached over the broken glass and touched her shoulder.

'Miss!'

She dropped her hands and shrank away from him. She was very frightened and he smelt of blood.

'Don't touch me!'

He looked hurt and dropped his hand. They stared at each other. She was very pretty and very young, and he wondered if she was an officer's girl, although Lil was as pretty. She was alone in the cab and he noticed that the windscreen was splintered and patterned like hoar frost.

He had not moved but she said again, 'Don't *touch* me!'

'What's the matter, miss?'

She didn't answer. She was looking at the blood on his blouse, the blood caked on his face, and he asked her again.

'Are you frightened?'

She wouldn't answer, but trembled.

'It's not safe here, miss. You'd better go home. There's a raid on.' And neither of them saw how funny it was for him to say a thing like that.

'I've got to serve tea to the firemen.'

'That's all right, miss. You serve tea, there's nothing much to be frightened of.'

'The bombs . . .'

'They make a lot of noise, that's all. Them chaps want some tea.' He placed one foot on the running board, and when he put his weight on it he heard the shifting of broken crockery inside the van. 'Shall we go down? Move over, miss, I can drive a truck. Let's go down and give them firemen some tea.'

Automatically she pulled her steel helmet down over her eyes. She didn't look at him. The soldier climbed into the cab and put it into reverse. It argued with him and would not move. He felt the old familiar friendliness of the wheel, the pedals beneath his feet, and he tried again. It was obedient this time. In an old gesture he raised a thumb silently before his face and pressed some invisible object with satisfaction.

He drove off the rubble and pointed the car towards the fire. The first floor of the public house fell into the flames and a shower of climbing sparks sped up to the shell-bursts. The soldier sat back and turned to the girl.

'I could do with a cup of tea myself,' he said.

The Prisoner's Bike

'WELL, I've got an Italian,' Mr McBride said to his wife when he came back from the Mart one Monday. 'I spoke to the Camp Labour Organizer and he said I could get one to billet.'

'And where are you going to billet him, pray?' Mrs McBride said belligerently.

'Oh, we'll easy get some place riggit up for him,' Mr McBride said. 'What aboot that little roomie at the foot o' the stairs? There's nothin' intil't just now but boxes and a lot o' auld junk.'

'There's no Italian comin' to bide in this house,' his wife said. 'Do ye want us all to be murdered in oor beds?'

'Dinna be daft, woman,' he said. 'They're quiet, inoffensive souls.'

'Quiet! Inoffensive! Frankie McBride, ha'e ye taken leave o' yer senses?'

'Well, well,' he said. 'If ye dinna want him in the hoose I'll get another place for him. But he's comin' here the morn, anyway. I've got to ha'e another man aboot the place, Italian or no Italian.'

'Can he nae stay at the Camp and come every day wi' the lorry the way the prisoners ging to other farms?' Mrs McBride said. 'That would be the best way. Ye'd ha'e no responsibility for him then.'

'They winna do it. This is too far for the lorry to come. We've got to billet him or do without him.'

'We'll all be murdered in oor beds,' Mrs McBride wailed. 'I tell ye nae good'll come out o' it. Dinna say I didna warn ye when ye find yersel' wi' a knife in yer back. A' thae Italians carry stilettos.'

She nagged about it all evening, but the next morning Mr McBride was up early and away to the Prisoner of War Camp. Mrs McBride and Mary the maid, a glaikit girl of fifteen were preparing the dinner when he came back. They peered out of the kitchen window at the Italian sitting beside Mr McBride in the front seat of the car. 'He's nae feared,' Mrs McBride cried. 'Wi' that villain cockit there aside him. The Tally could easy ha'e grabbed the wheel and coupit them baith oot in the ditch.'

Mr McBride barged into the kitchen, crying: 'Well, well, here he is!' The Italian followed him, grinning shyly. He was a tall, good-looking youth of about twenty-two with dark wavy hair. He bobbed his head amiably to everything Mr McBride said to him, and he kept saying: 'No compree, no compree.'

'I'd no compree him,' Mrs McBride said. 'He comprees fine. I'd like to gi'e him a right guid wallop wi' this dish-clout. I'd soon take the grin off his face!'

'Stop yer antics, Frankie,' she cried to her husband who was trying by pantomime to explain something to the prisoner. 'And get awa' oot o' here and take that grinnin' heathen wi' ye!'

'Get on wi' yer work, girl,' she said to Mary who had run to the window to watch the Italian follow Mr McBride across the court.

Mary went back sulkily to peel potatoes. 'Dinna you glower at me like that, girl,' Mrs McBride said. 'And if I catch ye makin' sheep's-eyes again at that dirty Tally I'll send ye packin' doon the road.'

At lousing-time Mr McBride came in and said: 'What aboot some dinner for the Tally?'

'He's gettin' nothin' to eat in this house,' Mrs McBride said firmly. 'If he gets anythin' it'll be ower ma dead body.'

'Well, ye'd better order yer coffin right now,' her husband said. 'He's here to work and he's here to bide, so ye'd better just make the best o' it.'

'He's eatin' nothin' in this hoose,' Mrs McBride said.

'Well, well, he can eat it in the barn. Get somethin' hot for him and I'll take it oot to him.'

Mrs McBride handed him a plate with some mince and potatoes. 'That's plenty for him.'

He handed it back. 'Ye'll put as much as that on again,' he said. 'The man's a guid worker and I'm goin' to see that he's fed properly.'

'Where's he goin' to bide?' Mrs McBride said. 'He's nae comin' here. As soon as he comes in that door I ging oot at the other ane.'

'Ye dinna need to pack yer kist just yet,' Mr McBride said, grinning, 'I've got a room for him wi' Jack Hutcheon. Mrs Hutcheon's nae feared for gettin' a stiletto in her back!'

'Nae that ye should worry yersel' aboot that,' he said as he went out. 'Yer stays make a guid enough armour!'

Jack Hutcheon's cottage was a mile from the steading and he

cycled to his work. 'Ye'll ha'e to get a bike for the Tally, too,' he said to Mr McBride. 'Ye canna expect him to walk a' that way.'

The farmer picked his fat big-pored nose and thought for a minute. 'I'll gi'e him mine,' he said after a while, and he looked down at his protruding stomach and chuckled. 'I doot ma ain cyclin' days are ower!'

The Italian grinned more than ever when he was given the bike at the end of the day. 'Beeceecle?' he said. 'Beeceecle!'

'Will he be able to ging it, dae ye think?' Mr McBride said to Jack Hutcheon.

But before Hutcheon could answer the prisoner had jumped on the bike and was pedalling round and round the court. He laughed and shouted, waving first one arm and then the other. Then he took both hands off the handlebars and leaned back, singing at the pitch of his voice. 'Good?' he cried, jumping off. 'Veree good, yes?'

'Very good,' Mr McBride said.

Guiseppe was a barber and came from Bologna. At first he had been scared and unhappy when he was told that he was to be billeted away from the Camp; he had not wanted to leave his friends and go amongst people to whom he could not make himself understood. But in a few days he had settled down on the farm. The Hutcheons were very kind to him. At nights Jack Hutcheon tried to teach him English. He and his wife and two children could not pronounce the Italian's name, so they changed it to Gee-up. The other men on the farm took up this. At first they chaffed him about the war, but in a good-natured way. 'Mussolini no good,' they would say, and Guiseppe would grin and say: 'Churchill no good.' But soon they stopped this. There was no fun in chaffing somebody who did not get angry. They saw that the Italian was a decent man like themselves even though he wore a magenta-coloured uniform with big round blue patches. They saw that he was glad to be out of the war, and that he had not wanted to be a soldier any more than they wanted to be soldiers themselves. In a vague sort of way they felt that there must be many more like him in Italy and that all Italians were not Mussolinis and Cianos.

Guiseppe made friends most quickly with the cottar children, and usually there were two or three of them hanging around him. Like their parents they delighted to tease him, saying 'You no good'. But he would just laugh and repeat this, and soon the children tired of the joke. He taught them the Italian for simple things, pointing at them and repeating the names again and again, laughing at the children's attempts to say them.

Mr McBride bought a small English-Italian dictionary, but he found that it was almost impossible to use it. Whenever he wanted to find a word to explain something to Guiseppe he would find that the dictionary was in the house. Or if he had it in his pocket it was usually much quicker to explain what he wanted by signs. Guiseppe always told him the Italian word for whatever he was wanting, and Mr McBride would repeat it several times, nodding his head and looking ponderous. But in a few minutes he would have forgotten it and the same pantomime would be gone through the next day. The only word he seemed able to remember was 'aqua'. 'And that's funny,' he said to his wife. 'I wasna just what ye'd call very bright at Latin at the school.'

The men, too, tried to learn Italian, but they did not learn nearly as quickly as Guiseppe learned certain Scottish words. Mrs McBride was horrified one day when she heard him speaking in the stable. 'If he was goin' aboot his work he wouldna ha'e time to say things like that,' she said. 'The men ha'e awfa little need to learn him thae words. He'll be sayin' them to the bairns next.'

'Ach, ye're nae needin' to worry yersel' aboot them,' Mr McBride said. 'It was the bairns that taught him maist o' the words, anyway!'

Everybody on the farm was interested in the Catholic medallion which Guiseppe wore on his wrist. It had a picture of the Virgin and Child on it. One day when he went into the Potato Shed Mr McBride found the men having an argument about the Italian word for 'baby'. 'I ken what it is, too,' Jack Hutcheon was saying, scratching his head. 'But I'm damned if I can mind it.'

'Here, Gee-up!' he cried.

The Italian came over grinning. Jack seized his wrist and pulled the medallion from under his sleeve. 'What's that?' he said, pointing to the Child in the Virgin's arms. But before Guiseppe could understand what was wanted of him, Jack suddenly remembered for himself.

'I mind on it now!' he cried. 'It's baboon! Baboon!'

Mr McBride was so amused by this rendering of 'bambino' (which he had not known himself) that he repeated the story everywhere. Only Mrs McBride was not amused. She was the only one on the farm who had not tried to learn Italian. She was quite untouched by the Italian's charm. She went out of her way to find fault with him, and she was always complaining about him to her husband. 'A pure rogue if ever there was one,' she said. 'He's as full of blarney as the very Devil.' When he was working near the house she watched him from the kitchen window, ready to pounce on the slightest fault. But even though there had been anything, her husband would not have listened to her; he was well pleased with the way Guiseppe worked. The only thing that Mrs McBride could get to complain about was the fact that when he was walking from one job to another Guiseppe sometimes took a comb from his pocket and passed it through his thick dark hair. 'D'ye see that, Frankie?' she said. 'If he was right busy he wouldna ha'e time to dae that. The muckle sissy!'

'I'm nae complainin',' Mr McBride said. 'I only wish I had a head o' hair like him so that I could use a comb! And anyway, the men are fell pleased wi' him. He's a grand barber. I wouldna be surprised if after the war he didna set up a wee shoppie doon in the village.'

But one day Mrs McBride thought that at last she had found the chance she had been waiting for. She was watching the men coming in from the fields at lousing-time. Guiseppe sitting on his horse's back was singing what she felt was an Italian love-song. Mary the maid was coming from the drying-green with a basket of clothes. Guiseppe smiled and waved to her, and Mary shouted: 'See and nae fall off the horse's back!'

Guiseppe grinned and patted the horse's neck as he slid off at the stable-door. 'Thees veree good horse,' he said, winking at the girl. 'By and by he speak Italian!'

He led the horse into the stable. Mary was loitering at the door, but Mrs McBride rapped angrily on the window. 'Come inside at once, ye shameless besom!' she called. 'If I catch ye at that again I'll send ye packin'.'

'Ach to hell,' Mary said. 'I wasna doin' any harm. I can speak to who I like, can't I?'

Mrs McBride put down the pot she was filling at the tap. 'What's that?' she said, turning off the water. 'Ye can speak to whae ye like, can ye? Well, well! Nae as long as I have anythin' to do wi' it!'

'Well, then, I'm leavin',' Mary said. 'I was for leavin' at the term, onywye. But I'll ging afore then.'

'Ging then,' Mrs McBride snapped. 'Ye can ging right now. I'll be glad to see the back o' ye, ye dirty shameless bitch!'

For the next few minutes Mrs McBride forgot about the Italian, but happening to glance out of the window while she was thinking of something else to say to Mary, who by this time was howling with rage, she saw Guiseppe come out of the stable, and come towards the dairy to get his pitcher of milk. 'Ye're just a dirty slut, onywye,' she said to the girl, though she kept looking out of the window.

She saw Guiseppe stop at the dairy door, take out his knife and begin to scrape the mud off his boots on to the strip of concrete between the dairy and the kitchen doors. 'Go to your room, girl!' Mrs McBride said, turning her back on Mary. 'I'll attend to you later.'

She lifted the curtain a bit, scowling out at the Italian. Now was her chance! Many a battle had she waged with the men about that very same bit of concrete, quarrelling them for bringing their carts over it. And if none of the farmworkers were to be allowed to dirty it, then no lousy heathen of an Italian was going to be allowed either!

'Ging to yer room and pack yer kist, girl,' she said over her shoulder. 'And bide there till I come up.'

'I'll get ma mither to ye,' Mary snivelled.

'Get her!' Mrs McBride said majestically. 'Get her! I'll gi'e her a right guid piece o' ma mind. I'm nane feared for her or for you either. I'll tell her exactly what I think o' ye baith – a dirty pair!'

'I'll get the bobby,' Mary shrieked, making for the back stairs. 'I'll have ye up for slander.'

'Just you daur! Just you daur!' Mrs McBride said, lowering her brows and half-smiling. 'Just you daur, and by the Lord Harry I'll see that there are a lot o' funny things come oot in the court.'

Mary gawked and retreated up the stairs. Mrs McBride wiped her nose on the back of her hand and went to the door. She pulled it open with a flourish and opened her mouth. But what she had been going to shout died away into a mumble.

Guiseppe had a brush in his hand and was sweeping away the dirt. He looked round at her and grinned. 'I sweep, Missis Boss! Veree good, yes?'

Mrs McBride stepped back and shut the door.

During the next few days Mrs McBride had not much time to worry about the Italian. As soon as Mary had gone she began to realize just how much work the glaikit creature had been able to do. She had always needed supervision; nevertheless, she had been able to do all the rough work which Mrs McBride now found she had to do herself. It was a scutter. 'I'm fair trauchled to death,' she complained one evening to her husband. 'The quicker we get another maid the better.'

'Well, who's fault is it?' he said. 'Ye should ha'e thought aboot that afore ye gave the quaen her notice. What do ye think I would do if I was aye castin' oot wi' ma men? I would be in a bonnie like mess if I sent them packin' every time I had a few words wi' them.'

'Huh, there's one I would send packin' double quick, onywye,' she said. 'And that's that dirty Italian. I widna ha'e him aboot ma place.'

'What's wrong wi' him?' Mr McBride said. 'He's a very pleasant obliging childe. And he's a right guid worker.'

'Worker!' Mrs McBride sniffed. 'A fat lot o' work he does as far as I can see. He's aye fleein' aboot on that bike. Just caperin'. It's a peety nor he widna break his neck!'

'Noo listen to me, woman, just you leave Gee-up and his bike alone. It's the only pleasure the puir devil has.' Mr McBride chuckled as he lit his pipe. 'Man, he's just like a bairn wi' a toy,' he said, puffing vigorously to get the pipe alight. 'He's a right caution the way he cleans and oils at it. He attends til't better than many a woman attends til her bairns. I doot he'd be fair heart-broken if onythin' happened til that bike.'

Mrs McBride smiled sarcastically. 'I widna mind puttin' a spoke in his wheel!' she said. 'What's a prisoner needin' wi' a bike, onywye? It's chains he should ha'e, and it's chains he *would* ha'e if I had my way o't.'

'Ye're a right nasty bitch sometimes, Peg,' he said. 'Ye dinna like to see onybody enjoyin' theirsels. It's a guid job that everybody on the farm isna like you, or we widna be able to live.'

'Oh, are they no'?' she snorted. 'I bet they like the Tally as little as I do. Only they're feared to say it to ye. They ken ye're that soft-hearted.'

'I dinna ken aboot that,' he said. 'I had Jack Hutcheon at me the day, wonderin' if it would be a' right if he took the Tally to the pictures in the village.'

'Pictures!' Mrs McBride leaned back in her chair. 'Pictures! Well,

I never heard the like! Wantin' to take a prisoner to the pictures! I must say I aye thought Jack Hutcheon had mair sense. I hope ye tellt him to ging hame and nae haver?'

'Ay, unfortunately,' Mr McBride sighed. 'I had to say that I didn't think the POW Camp would be very pleased aboot it if they heard. It's a pity, it would ha'e been a fine treat for him.'

'I'd treat him!' She stood up, preparing to go and get the supper. 'I'd treat him to a right guid wallop on the lug! It's a pity nor he hadna to dae some o' the hard work I have to dae – and a' because o' that glaikit cratur', Mary!'

It was when she was feeding the hens that Mrs McBride missed Mary most. The girl had always been there to run out in any kind of weather. And although she would hardly have admitted it to herself Mrs McBride sometimes found the heavy pails of mash just more than she could manage. But she struggled on with them. She was determined not to ask Mr McBride to get a woman from the cottar houses to help her; she knew that if she did the cottar women would gossip amongst themselves about it.

One morning a week after Mary had gone she was coming out of the back door with two heavy pails of mash when she met Guiseppe. She wished that she had not looked so trauchled. She was preparing to pass him, as she usually did, with her head in the air, but he stepped in front of her. 'Excuse, Missis Boss,' he said, smiling. 'I carry pail.'

'No, thank you,' she said coldly.

'Ah yes, yes!' he said, and he seized the pails. 'Veree heavy for *la padrona*.'

'I'll carry them myself,' she said, and she tried to pull them away from him. But he grinned and held tightly to them. 'Too heavy for woman,' he said. 'Guiseppe carry.'

Mrs McBride was thankful that none of the other men were about. What would they have thought! And what would they have gone home and told their wives! All the way to the hen-house she kept saying 'I'll manage fine myself', and she kept trying to take the pails away from him. But Guiseppe just grinned and shook his head. 'I carry, Missis Boss,' he said.

She was relieved when they got to the hen-house. She pulled the pails from him, muttered 'Thank you', and rushed inside.

The following morning when she went out with the pails he was waiting for her. He came forward, smiling, and took the pails. She protested as vigorously as she could, but he merely smiled and said: 'Too heavy for woman. Guiseppe carry.'

Mrs McBride did not know what to do about it. She had never been used to having men do things for her; men about farms were usually too busy to bother about courtesies. Frankie McBride had carried things for her only when they were courting and then in a shamefaced way. But all those foreigners were alike, she thought. There was something namby-pamby about them, aye running after women and slavering about them. It was just a lot of dirt!

'Ach, why should he nae do it?' she said to herself on the third morning when he came to the back door and stood waiting for the pails. 'It's just part o' his work.'

Mr McBride had known from the medallion on Guiseppe's wrist that he was a Roman Catholic, but he was surprised one day when the prisoner came and said: 'Boss! Please to listen to me, boss! Chapel in village, yes?'

'No,' Mr McBride said. 'No chapel.'

'Too bad,' Guiseppe said, laying his head almost on top of his right shoulder and spreading out his arms. 'I want confess. Go to Mass sometime. Mass in Campo, no Mass at Missis Hutcheon. Too bad.'

'I see.' Mr McBride scratched his chin. 'Well, there's a Chapel at Clovey, but it's ten miles awa'. Ye couldna very well ging there.'

'Bike,' Guiseppe said. 'Bike veree good.'

'Ach, it widna dae ava. We couldna ha'e ye cyclin' a' that distance.'

'Please, boss, I can manage fine.'

'Very well, if ye think ye can manage,' Mr McBride said, 'ye're welcome to try it.'

But after thinking it over Mr McBride thought that perhaps he'd better phone the Camp authorities before he allowed Guiseppe to go. After all the man was a prisoner and was in his care.

'It's impossible,' the Camp Labour Organizer said. 'It's ridiculous. The man shouldn't have a bike, anyway. You must take the bike away from him at once, Mr McBride. Didn't you get a notice to say that prisoners weren't to be allowed to ride on bikes?'

'Ay, I believe there was somethin' o' the kind came in,' Mr McBride said. 'But I dinna believe I ever read it right.'

'Good heavens, man, what do you think we send these notices

out for?' The Camp Labour Organizer was raising his voice so much that Mr McBride held the phone away from his ear, screwing up his face at the noise. 'Do you think we send these notices out for fun?'

'No, I just thought ye sent them to gi'e us puir farmers a lot o' work,' Mr McBride said. 'I have as many Government notices here as would paper a fair-sized room. Goodbye!'

'So that's that,' he said to his wife after dinner. 'If I dinna take the bike awa' frae him they'll take him awa' frae me.'

'Well!' Mrs McBride said.

She rattled the dirty dishes on to a tray. 'The idea!' she said. 'What a nerve thae fowk at the Camp have! Just a lot o' red tape, that's what it is. Tryin' to keep the poor Tally frae goin' to the kirk.'

She picked up the tray and held it like a shield in front of her. 'Frankie,' she said. 'Do we get petrol for goin' to the kirk?'

'Ay,' he said. 'We could if we wanted to.'

'What way?' he said, raising one eyebrow. Mrs McBride had not been through a church door for over three years. She had always maintained that it was unpatriotic to waste the nation's petrol on kirk-going, and that, speaking for herself, you could live a godly enough life at home without attending services.

She carried the tray to the door. 'Well, ye'd better apply for it right now,' she said. 'We're goin' to Clovey on Sunday. It's a long time since I was at the kirk and I dinna see why I shouldna get when other fowk ha'e the nerve to apply for petrol to go. We'll take Gee-up wi' us and he can ging to his Mass. That'll learn the Camp authorities for tryin' to take the poor Tally's bike awa' frae him!'

The Blanket

THE farmhouse lay by itself at the side of a cart-track, a mile or two from our billets. It was like the other houses in the neighbourhood, but somewhat larger than most.

A flight of steps led up the southern wall to an upper room; there was a small vineyard nearby, and a tall, conical haystack, which had been sliced into at need like a cake, and began to look top-heavy. With its white walls and rust-red pantiled roof, the house looked friendly and welcoming in the spring sunshine.

A small boy, playing in the yard, looked at us curiously. Presently he sidled up to us.

'*Sigaretti? Cioccolata?*' he asked hopefully.

'We go to ask some *vino*,' said Kurt.

There were three of us: Kurt Schlegel, the Austrian Jew enlisted in Palestine, Charlie Dacres, the Cockney, and myself. Kurt was teaching himself Italian, and usually acted as our interpreter.

'*Avete del vino?*' he asked now.

'*Si, si,*' the boy answered with a charming smile.

We followed him round to the doorway on the other side. A woman appeared at the door: tall, broad-bosomed, brown-faced, dressed in nondescript clothes which had once been gaily coloured, and still hung gracefully upon her straight, stalwart body. On her head was a bright-coloured kerchief.

'*Buon giorno,*' she said, with a curious, dramatic sweep of her arm: a stylized, almost operatic gesture of welcome, at once proud and humble, which seemed to imply that we were free to take possession, if we wished, of the entire farm, such as it was. She accompanied the movement with a broad, delightful smile, revealing two rows of strong, white teeth.

'*Dovè il padrone, Signora, per cortesia?*' asked Kurt.

'The *padrone* was out at work,' she replied. '*Cosa vuole?*'

'*Se avete un mezzo-litro di vino . . . ?*'

'*Si, si,*' she exclaimed, and immediately pushed forward three little wooden chairs for us.

'In moment her husband works in the fields,' Kurt explained to Charlie, whose Italian was almost non-existent. 'But she gives us wine.'

We sat down, and presently the woman returned with a jug of wine and three glasses. I poured out the wine, and we all said '*Saluti*'. The woman watched us as we drank; so did the little boy, still on the look-out for chocolate.

'*E buono?*' she asked.

'*Molto buono*', we said.

It was true: the wine was a *vino nero* – dark, sour, potent, with a purplish glint when held to the light; much better than most of the local wines, which were light and watery, like alcoholic lemonade.

We sat in the sunshine, drinking it slowly, and talking a little to the woman. Kurt did most of the talking: he spoke ungrammatically, but with the confidence of a Central European. I was shy, being British, and had to think up my phrases more carefully. Charlie contented himself with saying '*molto buono*' and playing with the child.

Presently other children appeared, stealing up like shy birds whom the sight of us had driven away: another little boy, a girl of fifteen strikingly like her mother, and another younger girl, perhaps eleven or twelve, blonde and uncannily beautiful.

We were introduced: the elder girl was called Assunta, the younger Graziella, the two boys Leonardo and Giovanni.

'*Quanti bambini?*' Kurt asked.

'*Cinque,*' the woman replied, holding up the five fingers of one hand; adding that one, the eldest son, was working with his father.

'She is beautiful,' Kurt remarked, of Graziella.

'Like a Botticelli,' I said.

'*Volete ancora?*' the woman asked.

'I think we drink some more,' Kurt said, with decision.

'Too bloody true we will,' said Charlie. 'Best *vino* I've had since we came to this place.'

Kurt asked the woman for more, explaining that we would pay for it.

'*Non fa niente,*' she assured us.

'We give her cigarettes,' Kurt suggested.

We pulled out our cases, and contributed ten each. Kurt handed them to the woman.

'*Per il padrone,*' he said.

'*Eh. . . Lei è molto gentile,*' she said, with a half-protesting gesture, and hurried to bring more wine. This time she brought, in addition, three pieces of bread, some cheese, and some sprouts of fennel.

Did we like *finocchio*? she asked.

We said we liked it.

It was not good to drink without eating, she added apologetically.

We sat over the second jug of wine, relaxed and happy in the warm sun. In front of the house, fields sloped down to a little wooded valley; beyond this, the country stretched away flatly to a range of low hills, capped by small villages. The landscape was like some formal vision of 'Spring' in a medieval missal: smooth, brightly-coloured, with a curious quality of *naïveté* and innocence. Two cypresses, a few yards from the house, divided the picture abruptly into sections, like the divisions of a triptych. In the middle-distance, figures moved across the fields, hoeing – perhaps the *padrone* was among them. The stooping forms of women showed as red and blue blobs, indistinct in the bright sunshine.

Presently the beautiful child, Graziella, who had wandered off, reappeared, carrying a little bunch of field-flowers: grape-hyacinths, narcissi, and small yellow tulips. These she presented to us, gravely smiling, then shyly backed away again.

'I've a feeling we're getting well in here,' Charlie said. 'What say we ask for some parster shooter?'

'She'd do it,' I said. 'Go on, Kurt. You ask her. Not today, though. I'm on at five o'clock, you know.'

'No, I don't ask. Always you want me to talk bloody Italian. You ask yourself.'

Finally Kurt and I together approached the topic with as much delicacy as our Italian allowed.

'*E possibile mangiare qui, alla vostra casa?*' we began, and, antiphonally, pressed our point: *pasta asciutta*, perhaps a salad, some eggs. We were so tired of Army food, we explained: we wanted to eat well, *mangiare bene all' Italiano.*

The woman shrugged her shoulders. They had so little food, now, in Italy; the *tedeschi* had taken everything – cattle, poultry, wine, anything they could carry – *e niente pagato.* It was different in peacetime; but now, *in tempo di guerra. . . .*

'Heavy going,' I said to Kurt. 'We'll have to use bribery. Jimmy'll give us a tin of bully out of the store, if we get him a bottle of *vino.*'

Kurt nodded, a glint coming into his eye.

'We make business,' he said.

At mention of *carne*, the *signora* obviously began to weaken. She would ask the *padrone*. I added that I would bring some clothes: I had some old civvy vests and pants in my kit which I never wore. The outlook began to seem more hopeful.

At that moment, the *padrone* himself appeared, with his eldest son. The father was short, with a pleasant, sharp-featured face and beady-black eyes; he wore a battered trilby, and a brightly-coloured handkerchief round his neck. The son, about sixteen, was beautiful. If Graziella was Renaissance, Umberto was something archaic: a faun from a Greek vase-painting.

The father was presented with the cigarettes. He immediately called for more wine, and we all sat down again, inside this time. Charlie came in, and the atmosphere became distinctly festive. I wished I wasn't on duty at five: I began to feel rather drunk, and refused any more wine. The bare, whitewashed room was very clean; bunches of drying tomatoes hung from the ceiling-beams, and a few *salami*. In the open stone hearth a fire of olive wood was blazing, and a vast cauldron hung over it, waiting for the *pasta*, which lay ready for cooking, in a floury pile, on the scrubbed wooden table.

The *padrone* was very friendly. He wanted to know all about the war: we were soldiers, we should know. We explained that we were medical orderlies, *croce rossa, non combattere*. He looked half-convinced. *Ieri sera molto boom-boom-boom*, he insisted: over there, beyond the mountains – beyond Pescara, on the way to Bologna. We were lucky, he said, not to fight. Had we many *feriti* in our hospital? No, we only dealt with medical cases, we said, *ammalati*. Our hospital was in the *Scuola Agricola* across the fields.

Time was getting short, and after a discreet interval we broached the subject of food again. Yes, certainly we must come, he said: next Sunday was Easter – *una grande festa*. It was also a special feast for the family – Leonardo, the second son, was to make his first communion. The cigarettes had done their work. We scraped up a few more for Umberto, and prepared to leave. This we were not allowed to do until we had drunk another glass of wine. We repeated, for the *padrone's* benefit, our promises to the *signora*: we would bring a tin of bully, some old clothes, some chocolate for the *bambini*. Sud-

denly made bold by our success with her husband, the *signora* took
me aside and half-whispered that if we could see our way to bring a
coperta as well . . .

'They want a blanket,' I said to Kurt.

'They've had it,' Kurt said. 'I don't go over the wall for two years,
that's sure.'

'We've all those buckshee ones from Foggia,' I pointed out.
'They've no check on them.'

'I'm not mad,' said Kurt.

'Plenty of blankets,' said Charlie, who had been putting back a
good deal of *vino* on the quiet. 'I'll bring her one.' He turned to the
signora. '*Si, si,*' he assured her, '*molto* blankets – what the ——ing
hell are blankets?'

'She understands all right.'

'Certainly she does,' said Kurt. 'Don't you be worried.'

'*Io portare molto* – you know, blankets,' Charlie insisted. 'Compree?'

'*Si, si. Lei è troppo gentile,*' the *signora* exclaimed, rewarding
Charlie with one of her broad, maternal smiles. She was like a
Demeter, an Earth-Goddess, I thought.

'See, she's taken a fancy to me,' Charlie said proudly. 'I told you
we'd get well in.'

We promised to come at two o'clock on Easter Sunday, and with
difficulty left the house. At the last minute, Assunta presented us
each with a little bunch of violets, and Umberto, no doubt on
instructions from the *padrone*, brought up a bottle of wine, which I
stuffed into the front of my battledress. The family watched us out
of sight. Looking back across the fields, we saw them standing in
the doorway, waving. The house, with its two dark cypresses, stood
out brilliantly against the sun-flooded landscape: it seemed like a
symbol of happiness, a vision of the good life.

The problem was to get the blanket out of the billets without being
seen.

'It is better if you take it at night,' Kurt advised.

'Is it ——,' retorted Charlie. 'Looks too bloody suspicious. Much
better to take it in daylight.'

'So then, Private Dacres, you go over the wall,' Kurt predicted
with morbid relish. 'That is sure.'

'And you ——ing come with me, Private ——ing Schlegel,

RAMC,' said Charlie with gusto. 'It's all right, mate, I wasn't born yesterday.'

We walked out of the billets just before two o'clock on Easter Sunday. Charlie had rolled up the blanket – one of a buckshee issue, unchecked, which we had acquired at Foggia – in a bundle, adequately disguised, to unsuspicious eyes, by several layers of dirty linen. Kurt also carried a bundle: he had compromised with his scruples sufficiently to part with a couple of KD shirts which weren't shown on his 1157. My own bundle, innocent enough to all appearances, contained the cast-off civvy underclothes which I'd bought in Cairo; in the front of my battledress was a tin of bully for which I had bargained with Jimmy James, the Ration Corporal.

We stepped jauntily out of the hospital entrance, looking rather consciously innocent, and walked straight into Staff-Sergeant Woolf, Acting Sergeant-Major for the Unit.

'Where're you blokes off to?' he said.

My heart sank like a stone. Just our luck, I thought. If Woolfy was in a bad mood, he might quite easily make things awkward. He flogged too much himself, as we all knew, to regard our bundles without suspicion.

'What's in all them ——ing bundles?' he asked.

I mentally decided to unroll my own first, if he pressed the point: there was nothing in mine he could pick on. I hoped he wouldn't ask to see Charlie's.

'We take our laundry to a farm,' Kurt explained.

'That's right,' Charlie agreed. 'The old *biancheria*, you know.'

The Staff grunted.

'Remember,' he said, 'if I find anyone in this unit flogging stuff, I'm coming down heavy on them. Very heavy.'

'Ain't got nothing to flog,' Charlie said, nervousness making him cheeky.

The Staff gave him a nasty look.

'Is anyone on duty in this joint?' he asked. 'Who's in the Clinic, eh?'

'Smudge is relieving me,' Charlie said. 'It's my half-day.'

'Who's in the Lab.?'

'Nobby does the Lab. in moment,' Kurt replied. 'He has two dark-grounds and one installation, then finish.'

'What about the office?'

'Mac's there,' I said. 'He's on long-trot today.'

'Well, don't get too pissed. If I had my way I'd have those bloody casas all put out of bounds. You'd think this was a bloody rest-camp, instead of a pox-joint.'

We escaped.

'Miserable old sod,' Charlie muttered. 'Just 'cos he doesn't like *vino*.'

'He likes *finocchio*,' I said. 'We might bring him some.'

'—— him.'

The day was brilliant and cloudless, hot but with a fresh breeze. We walked through a field breast-deep already with pink clover. In the little copse at the field's edge, nightingales were singing. In the meadow beyond the clover field the stream-side was fringed with white narcissi, their heavy scent evoking the atmosphere of English drawing-rooms in winter.

'It's a wonderful country,' Charlie said. 'Bloody wonderful. Garden flowers growing wild, and all.'

Kurt and I laughed.

'Three months ago you were saying how bloody awful it was,' I reminded him.

'I didn't know it then.'

'So now you stay in Italy *dopo la guerra* and marry a nice *signorina*, isn't it?' Kurt suggested.

'I might if I hadn't a wife and kids in Blighty,' Charlie agreed.

We came out on to the track, by a little row of houses. Some of the families were standing outside, wearing their best finery for Easter. They greeted us with smiles and welcoming gestures.

'*Buona Pasqua*,' they said; Christ might have risen, this very morning, for their special benefit: so happy did they seem. It was hard to believe there was a war on – and not so far away either. Even as we passed the houses, a muffled rumble came from over the mountains – away beyond the Maiella, white and austere on the horizon.

A family with whom we were friendly – we had treated the daughter for malaria – refused to let us pass without a glass of wine. Their neighbours followed suit. We were not allowed to go on till we had drunk a glass at each house in the row. When at last we arrived at the farmhouse where we were invited, we were, as Charlie said, 'Well away.'

We had been asked for two o'clock, but time in Italy is elastic, and dinner was far from being ready. The *signora* was busy with pots and pans; Assunta, the eldest daughter, was cutting up the *pasta* into long strips like tapeworms. The other children sat with the *padrone* just inside the door. At the hearth sat an ancient woman whom we had not met before: grey-haired, dressed in drab, ragged clothes, she looked like a benevolent witch. Introduced to us as *la nonna*, she croaked an unintelligible greeting, in dialect, and went on with her task of stoking the fire with olive wood. Leonardo, who had taken his first communion that morning, was the hero of the occasion: with his face scrubbed, and wearing a little suit of snow-white linen, he looked cherubic and very self-important. With immense pride he showed us his *Ricordo della prima communione* – a three-colour print showing an epicene Christ surrounded by very bourgeois-looking children, all with blond hair.

With many nods, gestures, and whispered thanks (as though the entire Corps of Military Police lay in ambush round the house) the blanket, the bully and the underclothes were secreted in a back room. A two-litre flask of wine appeared as though by magic: this was not good wine, the *padrone* explained; later we would drink good wine, *del vino tanto buono.*

It was good enough for us. We had had no dinner, and must have already drunk nearly a litre apiece on the way. We distributed cigarettes to the *padrone* and Umberto, and chocolate to the children. Leonardo received six bars all to himself, and Giovanni, who resented his brother's hour of glory, burst into tears. He was consoled with half a glass of wine.

'Wish I'd been brought up like that,' said Charlie.

'It's all for a cock, these bloody Catholic *festas*,' said Kurt, who, being both Jew and Communist, objected to Easter on religious and political grounds.

'Ah, you miserable old bugger,' exclaimed Charlie, and, lifting Giovanni on to his knee, consoled him further with an extra piece of chocolate.

Presently the meal began: the steaming, fragrant tomato juice was poured over the two enormous bowls of *pasta*, and we sat down round the table.

'*Ancora, ancora,*' the *padrone* insisted, before we had finished our first platefuls. '*Oggi festa – mangiamo molto alla Pasqua.*'

After the *pasta* there was chicken cooked with tomato and *peperoni*. This was followed by *salami* fried with eggs. Then came a dish of pork with young peas. Roast sparrows followed, and afterwards a salad. At about the *salami* stage, after several false alarms, the 'good' wine was produced: two bottles the size of magnums.

It was a Homeric meal. Kurt, who had been a student in Vienna before the war, quoted Homer very appropriately, but in German, which nobody understood. Charlie was trying to sing *Lilli Marlene* in Italian to Graziella, who sat on his knee. Umberto produced an ancient concertina and began to play it. Kurt, forgetting Homer, started to sing a very sad Austrian folk-song. The *padrone*, for my benefit, kept up a running commentary on the proceedings, comparing the occasion unfavourably with Easters before the war.

'*Prima la guerra era bella, bellissima,*' he insisted. Today, everyone was poor. '*E sempre la miseria.*' The Germans had taken everything. It could hardly be called a *festa* at all. He was ashamed: ashamed to offer such an Easter meal to his guests, and mortified, moreover, that Leonardo's first communion should be celebrated so wretchedly. '*Siamo poveri, poveri – noi contadini. Eh, la guerra – quando finirà?*'

I was not only extremely drunk by this time, but I had never eaten so much food in my life. So far as I was concerned, Leonardo's first communion party had been more than adequate.

Presently Umberto struck up a *tarantella*, and the whole family, as though at a given signal, took the floor. We all paired off, indifferent as to sex, and bobbed and jigged in time to the music. Charlie insisted on taking *la nonna* for his partner; I danced with the *signora*. I found to my surprise that I was perfectly steady on my feet. Moreover, it seemed that I had been dancing the *tarantella* all my life. Gravely, wearing her calm Demeter-like smile, the *signora* advanced and retreated, hands on hips, bobbed and circled and bowed, all with a goddess-like dignity. Her brown face, beneath her coloured kerchief, was as calm as though she were at Mass; only a beatific happiness irradiated it, as though Christ indeed were risen. She seemed immensely aware, too, of her own personal fulfilment: she had given pleasure to her man, borne him healthy children and (more recently) cooked a dinner fit for those Gods whose Olympian peer she seemed.

The music became faster, the dancing less restrained. The *padrone* whirled about like a ballet dancer; Giovanni, still taking a rather disgruntled view of the occasion, did a little dance by himself in the corner. Leonardo didn't dance at all: he stood at the doorway and watched the proceedings with the distant air of one who has, that very morning, eaten the body of Christ for the first time. The two girls, Assunta and Graziella, danced a little apart: separated, it seemed, from the rest by a mysterious barrier, a mutual understanding; it was as though they were priestesses, gravely celebrating the godhead of their mother. Umberto sat in a corner, with his concertina: an archaic, sculptured faun, younger and older than anybody else in the room.

At last we could bear it no longer, and staggered out into the late afternoon sun, to cool off. Charlie's face was scarlet, his battledress and shirt gaped open, showing a pink, damp expanse of skin. Kurt's hair had fallen over his square, heavy-browed face: he looked like Beethoven would have looked if he had ever got seriously drunk. I told him so.

'Ach, I could write great symphonies in moment,' he declared. 'I am great *Musiker*. Too bloody true I am, you old sod.'

'You're a fat Austrian c——,' Charlie remarked happily.

'It is pity I am not, my friend,' Kurt replied.

Umberto came out, his concertina still slung over his shoulder. He took my hand.

'*Sei felice?*' he asked, his teeth flashing white in his brown face.

'*Sono felice,*' I said.

Beyond the twin cypresses the country lay flooded in the warm, slanting light. Away on the horizon, hill upon hill lay revealed in the evening radiance, each topped with its fairy-tale village or castle. In the oak copse nearby, a chorus of nightingales shouted. Graziella had run into the field, and was gathering a bunch of white narcissi.

'*Eh, la guerra. Quando finirà?*'

It was the *padrone*. He looked sadly across the fields. '*Siamo poveri, poveri,*' he added, as if to himself.

There was a war, they were poor, the landlords in Naples or Rome ground them underfoot, their children were uneducated, the priests were paid to keep them in ignorance . . . I knew it all: I had heard Kurt, the Communist, expound it all – with conviction, with passion, and at length. Yet I knew also that with these people, on this Easter day, I had felt happier, I had felt a more genuine sense of the joy of living, than ever in my life before.

At last we prepared to leave. Farewells were protracted, and delayed by innumerable afterthoughts in the form of presents and souvenirs: a bottle of wine in case we were thirsty on the way, another for when we got home, one more because it was the 'good' wine, the special wine for Leonardo's first communion. A fourth bottle was added for some further, rather complicated, reason: perhaps it was to drink Leonardo's health tomorrow. A bundle of *finocchio* was produced for the Staff-Sergeant, whose partiality for it we had mentioned. Pieces of Easter-cake were pressed upon us for our friends who had not been to the party. A *salami* was offered by the *signora* in case we were hungry in the night – we had had a poor meal after all, she said. Bunches of narcissi and violets could not be refused. Umberto even offered a loaf of bread, in case we should have none with which to eat the *salami*. A pot of some conserve made of pig's blood was proffered by *la nonna*, because a pig had been killed recently.

Our tunics bulging with bottles, our hands clutching *finocchio* and narcissi, we started out across the fields. Half-way, we were overtaken by Umberto with a dozen new-laid eggs. When at last we reached the hospital and staggered across the yard in front of it, we observed Staff Woolf standing before the entrance exactly where we had left him. He was accompanied by MacDowd, the Corporal Clerk, and Smudger Smith. Their mouths opened, they stared. Then Smudge began to laugh; Mac began to laugh too. Only the Staff kept his countenance: he looked as black as thunder.

''Ere you are, Staff: 'ere's the mustard and ——ing cress for you,' Charlie bawled, and advanced towards the Staff-Sergeant proferring the bundle of *finocchio*. Unfortunately for the success of the gesture, he tripped over a stone and fell flat on his face: the bottle of wine secreted in his tunic smashed noisily, and spilt itself, like some sudden hæmorrhage, over the gravel.

A quiver which might have been a smile flickered over the Staff's prim grey face.

'You'd better get straight into your ——ing billets and get to ——ing bed before the old man sees you,' he said.

In the billets that night I said to Kurt:

'You can say what you like, these people know how to enjoy themselves. They may be politically uneducated and down-trodden and priest-ridden and all the rest of it, but they know how to live.'

'Too bloody true,' said Charlie, who was finishing off the bottle of 'good' wine.

Kurt sat up in bed, looking more than ever like Beethoven after a night out.

'So then, you have forgotten?' he asked, with the ominous air of a minor prophet. 'You think they give you all that for nothing? You are ——ing stupid, both of you.'

''Course I'm stupid. Who wouldn't be after all that?' Charlie commented, and let a satisfied fart.

'Do you not then realize to what you owe this *festa*?' Kurt pursued.

'Well, what?'

'To *una coperta*, one blanket, GS, property of the ——ing British Army. To that you owe your bloody *festa*, isn't it?'

'Too bloody true,' Charlie agreed. 'But it was cheap at the price. Wasn't it?' he appealed to me.

'Yes, it was cheap at the price,' I said: thinking of the *signora* dancing like a goddess, the wine and the sunshine and the flowers, and, beyond the dark cypresses, the sun-flooded country rolling away towards the distant hills.

Night Attack

IN the dark behind me I can hear the stumbling file of men coming
up the hill. Exhausted and dazed with lack of sleep they slip and fall
and are beyond swearing. In front of me the man carrying the
Vickers ammunition is almost tearful with anger as the boxes slip
again and again out of the Everest carrier. The silhouetted ridge
ahead of us is our start line, and we have to clear a further ridge
running out from it at right angles. We were told at CO's orders that
there are believed to be no enemy there, but we've heard that one
before. The path begins to turn to the left parallel with the start line
and a hundred feet below the crest. Sergeant Williams slips and
drops his tommy-gun. 'For Christ's sake quiet, Williams.' If there
should be any enemy on the reverse slope of the ridge they must
know we're here now.

It's still only a quarter to three – in twenty minutes the guns will
start. We lie down along the path listening. Sentries are above us
and below us. It's quiet and cold in the moonlight. So still that you
can hear a dog barking in a farm back towards the town. It's too
quiet. On other nights there have always been nervous bursts of
Spandau and Bren as patrols move about the defile and trees begin
to look like men. They must know we're coming. They're as quiet
as we are because they're waiting for us. They are lying there
listening now. I wonder where they are? Perhaps they are only just
across the skyline, a few yards away. Rather frightened perhaps,
certainly determined, wondering what the tommies are doing,
wondering how many of us there are. Investing us with a ruth-
lessness and strength of which we are not conscious as we wait for
zero. We are wondering the same about them too. Why do the
enemy always seem supernaturally strong up to the end so that it is
always a surprise when you find that they have suddenly turned
into a frightened and dirty group of prisoners? I suppose until you
see the men themselves, they only exist as bullets and shells and
mortar bombs . . . it must be after three now . . . yes, it's five past on

my watch. Our support from divisional mortars should start any minute now. The guns are on D's objective. There they go, they've started firing . . . about twenty seconds before they pitch. . . one . . . two . . . three . . . they should be coming down now . . . twenty-four, twenty-five. . . . Here they come. They are only just on the other side of the ridge. Hell, this one's close . . . get flat, get flat, for Christ's sake flat! . . . Jimmy, that last mortar is dropping short, can you tell them? Oh hell, I'd forgotten wireless silence. No one hurt? Here they come again. They're plastering the other side. Here's the short one. . . . Jesus, that was close. . . . Stretcher-bearers, stretcher-bearers? . . . Who's had it? . . . 14 platoon are you? Are you quite sure you can walk to the RAP? . . . you know where it is? Good lad, we shall want all our stretcher-bearers tonight, so as long as you can walk. . . . It's one of the reinforcements, sergeant, he's Mr White's platoon; in the shoulder . . . not too bad. I wonder how Dick will get on down at the bridge. We'll miss his platoon before the night's out. Still I'm glad I'm not on that job, I want to be alive tomorrow . . . another short. But I'd rather be here than on the other side. Paddy, my batman, is swearing quietly; the man next to him is huddled up and shuddering, pressed hard to the ground. I don't like the look of him at all. Lord, it's my mortar lance-corporal. If he breaks we'll be right up the creek. He's been getting shaky the last few days, perhaps I ought to have sent him down. It's too late now, I must watch him though. . . . It's twenty-five past. This will be the last lot of mortar. Pray god the short one doesn't hit me now. Well out of the way, thank god. . . . Here comes Jimmy. 'Are you ready, fifteen? Follow Company HQ.' . . . Now for it. The moon has risen and is very bright. I must remember to use the shadows. I wonder what the mortars have done over on the other side?

Tiredness has vanished; we all feel keyed up with a tight quivering feeling in our stomachs. At the skyline I see Company HQ going flat and crawling. In front of me two stretcher-bearers roll over the edge of the ridge into the bushes on the far slope. Just before I go over there's an outburst of firing from the right. There are Germans on D's objective all right, and from the sound of it on their start line too. We haven't time to worry about D though, we shall probably have enough on our own plate any minute now. I can see both sides of the ridge we are attacking. It can't be more than fifty yards wide and the sides are as steep as hell . . . if they have fixed lines down it. . . . Down to the left, against the black background of the big hill with the monastery, every house in Alessia seems to be burning, and the saucer of the valley is criss-crossed with tracer. On the other side there are fires in Dupino, but they look more like petrol and ammo. Far in the background where the mediums are firing are more red glows and flames. . . . The moon is strong and full, and we can see some distance along the ridge. Jack is keeping to the top and pushing straight on. Perhaps there are no enemy there after all. All the guns have stopped now. They are watching back at the Command Posts for green over white, our SOS flares. I hope we don't have to use them tonight.

Hullo, Jack's run into it. . . . 'Four section, here . . . five, left . . . six, right and rear . . . take over, sergeant . . . I'm going to see what's happened. . . . Hullo there, Jimmy, what's up?'

'Jack's overrun their outpost section and taken half a dozen prisoners – he's stuck now. They've got fixed lines down the ridge. Hell of a lot of guns, too . . . stay there a bit.'

As Jimmy goes off to recce I look around. The tracer is coming down the ridge from the far end, but only odd shots are going near where my chaps have gone to ground. There's deep shadow on the left . . . if I have to move that's my side. Here's Jimmy coming back now.

'Look, this is the form. Jack's stuck about one hundred and fifty yards further on, and he thinks the German is another hundred yards away. He will give you fire support. Will you have a crack? This is my plan. You'll have to flank them with Jack's support. Red light when you get on the objective, and then we'll all come in. I wish to God we had Dick's platoon to help you, it's a sod of a job. What's your idea?'

'Left flank in the shadow, crawl up the slope and get as close as I can without being seen. We'll have to go in up the hell of a slope though.'

'I'm afraid that's the same either way, get going as quick as you can. Good luck.'

The section leaders are told, and we move off down the flank of the ridge fifty feet below the crest. I lead the platoon slowly through the bushes. All the time my brain functions automatically, but beneath everything I feel 'This isn't me. It's someone else. This is only a night exercise at the battle school. It can't be me, it must be someone else. The enemy will fire at me soon. In two minutes I may be dead. Soon I may just cease to exist. It isn't me that may be killed, it's a different person. Suppose I'm blinded or shot in the guts like poor old Harrison . . . Oh God get it over, please God let it be tomorrow soon. I know I shall be hit . . . it must be a whole company dug in up there. Hermann Goering bastards too. We must be close now.' I give the sign to start moving up the slope. We're nearly at the crest of the ridge again. I sling my rifle and take the pin out of a grenade. We move quietly another few yards up the hill. I can hear my leading section commander breathing heavily next to me. Suddenly there is a shout in German and a burst of machine carbine from a few yards away. The corporal's tommy-gun fires from beside me and I throw my grenade and shout 'Go in'. Then without knowing how or why we all start scrambling for the top. Jack's Brens are firing like hell from where he's pinned down. Every weapon in the world seems to be firing, and then suddenly there's a blow on my arm as if from a stone, and I see my rifle sliding away down the slope. I've been hit and it hasn't hurt. I'm not much hurt though, so I must keep on up this damned hill. Where's my bloody rifle? Hell, I'll have to use my other grenade. All at once a confusion of noise and flash and my legs go from underneath me, and I'm rolling down the hill. God, I think my leg must have gone. . . . I must keep rolling to some cover. . . . Jesus, this hurts. I must be in a mess . . . at last I stop in the bushes again.

The firing has died down now and there are only odd bursts. I take stock of myself. I'm not bleeding very badly, but I can't feel my right leg below the knee. I can see the boot though. I try to move my knee and can feel the leg flopping about and the bones grating together. That's the answer, it's smashed. It must have been a grenade. My arm I can still move, though it feels odd and the wounds are throbbing.

Suddenly Sergeant Williams appears from below me. 'We had to pull out,' he whispers. 'I've sent 'em back, and we've got the wounded in. I'll go back and get 'em in position and then I'll come back for you. Where are you hit? . . . I'm afraid your leg has had it.'

He moves off and attracts a burst of fire. I feel scared and alone, for I'm still not more than forty yards from the enemy. Using my left arm and leg I do a sort of side stroke along the ground. I get tired and want to stop and go to sleep. Ahead of me I can see the silhouette of the start line ridge. It means safety. As I drag along the ground I keep saying to myself 'Over that ridge I'm in England, over that ridge I'm in England.' I get more tired. I must reach that ridge. I get the old

cross-country feeling – if I stop for a minute I'll run harder afterwards – and I know that it's an even bigger lie now than it was on
the battalion runs. If I stop I've had it. At last I'm too tired and have
to stop. I've forgotten Williams's promise to come for me. I don't
expect him to do such a damned silly thing anyhow. I feel very tired,
soon I shall go to sleep. I've lost interest in the battle, in my
wounds, in everything, and strangely I'm not so frightened now. It
seems inevitable that in a few hours this person who isn't me will
be dead and that the real me will wake up in my bed at home.

After about half an hour the tiredness starts getting less and I
want to live. I try to move, but my arm has stiffened and swollen.
Then I hear someone coming, I prickle with fear, it can only be a
German. But then I hear a whisper from above me where my
original place was. 'Where are you, Mr Grey, where are you?' I try to
answer and can't. The relief makes me weak. Then: 'Where are you,
you bloody fool?' Williams has come back, and until he hears my
answer he calls me every name he can think of in his anxiety. He
seems to be making a dreadful noise as he comes through the
undergrowth to me, the Germans must have heard him.

'I'll not move you until I've bound you,' he says; and then as he
binds my arm he tells me quietly that we've lost a lot, and some of
our best chaps. 'Corporal Lavers and three of the Jock reinforcements have been killed, sir, and young Newton has a burst through
his knees. Burrell's pretty bad and Lance-Corporal McIver too, but
the rest are all right except for a couple of cushy ones. I saw we
hadn't a chance after we had lost half the platoon, so I kept six
section back and pulled the rest out. You and four section went
under before the others had had time to get a shot in. . . . I can't
do anything for your leg. I'll get you under the shoulders and
pull.'

He pulls me along the ground through the bushes, and we get a
few yards nearer the company, but the noise makes the German
open up again. Now there's a good chance to live, I'm as scared as
hell. I don't want to be hit now. It's pretty awful for both of us, for
I'm no light weight in full equipment. After a hundred yards or so
one of my mortar team joins Williams, and it becomes easier. At
last we hear an English voice: 'Halt.' Quickly Williams replies:
'Williams and Mr Grey.' Jimmy comes up from Company HQ a few
yards away. 'Thank God, I thought you'd had it. Is it very bad?
You're not bleeding too much, you'll be all right, John. We'll get you

down to the RAP as soon as possible. Do you feel all right to tell me what you found?'

Six hours later two tired stretcher-bearers carried me into the Advance Dressing Station. A Scots doctor came to look at me.

'Compound right tib. and fib., severe,' he said, 'right arm gunshot wound and in the wrist. Bring a mug of tea here, shell dressings and a blanket. You'll be all right now, laddie, it could be a lot worse. Can you move your toes? Good. There's a little movement. What? I don't see why you should lose it.' He sprinkled sulphanilamide on it. 'Send him down on the next jeep, Wilson.'

With the morphia came relief. I couldn't do any more for my poor chaps now up on 532. I was alive, I was going to live, I was over the ridge. Soon I should wake up in my own bed in England.

All This is Ended

THE road turned in a half-circle through the middle of the battalion position. North of the road there was a wood, and in the wood they had built their Headquarters: two pits dug into the ground and connected by a crawl-trench. The wood was thin with trees: there was still a little snow left on the ground and the road was covered with an ice-sheet. Two motor-cyclists had been killed on it in the last week, skidding on the ice. And that was not a thing that should happen: if a dispatch-rider were killed by a bullet or by part of a shell then that would be all right: that is part of the business of fighting. It showed a lack of care to break your neck by skidding into a wall, as though you were coming back from Brighton on a Boxing Day.

Scotty was the Intelligence Officer with the face of a cherub: he was walking down the road along the line of the hedge with a map under his arm. The clouds were very low, and as he reached the edge of the wood he heard the top-heavy drone of bombers. Quick sharp whistle-blasts came from the wood and he heard men slushing through the snow that was becoming mud. He stood by the motor-cycle park and looked into the sky. The planes passed over: probably they were going to bomb the new positions behind the river. That didn't matter much now: no one was going to use those positions. 'Hold fast until the end,' they had said. Be blown to bloody pieces for democracy. And why not? The battle was going well elsewhere: it was just your own little bit that was rotten. A few distant thuds meant that the bombs were dropping on the trenches and pits behind the river. Clearly the enemy didn't know of the order to hold fast. He was wasting his bombs and risking the few aircraft he seemed to have these days. Long blasts on the whistles came from the wood. Men slushed back to their jobs. The cherubic Intelligence Officer entered the wood.

In the Orderly Room, roofed with two fifteen-hundredweight truck covers the CO was sitting by the telephone, his balaclava pulled down well over his ears. He was eating his day's chocolate ration, idly flicking two glucose toffees across the table from one hand to the other between the bites of chocolate. The Intelligence Corporal was writing up the log by the light of a tilley lamp. The colonel looked up when the Intelligence Officer entered. Saying nothing he looked down again, took a bite of chocolate and flicked one of the toffees so hard that it fell to the floor. The young officer put his map-case on the floor and began to search in the straw for the toffee.

'Never mind it. We get two each every day. I don't need them, anyway.'

The lamp began to pop. More aircraft flew overhead, and there were more sharp blasts on the whistle. The corporal began to pump the lamp. The planes passed over.

'It looks bad, sir.'

'I know it looks bad, Scotty. Find out anything?'

'Only substantiated what they said over the phone, sir. They're just as we thought. Fortieth in front and forty-second on the left. One interesting thing, sir. Apparently they're moving a whole artillery regiment from left to right.'

'They'll attack us on the left.'

'Missing us. Mopping us up afterwards. We haven't a hope staying here, sir, honestly, sir.'

'Are you funking?'

'Of course not, sir. But a brigade alive is of more use than a brigade dead . . .'

'Quite.' The colonel took another bite of chocolate, then he went on: 'I saw the Brigadier this morning. I'll tell you what's going to happen. Tonight will be normal patrolling. I'm going to send Teaser out to confirm what we suspect. Then at dawn we shall attack. The whole brigade, two battalions up and one back.'

'Against a brigade and a bit, sir.'

The whistles in the wood blew the all clear.

'Against two brigades near enough. It may put off their attack for a day, maybe. A few hours, anyway. It will cause of a lot of dislocation. It's bound to. Under no circumstances will we fall back from the wood. If they pass us then we still stay here. We attack at dawn, leaving a rear party here. The attack can't possibly succeed in the long run. We will be counter-attacked and driven back. Then we stay here. If there are only a few of us left then we exist as a guerrilla band.'

'It's suicide, sir.'

'I know. At least for us it's suicide. That is our job. We will make it easier for the rest of the Division and for Ninety Div. on our left. In under a week the Allied advance will continue. But probably we won't be there to see it.'

He picked up the phone.

'Exchange? Is the Signal Officer there? Hello? Charles? Yes. Look, Charles, CO here. Tell the usual people "O" Group at five o'clock. And bring the doctor this time.'

He put the receiver back slowly. It was quiet now in the office except for the scratching of the corporal's pen.

In the Signal Office Mr Mason took out a pad of notepaper and put away his Flaubert. He had joined the Army straight from Balliol: he had resolved to remain the complete intellectual in khaki. In order to appease the authorities he maintained a razor-edged crease in his battledress trousers and took care to be an efficient Signal Officer. He was regarded as an amiable eccentric, crackers but reliable. He had carried Volume II of Proust to the beaches of Dunkirk and then left it behind in the hope that it might prove enlightening to the enemy. He had studied Santayana at his OCTU and read the whole of *Anna Karenina* (for the fourth time) within the walls of Tobruk. He was now two-thirds the way through *L'Éducation Sentimentale*: but there were times when he found reading to be impossible. And this was one of those times. The CO was calling a conference and the MO was to be present. The MO was not always present but Stinky Lewis had his guts blown out shortly after the last conference that the MO attended. It was perhaps the thought of Stinky Lewis that now forced Mr Mason to close his Flaubert. Stinky Lewis turning a stirrup-pump on the Brigadier at his twenty-first birthday party: Stinky Lewis kidding that NAAFI girl that he was the fourth Baron Lewis of Swansea: Stinky Lewis on a weekend pass in London every weekend before the big show started: Stinky Lewis scattered in little pieces over the countryside, unrecognized because he always forgot to carry his identity discs.

Mr Mason took out his pad of notepaper and looked at the photograph of the girl on the office table. He hoped to marry her sometime. Sometime when he had a job and a bit of money and there wasn't much danger of the house falling in after a bomb had landed. Sometime when you could think farther ahead than the next cup of tea. Mr Mason began to write, confronted (as ever) by the paradox that his love letters seemed so childishly silly when he read them over again. (At his OCTU there had been Blacket, who began 'My very own dearest darling' and who amused him a lot because of it.) He wasn't going to be slushy: 'My darling Joan,' he began, then his pencil broke. 'I got your last letter,' he went on. 'I hope Dinky is still fun.' Dinky was a kitten, a present from the sub-editor of a farming weekly. It used to sleep on top of the eiderdown at night, and purr over their faces in the sun of the morning, purr uncontrollably as they lay together, purr as though it were about to explode and blow itself to pieces over their bodies. Pieces like Stinky Lewis: Stinky Lewis, who put in a three-inch mortar bomb upside down, causing Chalky White to have a stroke on the spot. Stinky Lewis. Mr Mason tore up the page and put the notebook in his pocket.

Outside it was still quiet. Two miles away a dispatch-rider, singing to himself as he went along, fell suddenly, shot through the head. His motor cycle charged on alone, then fell noisily on its side. It burst into flames. This was a common incident, of no importance except to the dozen people whose lives were the less full for the death of the man. The RSM would see that his name was entered in the Casualty Return for the day. The motor cycle would have to be replaced. Motor cycles were hard to obtain. They took up shipping space.

The CO's conference was very simple. For the past hour he had said his orders to himself over and over again. At three in the morning the battalion would leave the wood and form up in accordance with the brigade plan. On the code word Simplex the battalion on the right would advance up the hill to attack the enemy's left front. On the code word Duplex the battalion on the left would advance up the hill to attack the enemy's right front. 'On receipt of code word Triplex,' said the colonel, 'we leave the start point and begin our advance. Our objective is the Headquarters of the Fortieth Division.' There were details about communications: Mr Mason took them down diligently with a pencil sharpened at each end. There were medical details, issued and received with a grim smile. There were ammunition details. Anti-tank details. Carrier and mortar details. Details of food and details of consolidation. Details of times and details of transport. Details of aircraft, of artillery, of tanks. The colonel had it all clear-cut. If his unit had to die then at least its death would be accurate in all the administrative details. 'Any questions?' he snapped, as though it would be regarded as a breach of discipline if any of his company commanders dared to suggest any omissions. There were no questions. The conference split up with a series of uncoordinated salutes. The colonel saluted over-pompously. Then he shouted, as an afterthought, 'and best of luck, chaps, by the way'. He turned and entered the hole that was his office. He ate two of the glucose tablets in quick succession.

'Destroy all documents,' he said.

'Right, sir,' said Scotty.

'I'm going to get some sleep.'

'Right, sir. Good-night, sir.'

'Good-night.'

Darkness fell over the wood and the troops rested. Mr Mason resumed his letter. He wrote two more sentences and began to feel intolerably sentimental. This would never do. What would she think of him, of the hard-boiled intellectual, if he wrote what he was feeling now? Unable to face the thought, he tore up his letter and opened his Flaubert. But he could not concentrate. He opened a packet of biscuits and munched them miserably. Then he went to bed. But like so many men in that wood he was unable to sleep. Not that he was afraid of being killed. He liked sometimes to think that Joan was afraid of his being killed. Joan, professing to share his scepticism, still managed to pray for him every night. He did not know about this. But in any case he would not be killed in the morning. He was staying back in the wood during the attack. He was keeping in touch with the battalion by wireless and with brigade HQ by telephone: he was an important link in the brigade plan. But he was to stay in the wood. With him there would be a handful of signallers, batmen, and drivers. He tossed in his tent until the guard told him that it was half-past two.

Teaser Watson was out on a patrol that night. An ex-sergeant of the Coldstreams, now a captain, he was the most efficient, the fairest, and the most popular officer in the unit. He told the dirtiest stories ever heard in the Mess but he was devoted to his pretty dark-haired wife. He used words of the most astonishing blasphemy but he was the gentlest of men. He had made a profession of the Army but he was not pugnacious. However, if anybody insulted him he would lay them out in order to save words.

He left the wood with two men at ten o'clock. His job was simple in aim, difficult in execution. He had to see if the enemy HQ was where it was thought to be. If it was not there, if it had been moved, half an hour before the attack was to go in, he was to cut the telephone lines and tie the wrong ends together, throwing the communications into chaos at the vital moment. For the whole of that night he thought only of the job on hand; he even failed to think of his pretty wife. He thought of the ground, of the enemy, of concealment, of silence, of time, of cunning, of laying men out. At dawn he was within fifty yards of the enemy HQ: it had been pin-pointed exactly. Good old Scotty. He lay down and looked at his watch. When the moment came he would crawl forward with a pair of pliers to a tree where all the telephone lines seemed to converge. Had he been able to see his own face it would have astonished him. It was lined, like an old oak. His two men lay behind him, afraid but not showing that they were afraid, not showing Teaser, not even showing each other. Unfortunately one of them chanced to disturb a telephone cable, which in its turn disturbed a sentry. The sentry grabbed a grenade and threw it at the three men where they lay. The explosion was very loud and the sentry was later admonished for making such a noise. Captain Watson's pretty little wife threw herself into the Thames a month later. And during the attack the enemy's communications worked extremely well.

The men lying in the wood were unaware of what was happening to Captain Watson: a few of them had been told what he was trying to do. They had soon told the others. And as Captain Watson was a good man in whom everyone had complete faith it was encouraging in the early hours of the morning to think that the enemy communications would be destroyed at the vital moment. A few of the troops slept a little, especially the old soldiers, men who had slept soundly from Bengal to Palestine, in the desert, in Sicily, in Italy. They had slept in ditches, under trucks, in the open. They had slept in the rain and in the heat; they had slept when the desert was silent and they had slept when the air was full of the noise of shells. To some of them the wood was luxurious: they had a blanket and a cover over their heads. But some did not sleep. Some did not sleep at all. It was only the second time that they had fought. They had been bombed, but in 1940 most of them had been bombed at home. Sometimes a shell had been close to them. Now and then a man would fall suddenly dead, like the motor-cyclist. But this was not like fighting with your own rifle and your own bayonet, supported by your own mortars and your own carriers and your own anti-tank guns. This was like nothing you had been training for, getting the battalion into a precision machine of the highest order. All that training was now going to be tested thoroughly for the first time. And as a result of that testing some of them would die. The CO knew that most of them would die, that the unit he had trained for three years would be obliterated in a single morning. He was worried by this. But it was the luck of war. He had some good men: it was a pity. It was a very great pity indeed.

At dawn Mr Mason was in his office. It was cold, and some more snow had fallen in the night. He stayed in his office while the battalion went away, crunching the snow, down to the road and along to the start line. The CO put his head in the doorway before leaving.

'Got it all taped, Mason, have you?'

'Yes, sir. Best of luck, sir.'

'Thanks. We'll need it. You're a good fellow, Mason. Damn silly books you read, but you're a good chap.'

'Thank you, sir. Goodbye, sir.'

'Goodbye, Mason.'

Mr Mason was not in the mood to read Flaubert, not in the mood to write a letter to Joan. He broke into a bar of chocolate and passed it round the office. The signallers, pale and in need of a shave, munched in silence. Then they tested all the telephone lines. The lines were in order. They rang up brigade and checked their watches. Joan's picture looked round at the office. It was a picture full of sunshine, taken on a punt. Joan, standing on the end of the punt, had grabbed a tennis racket. She looked like an overgrown schoolgirl, all health and innocence. Mr Mason sighed, and then he checked himself. He had no right to indulge in such thoughts. He must stamp them completely out of his mind. They hampered his efficiency. And if he didn't survive? Then she would stand on the back of another punt and let someone else take her photograph. Mr Mason could not bring himself to believe this: despite all his other affectations he knew perfectly well that Joan would do no such thing. It was not a piece of knowledge that gave him pleasure at the moment. It prevented him from getting on with the job in hand. He knocked these thoughts from his mind, left the little office, and arranged his small group of men in a defensive position round the wood. Then he returned to the office.

Only the second time they had fought. And Stinky Lewis had been blown to pieces the first time. How silly he had been not to wear his identity discs. Stinky Lewis, who had been so certain of living through the war and had survived five years of it without a scratch.

'Code word SIMPLEX' came from brigade. Mr Mason passed it over the wireless to the adjutant. From the wood they could hear the gunfire, the shells of the barrage as they whistled over the trees. The aircraft were swooping low over the troops. Then came 'Code word DUPLEX': Mr Mason passed it to the adjutant. Then came code word TRIPLEX, and he knew that the battalion was moving forward. Some were wondering what had happened to Captain Watson. Captain Watson who was lying dead near the enemy wire, blown into little pieces like Stinky Lewis. The noise and whistling of the shells increased.

The whole operation lasted only two hours. Their objective was behind the railway line and most of the fighting took place on the line itself. It was in the vicinity of the railway that 'C' Company was wiped out: 'B' Company crossed the line, took part of the enemy HQ, but was wiped out twenty minutes later: 'A' Company managed to evacuate a section to the wood: 'D' Company, in the rear, found itself surrounded. By midday the battalion was obliterated.

Back in the wood Mr Mason saw that the log was kept accurately. He took down all the messages and passed them on to brigade. When the last message had come through he closed the bag. The enemy, he concluded, would pass by on either side of the wood. In a few days they would send out parties to wipe out his little band. He no longer mattered. Unless the divisional offensive swept forward before the wood had been touched: that was a hope, the only hope now. He gathered his men together and told them what had happened. The gunfire had died down. He could hear the rumble of enemy tanks on either flank. He retired to the office. Then he took out a piece of notepaper and began to write. Filled with a power that he could not control he wrote a letter to Joan. It was the sort of letter he had never dared to write before. The knowledge that it might never be posted, that Joan might never receive it, did not prevent him from writing. He filled ten pages. His batman gave him a cup of tea with some jam and biscuits.

Stinky Lewis. Mr Mason went into his bivouac and put his hands into the pockets of his greatcoat. Stinky Lewis, blown to hell in unrecognizably little pieces. Mr Mason felt that this was more or less the end. From the pockets of his greatcoat he pulled out two identity discs fastened to a piece of string. They contained his Army number, his name, and his official religion. Stinky Lewis had forgotten to wear his identity discs.

He put them round his neck and walked slowly round the wood.

Ward 'O' 3 (b)

WARD 'O' 3 (b) was, and doubtless still is, a small room at the end of
the Officers' Convalescent Ward which occupies one wing of the
rectangle of one-storeyed sheds that enclose the 'lily-pond garden'
of No. X British General Hospital, Southern Army, India. The other
three wings contain the administrative offices, the Officers' Surgical Ward and the Officers' Medical Ward. An outer ring of buildings
consist of the various ancillary institutions, the kitchens, the
laboratory of tropical diseases, the mortuary, the operating theatres
and the X-ray theatre. They are all connected by roofed passage-
ways; the inner rectangle of wards has a roofed veranda opening
on the garden whose flagstones have a claustral and enduring aura.
The garden is kept in perpetual flower by six black, almost naked
Mahratti gardeners who drench it with water during the dry season
and prune and weed it incessantly during the rains. It has tall
flowering jacquarandas, beds of hollyhock and carnation and stock,
rose trellises and sticks swarming with sweet peas; and in the arid
months of burning heat the geraniums bud with fire in red earthen-
ware pots. It is, by 1943 standards, a good place to be in.

At the time of which I am writing, autumn 1942, Ward 'O' 3 (b),
which has four beds, was occupied by Captain A. G. Brownlow-
Grace, Lieut.-Quartermaster Withers, Lieut. Giles Moncrieff and
Lieut. Anthony Weston. The last-named was an RAC man who had
arrived in India from home four months previously and had been
seriously injured by an anti-tank mine during training. The other
three were infantrymen. Brownlow-Grace had lost an arm in Burma
six months earlier, Moncrieff had multiple leg injuries there and
infantile paralysis as well. 'Dad' Withers was the only man over
twenty-five. He was forty-four, a regular soldier with twenty-five
years in the ranks and three in commission; during this period
he had the distinction of never having been in action. He had spent
all but two years abroad; he had been home five times and had,
five children. He was suffering from chronic malaria, sciatica and

rheumatism. They were all awaiting a medical board, at which it is decided whether a man should be regraded to a lower medical category, whether he is fit for active or other service, whether he be sent home, or on leave, or discharged the service with a pension. They were the special charge of Sister Normanby, a regular QAIMNS nurse with a professional impersonality that controlled completely the undoubted flair and 'it' which distinguished her during an evening off at the Turf Club dances. She was the operating-theatre sister; the surgeons considered her a perfect assistant. On duty or off everybody was pleased about her and aware of her; even the old matron whose puritan and sexless maturity abhorred prettiness and romantics had actually asked Sister Normanby to go on leave with her, Sister deftly refusing.

II

The floor is red parquet, burnished as a windless lake, the coverlets of the four beds are plum red, the blankets cherry red. Moncrieff hates red, Brownlow-Grace has no emotions about colours, any more than about music or aesthetics; but he hates Moncrieff. This is not unnatural. Moncrieff is a University student, Oxford or some bloody place, as far as Brownlow-Grace knows. He whistles classical music, wears his hair long, which is impermissible in a civilian officer and tolerated only in a cavalry officer with at least five years' service in India behind him. Brownlow-Grace has done eight. Moncrieff says a thing is too wearing, dreadfully tedious, simply marvellous, wizard. He indulges in moods and casts himself on his bed in ecstasies of despair. He sleeps in a gauzy veil, parades the ward in the morning in chaplies and veil, swinging his wasted hips and boil-scarred shoulders from wash-place to bed; and he is vain. He has thirty photographs of himself, mounted enlargements, in SD and service cap, which he is sending off gradually to a network of young ladies in Greater London, Cape Town where he stayed on the way out, and the chain of hospitals he passed through on his return from Burma. His sickness has deformed him; that also Brownlow-Grace finds himself unable to stomach.

Moncrieff made several attempts to affiliate himself to Brownlow-Grace; came and looked over his shoulder at his album of photographs the second day they were together, asked him questions about hunting, fishing and shooting on the third day, talked to

him about Burma on the third day and asked him if he'd been afraid
to die. What a shocker, Brownlow-Grace thought. Now when he
saw the man looking at his mounted self-portraits for the ump-
teenth time he closed his eyes and tried to sleep himself out of it.
But his sleep was liverish and full of curses. He wanted to look at his
watch but refused to open his eyes because the day was so long and
it must be still short of nine. In his enormous tedium he prays Sister
Normanby to come at eleven with a glass of iced nimbo pani for
him. He doesn't know how he stands with her; he used to find
women easy before Burma, he knew his slim and elegant figure
could wear his numerous and expensive uniforms perfectly and he
never had to exert himself in a dance or reception from the Savoy in
the Strand through Shepheard's in Cairo to the Taj in Bombay or the
Turf Club in Poona. But now he wasn't sure; he wasn't sure
whether his face had sagged and aged, his hair thinned, his ampu-
tated arm in bad taste. He had sent an airgraph to his parents and his
fiancée in Shropshire telling them he'd had his arm off. Peggy
sounded as if she were thrilled by it in her reply. Maybe she was
being kind. He didn't care so much nowadays what she happened to
be feeling. Sister Normanby, however, could excite him obviously.
He wanted to ask her to go to a dinner-dance with him at the Club
as soon as he felt strong enough. But he was feeling lonely; nobody
came to see him; how could they, anyway? He was the only officer
to come out alive. He felt ashamed of that sometimes. He hadn't
thought about getting away until the butchery was over and the
Japs were mopping up with the bayonet. He'd tried like the devil
then, though; didn't realize he had so much cunning and desperation in him. And that little shocker asking him if he'd been afraid to
die. He hadn't given death two thoughts.

There was Mostyn Turner. He used to think about Death a lot.
Poor old Mostyn. Maybe it was just fancy, but looking at some of
Mostyn's photographs in the album, when the pair of them were on
shikari tiger-hunting in Belgaum or that fortnight they had together
in Kashmir, you could see by his face that he would die. He always
attracted the serious type of girl; and like as not he'd take it too far.
On the troopship to Rangoon he'd wanted Mostyn to play poker
after the bar closed; looked for him everywhere, couldn't find him
below decks, nor in the men's mess-deck where he sometimes
spent an hour or two yarning; their cabin was empty. He found him
on the boat deck eventually, hunched up by a lifeboat under the

stars. Something stopped him calling him, or even approaching him; he'd turned away and waited by the rails at the companionway head till Mostyn had finished. Yes, finished crying. Incredible, really. He knew what was coming to him, God knows how; and it wasn't a dry hunch, it was something very moving, meant a lot to him somehow. And by God he'd gone looking for it, Mostyn had. He had his own ideas about fighting. Didn't believe in right and left boundaries, fronts, flanks, rears. He had the guerrilla platoon under his command and they went off into the blue the night before the pukka battle with a roving commission to make a diversion in the Jap rear. That was all. He'd gone off at dusk as casually as if they were on training. No funny business about Death then. He knew it had come, so he wasn't worrying. Life must have been more interesting to Mostyn than it was to himself, being made that way, having those thoughts and things. What he'd seen of Death that day, it was just a bloody beastly filthy horrible business, so forget it.

His hand was long and thin and elegant as his body and his elongated narrow head with the Roman nose and the eyes whose colour nobody could have stated because nobody could stare back at him. His hand crumpled the sheet he was clutching. He was in a way a very fastidious man. He would have had exquisite taste if he hadn't lacked the faculty of taste.

'Messing up your new sheets again,' Sister Normanby said happily, coming into the room like a drop of Scotch. 'You ought to be playing the piano with those hands of yours, you know.'

He didn't remind her that he only had one left. He was pleased to think she didn't notice it.

'Hallo, Sister,' he said, bucking up at once. 'You're looking very young and fresh considering it was your night out last night.'

'I took it very quietly,' she said. 'Didn't dance much. Sat in the back of a car all the time.'

'For shame, my dear Celia,' Moncrieff butted in. 'Men are deceivers ever was said before the invention of the internal combustion engine and they're worse in every way since that happened.'

'What is my little monkey jabbering about now,' she replied, offended at his freedom with her Christian name.

'Have you heard of Gipsy Rose Lee?' Moncrieff replied inconsequentially. 'She has a song which says "I can't strip to Brahms! Can you?"'

'Course she can,' said Dad Withers, unobtrusive at the door, a wry old buck, 'so long as she's got a mosquito net, isn't it, Sister?'

'Why do you boys always make me feel I haven't got a skirt on when I come in here?' she said.

'Because you can't marry all of us,' said Dad.

'Deep, isn't he?' she said.

She had a bunch of newly cut antirrhinums and dahlias, the petals beaded with water, which she put into a bowl, arranging them quietly as she twitted the men. Moncrieff looked at her quizzically as though she had roused conjecture in the psychoanalytical department of his brain.

'Get on with your letter-writing, Moncrieff,' she said without having looked up. He flushed.

'There's such a thing as knowing too much,' Dad said to her paternally. 'I knew a girl in Singapore once, moved there from Shanghai wiv the regiment, she did. She liked us all, the same as nurses say they do. And when she found she liked one more than all the others put together, it come as a terrible shock to her and she had to start again. Took some doing, it did.'

'Dad, you're crazy,' she said, laughing hard. 'A man with all your complaints ought to be too busy counting them to tell all these stories.' And then, as she was about to go, she turned and dropped the momentous news she'd been holding out to them.

'You're all four having your medical board next Thursday,' she said. 'So you'd better make yourselves ill again if you want to go back home.'

'I don't want to go back "home",' Brownlow-Grace said, laying sardonic stress on the last word.

'I don't know,' Dad said. 'They tell me it's a good country to get into, this 'ere England. Why, I was only reading in the *Bombay Times* this morning there's a man Beaverage or something, made a report, they even give you money to bury yourself with there now. Suits me.'

'You won't die, Dad,' Brownlow-Grace said kindly. 'You'll simply fade away.'

'Well,' said Sister Normanby. 'There are your fresh flowers. I must go and help to remove a clot from a man's brain now. Goodbye.'

'Goodbye,' they all said, following her calves and swift heels as she went.

'I didn't know a dog had sweat glands in his paws before,' Brownlow-Grace said, looking at his copy of *The Field*.

The others didn't answer. They were thinking of their medical board. It was more interesting really than Sister Normanby.

III

Weston preferred to spend the earlier hours in a deck-chair in the garden, by the upraised circular stone pool, among the ferns; here he would watch the lizards run like quicksilver and as quickly freeze into an immobility so lifeless as to be macabre, and the striped rats playing among the jacquaranda branches; and he would look in vain for the mocking-bird whose monotony gave a timeless quality to the place and the mood. He was slow in recovering his strength; his three operations and the sulphanilamide tablets he was taking had exhausted the blood in his veins; most of it was somebody else's blood, anyway, an insipid blood that for two days had dripped from a bottle suspended over his bed, while they waited for him to die. His jaw and shoulder-bone had been shattered, a great clod of flesh torn out of his neck and thigh, baring his wind-pipe and epiglottis and exposing his lung and femoral artery; and although he had recovered very rapidly, his living self seemed overshadowed by the death trauma through which he had passed. There had been an annihilation, a complete obscuring; into which light had gradually dawned. And this light grew unbearably white, the glare of the sun on a vast expanse of snow, and in its unbounded voids he had moved without identity, a pillar of salt in a white desert as pocked and cratered as the dead face of the moon. And then some mutation had taken place and he became aware of pain. A pain that was not pure like the primal purity, but polluted, infected, with racking thirsts and suffocations and writhings, and black eruptions disturbed the whiteness, and coloured dots sifted the intense sun glare, areas of intolerable activities appeared in those passive and limitless oceans. And gradually these manifestations became the simple suppurations of his destroyed inarticulate flesh, and the bandaging and swobbing and probing of his wounds and the grunts of his throat. From it he desired wildly to return to the timeless void where the act of being was no more than a fall of snow or the throw of a rainbow; and these regions became a nostalgia to his pain and soothed his hurt and parched spirit. The two

succeeding operations had been conscious experiences, and he had
been frightened of them. The preliminaries got on his nerves, the
starving, the aperients, the trolley, the prick of morphia, and its
false peace. The spotless theatre with its walls of glass and massive
lamps of burnished chrome, the anaesthetist who stuttered like a
worn gramophone record, Sister Normanby clattering the knives in
trays of lysol, the soft irresistible waves of wool that surged up
darkly through the interstices of life like water through a boat; and
the choking final surrender to the void his heart feared.

And now, two and a half months later, with his wounds mere
puckers dribbling the last dregs of pus, his jaw no longer wired up
and splinted, his arm no longer inflamed with the jab of the needle,
he sat in the garden with his hands idle in a pool of sunlight, fretting
and fretting at himself. He was costive, his stockings had holes in
the heel that got wider every day and he hadn't the initiative to ask
Sister for a needle and wool; his pen had no ink, his razor-blade was
blunt, he had shaved badly, he hadn't replied to the airmail letter
that lay crumpled in his hand. He had carried that letter about with
him for four days, everywhere he went, ever since he'd received it.

'You look thrillingly pale and Byronic this morning, Weston,'
Moncrieff said, sitting in the deck-chair opposite him with his
writing-pad and a sheaf of received letters tied in silk tape. 'D'you
mind me sharing your gloom?'

Weston snorted.

'You can do what you bloody well like,' he said, with suppressed
irritation.

'Oh dear, have I gone and hurt you again? I'm always hurting
people I like,' Moncrieff said. 'But I can't help it. Honestly I can't.
You believe me, Weston, don't you?'

Disturbed by the sudden nakedness of his voice Weston looked up
at the waspish intense face, the dark eyebrows and malignant eyes.

'Of course I believe you, monkey,' he said. 'If you say so.'

'It's important that you should believe me,' Moncrieff said moo-
dily. 'I must find somebody who believes me wherever I happen to
be. I'm afraid otherwise. It's too lonely. Of course I hurt some
people purposely. That dolt Brownlow-Grace for example. I enjoy
making him wince. He's been brought up to think life should be
considerate to him. His mother, his bank manager, his batman, his
bearer – always somebody to mollycoddle him and see to his wants.
Christ, the fellow's incapable of wanting anything really. You

know he even resents Sister Normanby having to look after other people beside himself. He only considered the war as an opportunity for promotion; I bet he was delighted when Hitler attacked Poland. And there are other people in this world going about with their brains hanging out, their minds half lynched – a fat lot he understands.' He paused, and seeming to catch himself in the middle of his tirade, he laughed softly, 'I was going to write a letter-card to my wife,' he said. 'Still, I haven't got any news. No new love. Next Thursday we'll have some news for them, won't we? I get terribly worked up about this medical board, I can't sleep. You don't think they'll keep me out in India, Weston, do you? It's so lonely out here. I couldn't stay here any longer. I just couldn't.'

'You are in a state, monkey,' Weston said, perturbed and yet laughing, as one cheers a child badly injured. 'Sit quiet a bit, you're speaking loudly. Brownlow'll hear you if you don't take care.'

'Did he?' Moncrieff said suddenly apprehensive. 'He didn't hear me, did he? I don't want to sound as crude as that, even to him.'

'Oh, I don't know. He's not a bad stick,' Weston said. 'He's very sincere and he takes things in good part, even losing his arm, and his career.'

'Oh, I know you can preach a sermon on him easily. I don't think in terms of sermons, that's all,' Moncrieff said. 'But I've been through Burma the same as he has. Why does he sneer at me?' He was silent. Then he said again, 'It's lonely out here.' He sighed. 'I wish I hadn't come out of Burma. I needn't have, I could have let myself go. One night when my leg was gangrenous, the orderly gave me a shot of morphia and I felt myself nodding and smiling. And there was no more jungle, no Japs, no screams, no difficulties at home, no nothing. The orderly would have given me a second shot if I'd asked him. I don't know why I didn't. It would have finished me off nicely. Say, Weston, have you ever been afraid of Death?'

'I don't think it's as simple as that,' Weston said. 'When I was as good as dead, the first three days here, and for a fortnight afterwards too, I was almost enamoured of death. I'd lost my fear of it. But then I'd lost my will, and my emotions were all dead. I hadn't got any relationships left. It isn't really fair then, is it?'

'I think it is better to fear death,' Moncrieff said slowly. 'Otherwise you grow spiritually proud. With most people it's not so much the fear of death as love of life that keeps them sensible. I don't love life, personally. Only I'm a bit of a coward and I don't want to die again. I loathe Burma, I can't tell you how terribly. I hope they send me home. If you go home, you ought to tell them you got wounded in Burma, you know.'

'Good God, no,' Weston said, outraged. 'Why should I lie?'

'That's all they deserve,' Moncrieff said. 'I wonder what they're doing there now? Talking about reconstruction, I suppose. Even the cinemas will have reconstruction films. Well, maybe I'll get a job in some racket or other. Cramming Sandhurst cadets or something. What will you do when you get home?'

'Moncrieff, my good friend,' Weston said. 'We're soldiers, you know. And it isn't etiquette to talk about going home like that. I'm going in where you left off. I want to have a look at Burma. *And I don't want to see England.*'

'Don't you?' Moncrieff said, ignoring the slow emphasis of Weston's last words and twirling the tassel of his writing-pad slowly. 'Neither do I, very much,' he said with an indifference that ended the conversation.

IV

The sick have their own slightly different world, their jokes are as necessary and peculiar to them as their medicines; they can't afford to be morbid like the healthy, nor to be indifferent to their environment like the Arab. The outside world has been washed out; between them and the encircling mysteries there is only the spotlight of their obsessions holding the small backcloth of ward and garden before them. Anyone appearing before this backcloth has the heightened emphasis and significance of a character upon the stage. The Sikh fortune-tellers who offered them promotion and a fortune and England as sibilantly as panders, the mongoose-fight-snake wallahs with their wailing sweet pipes and devitalized cobras, the little native cobblers and peddlers who had customary right to enter the precincts entered as travellers from an unknown land. So did the visitors from the Anglo-India community and brother officers on leave. And each visitor was greedily absorbed and examined by every patient, with the intenser acumen of disease.

Brownlow-Grace had a visitor. This increased his prestige like having a lot of mail. It appeared she had only just discovered he was here, for during the last four days before his medical board she came every day after lunch and stayed sitting on his bed until dusk and conferred upon them an intimacy that evoked in the others a green nostalgia.

She was by any standards a beautiful woman. One afternoon a young unsophisticated English Miss in a fresh little frock and long hair; the next day French and exotic with the pallor of an undertaker's lily and hair like statuary; the third day exquisitely Japanese, carmined and beringed with huge green amber stones, her hair in a high bun that only a great lover would dare unloose. When she left each evening Sister Normanby came in with a great bustle of fresh air and practicality to tidy his bed and put up his mosquito net. And he seemed equally capable of entertaining and being entertained by both ladies.

On the morning of the medical board Brownlow-Grace came and sat by Anthony among the ferns beside the lily pool; and this being a gesture of unusual amiability in one whom training had made rigid, Weston was unreasonably pleased.

'Well, Weston,' he said. 'Sweating on the top line over this medical board?'

'What d'you mean?' Weston asked.

'Well, do you think everything's a wangle to get you home or keep you here like that little squirt Moncrieff?'

'I don't think along those lines, personally,' Weston said. He looked at the long languid officer sprawled in the deck-chair. 'The only thing I'm frightened of is that they'll keep me *here*, or give me some horrible office job where I'll never see a Valentine lift her belly over a bund and go grunting like a wild boar at – well, whoever happens to be there. I got used to the idea of the Germans. I suppose the Japs will do.'

'You're like me; no enemy,' Brownlow-Grace said. 'I didn't think twice about it – till it happened. You're lucky, though. You're the only one of us four who'll ever see action. I could kill some more. What do I want to go home for? They hacked my arm off, those bastards; I blew the fellow's guts out that did it, had the muzzle of my Colt rammed into his belly, I could feel his breath, he was like a frog, the swine. You, I suppose you want go home, haven't been away long, have you?'

'Six months.'

'Six months without a woman, eh?' Brownlow-Grace laughed, yet kindly.

'Yes.'

'I'm the sort who'll take somebody's else's,' Brownlow-Grace said. 'I don't harm them.'

Weston didn't reply.

'You've got a hell of a lot on your mind, haven't you, Weston? Any fool can see something's eating you up.' Still no reply. 'Look here, I may be a fool, but come out with me tonight, let's have a party together. Eh?' Surprisingly, Weston wasn't embarrassed at this extreme gesture of kindness. It was ingenuously made. Instead he felt an enormous relief, and for the first time the capacity to speak. Not, he told himself, to ask for advice. Brownlow-Grace wasn't a clergyman with a healing gift; but it was possible to tell him the thing simply, to shift the weight of it a bit. 'I'm all tied up,' he said. 'A party wouldn't be any use, nor a woman.'

'Wouldn't it?' Brownlow-Grace said drily, standing up. Weston had a feeling he was about to go. It would have excruciated him. Instead he half turned, as if to disembarrass him, and said, 'The flowers want watering.'

'You know, if you're soldiering, there are some things you've got to put out of bounds to your thoughts,' Weston said. 'Some things you don't let yourself doubt.'

'Your wife, you mean?' Brownlow-Grace said, holding a breath of his cigarette in his lungs and studying the ants on the wall.

'Not only her,' Weston said. 'Look. I didn't start with the same things as you. You had a pram and a private school and you saw the sea, maybe. My father was a collier and he worked in a wet pit. He got rheumatism and nystagmus and then the dole and then parish relief. I'm not telling you a sob story. It's just I was used to different sounds. I used to watch the wheel of the pit spin round year after year, after school and Saturdays and Sundays; and then from 1926 on I watched it not turning round at all, and I can't ever get that wheel out of my mind. It still spins and idles, and there's money and nystagmus coming into the house or no work and worse than nystagmus. I just missed the wheel sucking me down the shaft. I got a scholarship to the county school. I don't know when I started rebelling. Against that wheel in my head. I didn't get along very well. Worked in a grocer's and a printer's, and no job was good enough for me; I had a bug. Plenty of friends too, plenty of chaps thinking the same as me. Used to read books in those days, get passionate about politics, Russia was like a woman to me. Then I did get a job I wanted, in a bookshop in Holborn. A French woman came in one day. I usually talked to customers, mostly politics; but not to her. She came in several times, once with a trade union man I knew. She was short, she had freckles, a straight nose, chestnut hair, she looked about eighteen; she bought books about Beethoven, Schopenhauer, the Renaissance, biology – I read every book she bought, after she'd gone back to France. I asked this chap about her. He said she was a big name, you know the way revolutionary movements toss up a woman sometimes. She was a Communist, a big speaker in the industrial towns in North France, she'd been to Russia too. And, well, I just wanted her, more and more and more as the months passed. Not her politics, but her fire. If I could hear her addressing a crowd, never mind about wanting her in those dreams you get.

'And then the war came and most of my friends said it was a phoney war, but I was afraid from the beginning that something would happen to France and I wanted to hear her speaking first. I joined up in November and I made myself such a bloody pest that they posted me to France to reinforcements. I got my war all right. And I met her, too. The trade unionist I told you about gave me a letter to introduce myself. She lived in Lille. She knew me as soon as the door opened. And I was just frightened. But after two nights there was no need to be frightened. You get to think for years that life is just a fight, with a flirt thrown in sometimes, a flirt with death or sex or whatever happens to be passing, but mostly a fight all the way along. And then you soften up, you're no use, you haven't got any wheel whirring in your head any more. Only flowers on the table and a piano she plays sometimes, when she wants to, when she wants to love.'

'I've never been to France,' Brownlow-Grace said. 'Hated it at school, French I mean. Communists, of course – I thought they were all Bolshies, you know, won't obey an order. What happened after Dunkirk?'

'It was such burning sunny weather,' Weston said. 'It was funny, having fine weather. I couldn't get her out of my mind. The sun seemed to expand inside the lining of my brain and the whole fortnight after we made that last stand with Martel at Cambrai I didn't know whether I was looking for her or Dunkirk. When I was most exhausted it was worse, she came to me once by the side of the road, there were several dead Belgian women lying there, and she said "Look, Anthony, I have been raped. They raped me, the

Bosche." And the world was crashing and whirring, or it was doped, wouldn't life a finger to stop it, and the Germans crossing the Seine. A year before I'd have said to the world, "Serve you right." But not now, with Cecile somewhere inside the armies. She'd tried.'

'And that was the end?' Brownlow-Grace said.

'Yes,' said Weston. 'Just about. Only it wasn't a beautiful end, the way it turned out. I had eight months in England, and I never found out a thing. The Free French didn't know. One of them knew her well, knew her as a lover, he told me; boasted about it; I didn't tell him; I wanted to find her, I didn't care about anything else. And then something started in me. I used to mooch about London. A French girl touched me on the street one night. I went with her. I went with a lot of women. Then we embarked for overseas. I had a girl at Durban, and in Bombay: sometimes they were French, if possible they were French. God, it was foul.'

He got up and sat on the edge of the pool; under the green strata of mosses the scaled goldfish moved slowly in their palaces of burning gold. He wiped his face which was sweating.

'Five days ago I got this letter from America,' he said. 'From her.'

Brownlow-Grace said, 'That was a bit of luck.' Weston laughed.

'Yes,' he said. 'Yes, it was nice of her to write. She put it very nicely, too. Would you like to read it?'

'No,' said Brownlow-Grace. 'I don't want to read it.'

'She said it often entered her mind to write to me, because I had been so sweet to her, in Lille, that time. She hoped I was well. To enter America there had been certain formalities, she said; she'd married an American, a country which has all types, she said. There is a Life, she said, but not mine, and a war also, but not mine. Now it is the Japanese. That's all she said.'

'She remembered you,' Brownlow-Grace said.

'Some things stick in a woman's mind,' Weston said. 'She darned my socks for me in bed. Why didn't she say she remembered darning my socks?'

Brownlow-Grace pressed his hand, fingers extended, upon the surface of the water, not breaking its resistance, quite.

'I don't use the word,' he said. 'But I guess it's because she loved you.'

Weston looked up, searching and somehow naïve.

'I don't mind about the Japanese,' he said, 'if that were so.'

v

Dad Withers had his medical board first; he wasn't in the board room long; in fact he was back on the veranda outside 'O' 3 (b) when Weston returned from sending a cable at the camp post office.

'Did it go all right, Dad?' Weston asked.

'Sure, sure,' Dad said, purring as if at his own cleverness. 'Three colonels and two majors there, and the full colonel he said to me "Well, Withers, what's your trouble? Lieutenant-Quartermaster, weren't you?" And I said "Correct, sir, and now I'm putting my own body in for exchange, sir. It don't keep the rain out no more, sir." So he said, "You're not much use to us, Withers, by the look of you." And I said, "Not a bit of use, sir, sorry to report." And the end of it was they give me a free berth on the next ship home wiv full military honours and a disability pension and all. Good going, isn't it now?'

'Very good, Dad. I'm very pleased.'

'Thank you,' Dad said, his face wrinkled and benign as a tortoise. 'Now go and get your own ticket and don't keep the gentlemen waiting. . . .'

Dad lay half asleep in the deck-chair, thinking that it was all buttoned up now, all laid on, all made good. It had been a long time, a lifetime, more than twenty hot seasons, more than twenty rains. Not many could say that. Not many had stuck it like him. Five years in Jhansi with his body red as lobster from head to toe with prickly heat, squirting a water pistol down his back for enjoyment and scratching his shoulders with a long fork from the bazaar. Two big wars there'd been, and most of the boys had been glad to go into them, excited to be posted to France, or embark for Egypt. But he'd stuck it out. Still here, still good for a game of nap, and them all dead, the boys that wanted to get away. And now it was finished with him, too.

He didn't know. Maybe he wasn't going home the way he'd figured it out after all. Maybe there was something else, something he hadn't counted in. This tiredness, this emptiness, this grey blank wall of mist, this not caring. What would it be like in the small council house with five youngsters and his missus? She'd changed a lot, the last photo she sent she was like his mother, spectacles and fat legs, full of plainness. Maybe the kids would play with him, though, the two young ones?

He pulled himself slowly out of his seat, took out his wallet, counted his money; ninety chips he had. Enough to see India just once again. Poor old India. He dressed hurriedly, combed his thin hair, wiped his spectacles, dusted his shoes and left before the others came back. He picked up a tonga at the stand outside the main gates of the hospital cantonment, just past the MD lines, and named a certain hotel down town. And off he cantered, the skinny old horse clattering and letting off great puffs of bad air under the tonga wallah's whip, and Dad shouting 'Jillo, jillo,' impatient to be drunk.

Brownlow-Grace came in and went straight to the little bed table where he kept his papers in an untidy heap. He went there in a leisurely way, avoiding the inquiring silences of Weston and Moncrieff and Sister Normanby, who were all apparently doing something. He fished out an airgraph form and his fountain-pen and sat quietly on the edge of his bed.

'Oh damn and blast it,' he said angrily. 'My pen's dry.'

Weston gave him an ink-bottle.

He sat down again.

'What's the date?' he said after a minute.

'12th,' Moncrieff said.

'What month?' he asked.

'December.'

'Thanks.'

He wrote slowly, laboriously, long pauses between sentences. When he finished he put his pen away and looked for a stamp.

'What stamp d'you put on an airgraph?' he said.

'Three annas,' Moncrieff said patiently.

Sister Normanby decided to abolish the embarrassing reticence with which this odd man was concealing his board result. She had no room for broody hens.

'Well,' she said, gently enough. 'What happened at the board?'

He looked up at her and neither smiled nor showed any sign of recognition. Then he stood up, took his cane and peaked service cap, and brushed a speck of down off his long and well-fitting trousers.

'They discharged me,' he said. 'Will you post this airgraph for me, please? '

'Yes,' she said, and for some odd reason she found herself unable to deal with the situation and took it from him and went on with her work.

'I'm going out,' he said.

Weston followed him into the garden and caught him up by the lily pool.

'Is that invitation still open?' he asked.

'What invitation?' Brownlow-Grace said.

'To go on the spree with you tonight?' Weston said.

Brownlow-Grace looked at him thoughtfully.

'I've changed my mind, Anthony,' he said – Weston was pleasurably aware of this first use of his Christian name – 'I don't think I'd be any use to you tonight. Matter of fact, I phoned Rita just now, you know the woman who comes to see me, and she's calling for me in five minutes.'

'I see,' Weston said. 'OK by me.'

'You don't mind, do you?' he said. 'I don't think you need Rita's company, do you? Besides, she usually prefers one man at a time. She's the widow of a friend of mine, Mostyn Turner; he was killed in Burma, too.'

Weston came back into the ward to meet Sister Normanby's white face. 'Where's he gone?' she said.

Weston looked at her, surprised at the emotion and stress this normally imperturbable woman was showing.

He didn't answer her.

'He's gone to that woman,' she said, white and virulent. 'Hasn't he?'

'Yes, he has,' he said quietly.

'She always has them when they're convalescent,' she said, flashing with venom. She picked up her medicine book and the jar with her thermometer in it. 'I have them when they're sick.'

She left the ward, biting her white lips.

'I didn't know she felt that way about him,' Weston said.

'Neither did she,' said Moncrieff. 'She never knows till it's too late. That's the beauty about her. She's virginal.'

'You're very cruel, Moncrieff.'

Moncrieff turned on him like an animal.

'Cruel?' he said. 'Cruel? Well, I don't lick Lazarus's sores, Weston. I take the world the way it is. Nobody cares about you out here. Nobody. What have I done to anybody? Why should they keep me here? What's the use of keeping a man with infantile paralysis and six inches of bone missing from his leg? Why didn't the board let me go home?'

'You'll go home, monkey, you'll go home,' Weston said gently. 'You know the Army. You can help them out here. You're bound to go home, when the war ends.'

'Do you think so?' Moncrieff said. 'Do you?' He thought of this for a minute at least. Then he said, 'No, I shall never go home. I know it.'

'Don't be silly, monkey. You're a bit run down, that's all.' Weston soothed him. 'Let's go and sit by the pool for a while.'

'I like the pool,' Moncrieff said. They strolled out together and sat on the circular ledge. The curving bright branches held their leaves peacefully above the water. Under the mosses they could see the old toad of the pond sleeping, his back rusty with jewels. Weston put his hand in the water; minnows rose in small flocks and nibbled at his fingers. Circles of water lapped softly outwards, outwards, till they touched the edge of the pool, and cast a gentle wetness on the stone, and lapped again inwards, inwards. And as they lapped inwards he felt the ripples surging against the most withdrawn and inmost ledges of his being, like a series of temptations in the wilderness. And he felt glad tonight, feeling some small salient gained when for many reasons the men whom he was with were losing ground along the whole front to the darkness that there is.

'No,' said Moncrieff at last. 'Talking is no good. But perhaps you will write to me sometimes, will you, just to let me know.'

'Yes, I'll write to you, monkey,' Weston said, looking up.

And then he looked away again, not willing to consider those empty inarticulate eyes.

'The mosquitoes are starting to bite,' he said. 'We'd better go now.'

East is West

IT was the first day he had been able to get around without his crutch and so the sergeant was rather pleased with himself. In fact, although it was still an hour to midday, he thought he deserved a beer. The Sudanese barman gave him a bottle of Stella and a glass and he hobbled back to the table where he had left his writing things. He put down the bottle and glass and then, supporting himself with his left hand on the chair, swung his left leg under the table. He lowered himself carefully on to the seat, with his weight on his good leg. The other one stuck out under the table and the heavy plaster rested on the iron bar that did duty for a heel.

It was still winter; so, though the sun outside was hot on the empty parade-ground, in here it was cool and there was no need to shut the windows or draw the blinds. As he looked out to the desert beyond the barrack huts he smiled. It wasn't so bad. This was one rest camp where they really did leave you alone. If only he didn't have this letter to write.

He poured the beer out slowly and watched the bubbles spring to the surface in a fine froth.

Two other chaps came in and began to play ping-pong in the far corner. Before long they had their shirts off and were playing only in their shorts. They still hadn't quite got rid of the yellow stage of jaundice.

The sergeant sipped his beer, then lit a cigarette and took a couple of draws, rather fast. A fly flicked at his mouth, thirsty, came back and flicked again. He brushed it away every time it came till it gave up and settled on his writing pad. It crawled till it found the place where the sweat of his hand had moistened the paper. Fingers spread so as not to give it the advantage of the draught, his hand smacked down. He brushed the squashed body aside and tore off that sheet. But there was another sheet beneath it, just as blank. He picked up his pen, suddenly.

'Dear Mrs Curtis,' he wrote. Then he put the pen down again.

What the hell was he going to say? He'd written these letters before and it hadn't been easy. But this one seemed to be impossible altogether. What could he say? He could feel sorry for Curtis all right, poor sod. He was dead now, anyway, and it didn't matter much what sort of bloke he'd been. But that was no good. You couldn't very well say that to his mother. Was there anything in the whole rotten business you could say to her?

What did it have to happen for anyway? Why should he have to write the bloody letter? It was only a bit of bad luck he'd come across Curtis at all.

Only it had looked like good luck then. Or it would have if he hadn't been so bomb-happy at the time that he took everything for granted. You took everything for granted at a time like that, when you'd just had your tank brew up under you and seen the only other bloke who managed to get out take a burst of Spandau in the chest and face before he even hit the ground.

He'd dragged George Black for a few yards until he saw there was no future in it. George was dead. The bullets were flying and the ammo in the tank would go up any minute. George slumped back when he let go. His shirt had ridden up the back and you could see where the bullets had come out.

Smoke, very dense and black, was pouring out of the tank. There was a terrific stink of oil and petrol and explosive. It wasn't the only tank either. You could see others of them going up in the same way all over the ridge.

He'd got his breath and his nerve back now. Without looking at George he jumped to his feet and bolted into the smoke, going down wind with it. Anything to get away before she went up for good.

So it didn't seem surprising when he found himself being hauled into the cab of a Dodge pick-up. Or even when he saw it was Curtis and him with a captain's pips up, though the last time he'd seen him was in camp when they were Territorials and Curtis had only one stripe.

Curtis leaned across him and slammed the door to. The driver got back into gear and the truck went on, hell for leather.

'What happened, Sergeant? You all right?'

That brought him to a bit. Sergeant. It used to be Bob in the old days.

'OK, thanks. Tank went up. Only me and George got out. And they got George.'

He felt dopey and at the same time he wanted to talk. But he couldn't bring himself to call Curtis 'sir'. And he wasn't the sort of chap you could talk to about old George.

After a while he pulled himself together. 'Where are we off to?'

'B Ech HQ at Brigade,' Curtis said.

As good as anywhere else. It'd been a good tank. You'd never get a pal like old George again.

But B Ech was pulling out when they got there. There was a fat major stamping round, giving all sorts of orders. A bit of a flap on.

'Get your truck into the convoy, Curtis,' said the major. 'There's a column of Jerry armour coming along Trigh Capuzzo. We'll all be overrun and in the bag, if we don't get out of this a bit more smartly. Haven't you got that kit aboard yet, Rumbold?' He had turned towards a little fellow who was trying to shoulder a valise as big as himself into the back of a staff-car.

The sergeant couldn't see any sign of a Jerry column. But he didn't care. It was their show now. They were officers. Let them handle it. None of his business. He'd had enough for just now.

'Come on, Grace, get a move on,' said Curtis.

The driver took the Dodge into the column. It was in desert formation but pretty ragged. The front vehicles began to move off without waiting. Those behind started off as best they could and began to find their places. The staff-car was the last to get away, the major even helping Rumbold with the camp-bed he was in such a hurry. He cut across the Dodge's bows as he went up to the front. The sand behind him swirled in their open window.

'Put up that window, will you, Sergeant?' said Curtis.

'It looks as if we're going east,' said the sergeant.

'Where else? The show's a wash-out. You tankies have let him run all over you.'

The sergeant flushed. This from a man who wore the black beret, even if he was in B Ech. But he said nothing.

Behind them, half left, on the ridge, they saw the flying sand of a column. Curtis opened the trap in the roof and looked through his glasses.

'Jerry,' he said, bending his knees and coming down. 'Put your foot on it, Grace.'

The driver went on at the same pace. He had to keep in formation.

A black gusher of smoke came up between two of the trucks in front. The convoy kept on. Another and another. One of the leading trucks, apparently unhit, began to blaze all the same. Men spilled over the tailboard on to the sand.

'Shall we pick some of them up, sir?' said Grace.

'No time. Let one of the three-tonners do it. They've got more room.'

But he felt the sergeant's stare. 'All right. Stop.'

'Only three of you. In the back. Hurry.'

Another truck, a fifteen-hundredweight, pulled up. A young lieutenant got out of the cab.

'Pile in with my blokes, the rest of you,' he said. 'Come on, you're not out blackberrying.' He watched them aboard, smiling. The sergeant began to feel better.

'They're all aboard, Grace,' Curtis said. 'What are you waiting for? They're bound to get us if we hang round any longer.'

As they moved off there was a crash behind them.

The sergeant looked back. At first there was nothing but smoke. When it cleared he saw the other truck coming on. The officer was standing with his head and shoulders halfway out of the trap, his binoculars resting on the roof of the cab in front. He waved. The sergeant waved back. A good bloke.

The convoy had become a single column now with wide intervals between trucks. You could feel all they had in common was that they wanted to go fast and in the same direction.

B Ech bastards, the sergeant thought. He was already homesick for his squadron. What had happened to them all? Were things really as bad as this?

'Step on it, Grace.'

'Yes, sir,' said the driver. He drove at the same steady pace. He's all right, that chap, the sergeant thought.

'Any idea where we are?' he asked.

'El Gubbi is on the right somewhere,' said Curtis. 'We should get to the wire soon.'

The way he said it it didn't sound as if he had much idea. They seemed to be going south-east now. So they'd probably strike the wire all right. Anyhow, it was Curtis's business. He was the officer. And didn't he know it? But he was the officer all the same. You couldn't get past that. But the sergeant couldn't help remembering they used to call him Blanco in the Terries.

Curtis took out a packet of Players. The sergeant hadn't had a smoke since the battle began that morning. But he was damned if he was going to ask for one. He looked straight ahead through the windscreen. The sand from the truck in front uncoiled and expanded towards them, like a spring. Curtis was tapping a cigarette against the packet.

'Have one?'

'Thanks,' said the sergeant and took it. There were tears of relief in his eyes. The driver's face looked very set.

'What about the driver?' the sergeant said.

'Have one, Grace?' said Curtis, quite amiably.

'Thanks very much, sir,' said the driver.

It was getting on towards four when they came to the gap in the wire. There were no MPs there. Trucks had converged on it from all directions. You could see from all the different unit signs mixed up together, odds and sods of all sorts, that there'd been a pretty fair MFU, a real balls-up. Even if everyone hadn't been going the wrong way.

'We'll be hours getting through at this rate,' said Curtis.

The sergeant got out of the truck.

'I'll have one too,' Curtis said. He got out and began to unbutton his fly. But the sergeant was walking towards the gap.

'Where are you off to?' called Curtis.

'Must try and help straighten this out,' said the sergeant.

All it needed was someone to see that too many didn't try to get through at once. Soon he had the traffic going in a steady stream. Luckily no Jerry planes had turned up in time.

The Dodge came up. 'No point in staying there all night,' Curtis said. 'You might as well jump aboard. Let some other mug take a turn.'

On the other side the trucks had streamed away as fast as they got through. No one had any notion where the leading truck had got to. The convoy was well scattered, disorganized.

After a while the sergeant saw they might as well give up trying to keep in convoy. 'Let's pull out and have something to eat,' he said. 'If you've got any grub, that is.'

'There's plenty in the back,' Curtis said. 'But do you think it's all right? He might be pretty close behind us.' He seemed rather subdued.

'Might as well take a chance. We can always bolt for it.'

They got out and went round to the back of the truck. Curtis undid the flap. The three men who'd got aboard and his batman were sitting there, with knees drawn up. Their faces were caked with the fine sand that had got through the flap. They climbed out stiffly. One of them was a corporal.

The batman got some biscuits and bully and a tin of cheese. 'Here you are, sir.' Curtis took some.

'Have some, Sergeant?' said the batman.

'Thanks, chum.'

'There you are now, Corp.' The batman passed what was left to the corporal and he began to share it out.

'Think I should brew up and make a cup of char, sir?' said the batman.

'Christ, no. No time.'

The others all looked glum.

'What's the next move?' said the sergeant.

'There's nothing to stop the Jerries between here and Mersa. We'll have to go south-east a good bit before we turn up to join the reserves there.'

'Nothing between us and Mersa?' said the sergeant.

'I know what I'm talking about.'

The sergeant shrugged. Perhaps he did know. His own unit had been fighting off and on for three days. He had no idea what had been happening anywhere beyond what you could see from the tank. And not much about that either. But if Curtis was right things were pretty bad.

'Planes,' said one of the men.

There were three of them, coming out of the sun.

The sergeant had noticed a Bren in the back of the truck. He grabbed it and fitted a magazine.

'Put her on my shoulder,' said the corporal, running round to his front.

'OK, Corp.' He rested the barrel on the corporal's shoulder and waited.

'What's your unit?' he asked.

'I was orderly room corporal at B Ech HQ.'

'Good for you.' He wasn't sure what he meant. But he liked the corporal.

'Just as well the traffic's mostly through the gap,' the corporal said. 'What a target it was.'

The planes curved away and down towards a column of transport that had followed them through the gap and was now dispersed on the ridge opposite. They peeled off and dived, machine-gunning and bombing. There was some scattered AA fire.

When the planes had dropped their stuff and wheeled off west again, the sergeant and the corporal walked back to the truck.

'That sounded like Jerry AA to me,' said the sergeant.

'Rubbish, Sergeant,' Curtis said. He got up and brushed the sand from his battledress. 'It can't be. They can't have got here already.'

'The planes did look a bit like Tomahawks,' said the corporal.

'Nonsense.' Contradicting them made Curtis feel more confident. 'We'll drive over and see what the news is.'

This time the sergeant kept a look out from the trap.

'Could I borrow your glasses?' he called down.

Curtis got them out of their case. But already the truck was close enough.

'Jerries,' the sergeant said as he shot down through the trap. 'Quick, driver, left hand down.' They were no more than a couple of hundred yards away.

'We'll have to turn it in,' Curtis said.

The sergeant stared at him. His mouth was slightly open, face pale. He did not meet the sergeant's eye.

'Flat out,' said the sergeant across Curtis to the driver. There was a slight flush on the driver's cheekbone and a little ridge of cartilage riding up and down where the jaws joined. The truck righted itself as it came out of the swerve, the driver's foot hard on the accelerator.

They were running across the enemy's front now, a good target. The sergeant could see Jerries at the turrets of a few tanks which had been hidden behind the ridge. Resting up or getting ready to laager for the night.

A rip of bullets smashed through glass.

'It's no go,' said Curtis. 'We'd better turn it in.'

The bullets had smashed diagonally through the right-hand window, above the driver's head. The sergeant stared through the windscreen to the front, watching the desert come flying to meet them and waiting for the finishing burst. If he were driving he would hardly have had the spare energy to feel like this. He did not want to look at Curtis.

He got up and peered over the edge of the trap, looking back. The enemy trucks were well behind, perhaps already out of effective range. He came down into the cab again.

'I knew we shouldn't have stopped there,' Curtis said.

They drove on and didn't stop till it was safe to take a bearing.

'Don't you think we should head up towards the coast?' the sergeant said.

'They're probably all along the coast road by now,' Curtis said. 'They'll have come down Halfaya Pass, I'll bet.'

He had the compass and the sergeant was too tired to argue. But he suspected the navigation was very much by guess and by God. It would have been more comfortable if they'd had the coast road to guide them.

Last light came.

'I think it's safe to turn more to the north now,' Curtis said.

'Or perhaps brew up and bed down for the night?' suggested the sergeant. There didn't seem much sense in just plunging on through the night. And it was risky, too.

'We must try and join up with the rest at Mersa as soon as we can.'

But he told the driver to stop all the same and they had some more bully and biscuits. The men were getting a bit jittery. They'd obviously got Curtis pretty well summed up already. They sat off in a group by themselves in the sand and talked in low voices. The driver was evidently telling them how close they'd been to the bag. The batman skipped about, puttings things away. The sergeant was left with Curtis. Curtis didn't talk much. He had become more and more the officer as he felt his prestige going down.

'Come on, men,' he said at last. 'No time to waste. All aboard.'

The sergeant drove for a while. Then Curtis took over. The driver was supposed to be having a sleep. But it was his truck and, though both Curtis and the sergeant drove well, he was uneasy till it was his turn again. The sergeant dozed, waking at heavier jolts, then going off again. Once he was back in his tank just after it caught fire. Only this time the hatch had jammed. After that he didn't sleep for quite a while and even managed to ask Curtis for a cigarette. When it was finished he slept again.

A shell had smashed the tank track. Yet it seemed to be going on clanking.

'Sounds like a bit of wire or something caught in the mudguard,' he woke to hear the driver saying. 'We'd better stop and have a look.'

They got out and had a look. The truck had hit a single strand of wire and dragged it along.

'A minefield,' said the sergeant.

'It can't be,' Curtis said. 'They've never got as far as this.'

'It might be one of ours. We'd be wiser to stop where we are till first light. There's not even a moon.'

'Look,' said the driver. 'Flares.'

They turned round. Back the way they had come the flares were shooting up into the sky, lingering, then dropping slowly to a darkness that closed on them before they reached the ground.

'Jerries,' said Curtis.

'Might be our chaps.'

'I tell you, Sergeant, there's nothing to stop them between where they are and Mersa. We've got to get on.'

'I think we should stop where we are till first light. We'll be able to see then whether we're in a minefield or not.'

'And get picked up by the Jerries in the morning just for fear of a few imaginary mines? I thought you had more guts than that, Sergeant.' This was his revenge for the afternoon.

'I still think it's crazy.'

'It doesn't matter what you think. I'm the superior officer here and I say we're going on.' There had been a fresh outbreak of flares.

The driver had unwound the wire from the axle. They went back to the cab.

'I'll tell you what,' Curtis said, amiable again. 'You take a spell at the wheel and I'll get out on the mudguard, just to please you.'

The sergeant took her along slowly. The driver sat beside him, very uneasy, and then after a bit climbed out on the left. The sergeant's eyes strained out through the windscreen to the moving glimmer of desert in front. He thought how thin the flooring was that separated him from the upward blast that might come at any moment.

When it came it flung him through the door and out on his face. The flash left his eyes and he was staring at the sand, his ears singing on this side of a wall of deafness. He got up still stupid, and staggered out of the black fumes. He found himself at the back of the truck.

'Mines,' he said to the faces that stared out at him.

Then he remembered Curtis and the driver. He came round to the front again. Curtis seemed to be trying to raise himself on his hands and each time falling on his face, half-sideways. The driver was coming round the bonnet from the other side. He seemed all right.

Curtis was lying on his face when they got to him, no longer trying to get up. The sergeant turned him on his back. His right leg was gone, from the thigh. The left foot was hanging from the shinbone by a few ragged strands.

'Get out your field-dressings,' the sergeant said to the others who had all come up. He got out his own as well.

Curtis was beginning to struggle again. 'Sit on him,' said the sergeant to the driver. 'He mustn't see his legs.'

The driver sat on Curtis and lit him a cigarette. The corporal knelt and kept his fingers pressed down on the artery just below where it joined the groin. The sergeant from the other side tried to find enough thigh to get a purchase for the tourniquet. Curtis had begun to scream now and heaved from time to time. Each time the blood gulped out more swiftly than ever. The dressings were soaking already. The sergeant did his best with the tourniquet and then turned to the left leg. The ragged trouser was in the way.

'Anyone got a knife?'

Nobody had, but the sergeant remembered seeing one in the cab. Quicker to find it himself. His own foot was giving trouble now but he got to the cab, fumbled for the jack-knife which had slipped down behind the seat, got it and came back. He got on a second tourniquet and dressings.

Suddenly the corporal flopped. He had fainted. Curtis gave a sort of final heave and sat up. He saw what had happened to his legs.

'My legs,' he said, 'Jesus Christ, my legs.'

The blood was still coming from the right thigh, in spite of the tourniquet. Curtis got weaker and his voice quieter. 'Why did it have to be me?' he kept moaning. 'Oh, sweet Jesus Christ, why did it have to be me?'

The corporal came to and tried to stop the bleeding with his fingers on the artery again.

'Shall I make a cup of char on the Primus, Sergeant?' said the batman.

'OK. Here, corporal, give us a strain on this, will you?'

But it was no good. The blood kept getting away, soaking the dressings, the sand. And the pain was getting worse as the shock passed off. Curtis seemed to be going out of his mind with it. Sometimes he cried like a baby and called out for his mother.

Then he seemed to get himself under control again. He recognized the sergeant.

'Bob,' he said, 'shoot me, Bob, for Christ's sake. I can't stand it. Shoot me.'

The sergeant crouched beside him.

He did not know whether it was a long time or a short time before Curtis died.

He had to cut away the boot from his own foot then. Its aching did not let him sleep and he kept hearing Curtis and seeing Curtis, though Curtis was silent now under his last blanket. He was glad when first light came.

The corporal and he stabbed about with bayonets till they found a spot where there were no mines. They dug a grave and buried Curtis. His body was the colour of skimmed milk.

The batman made tea and they had breakfast, bully and biscuit. The driver stood with his mug in his hand, looking at the wrecked wheel and mudguard and shaking his head. The sergeant's foot was too swollen now for him to walk.

When the column of Indians who had leaguered a mile away that night rescued them from the minefield the sergeant had to be carried.

If it had been poor old George that had asked me I'd have done it for him, the sergeant was thinking now. I'd have known it was all right if it'd been a pal like George.

He hobbled up to the bar to get another beer. 'Dear Mrs Curtis,' was as far as he'd got. It was as far as he'd got yesterday, and the day before.

Not Substantial Things

A FEW miles beyond the village we came to a blown bridge the way Amedeo had said we would. So we began to have some confidence in him. Perhaps he did know a way through the minefields and round the demolitions after all.

But it was well after midday by now and we thought we might as well stop here as anywhere else and have something to eat. So Terry and I helped Ned get out the scran-box and then we left him to master the Primus and brew up while we took another look at the map. Amedeo skipped round helpfully at first. But we'd worked out a technique of putting a feed together in the past few years which didn't allow for spare parts like Amedeo and so in the end there was nothing to do for Amedeo but sit sadly on a stone while Ned brought the billy to the boil.

I still didn't really feel as if my heart was in the business. When Terry drove into HQ that morning and suggested a day's liberating I'd jumped at the idea, thinking it would be a change from just hanging round and chafing at the bit. Jerry had pulled out a couple of days before and was going north hell for leather to shape up on his new line above Rome. But the Div. wasn't being allowed to follow. The big shots were cooking up some new job for us and according to current latrino-gram we were going to be given a rest and then put in to crack a hole in the next line. Whatever it was we were all pretty browned off. We weren't allowed to follow up now we had him on the run, there was nothing much to do and there was no leave yet to Rome.

In fact, liberating in the territory old Jerry had vacated was about the only diversion there was and everyone who could lay his hands on a vehicle was cruising round looking for some village that hadn't been spoiled by other liberators getting in first. That would have been enough by itself to make Terry welcome when he and Ned turned up in the Brigadier's car.

But there was another reason. I'd thrown a farewell party the night before for my batman, Bandy Grimm. He and I had been together a long time. And now he was off to New Zealand on his three months' leave. With the Jerries rocking on their heels the way they were the odds were they'd have taken the count before he got back. Somehow it wasn't the way you expected to see the last of a bloke in this war. You got used to them pushing off for a while to Base or a hospital, but you knew they'd turn up again. And you got used to them setting out on some offensive when you knew there was a good chance they wouldn't turn up again. But somehow to realize all of a sudden that a chap you'd got as used to as Bandy was going for keeps, and going home at that, was different. It meant times were changing. Change and decay, in fact. You had to face up to it that you were probably going to survive after all. All these years you'd been thinking that as long as you hung on and didn't let your cobbers down and took the rough with the smooth, it didn't make much odds what else you did because there was no guarantee you wouldn't go back to the battalion any time, and then you'd soon reach the end of your ration of tomorrows. You'd have had your firkin, in fact.

But if blokes like Bandy were getting out of it alive, going home and all, then the chances were you would yourself. And then what the hell would you do?

So when we saw Bandy off in the jeep for Rear Div., all his traps along with him, and he leaned out and shook hands and the jeep roared out with Bandy looking at the HQ sign and the serial number for the last time, and raising a last crack for the Provost on point duty, I turned back to the mess-tent feeling pretty low. And breakfast didn't help any. It just reminded me I had a hangover as well and that I'd been pretty offensive to the G2 at the party, calling him a bank clerk in battledress. Which he was, but that's another story.

So Terry's arrival couldn't have been better timed.

All the same, the hangover, or whatever it was, wasn't as easy to shake off as all that. And Avezzano, our first stop, didn't help. There were a couple of armoured cars in the main square and the Div. Cav. had roped off a section for themselves. A few blokes were sitting on top of the cars reading the NZEF *Times* and a few more were brewing up alongside. The Ites were crowded round the ropes, gaping. The usual kids had got to close quarters and were cadging biscuits. Wally Riddell was in charge.

'Hallo,' he said, 'you bloody base-wallopers. Is the war over? Or are you doing an advance guard for AMGOT?'

'No, Wally,' Terry said, 'just showing ourselves to keep up the morale of the forward troops. AMGOT'll be along when the mines are lifted.'

'Poor old Ites,' said Wally. 'They've had everything. Ostrogoths, Visigoths, and all the rest. And now AMGOTS.'

'Don't blame us, Wally,' Terry said. 'We're just a couple of liberators like yourself.'

Wally gave us a bit of a look, as if to say: Not so like as all that, you come along afterwards. But he didn't need Terry's MC ribbon to remind him we'd had our share and he said nothing. Besides, a hell of an uproar broke out in a side street just then and so we all strolled over to have a look.

A crowd of Ites was struggling down the middle of the road. In the centre we got a glimpse of a woman they were dragging along and she was certainly getting a rough spin. She must have been quite good-looking, but her face was all scratched now and one old dame in particular kept grabbing her by the hair, peroxided it was with the peroxide beginning to fade, and trying to yank it out by the handful. The equivalent number of Gyppos could hardly have made more noise than this crowd.

'You speak Itie, don't you, Mick?' Wally said. 'What the hell's it all about?'

One of those bright kids you always find on the edge of a crowd explained.

'Well, what's he say?'

'Seems she and the local Jerry commandant went in for a bit of horizontal collaboration. He dropped her in the getaway and she's been hiding out. The general idea is to tear her to bits.'

'Oh, Jesus, here we go again. That's the second today. Where the hell's that Field Security bloke? I have to do all his dirty work.'

'Well, you'd better get cracking, Wally, on your errand of mercy,' Terry said. 'Remember her only sin is that she has loved too much.'

Wally glowered at him and shouldered his way into the mob, a couple of his men after him.

There was no point in hanging around and so we went back to the car where Ned was waiting for us.

'Popular as a bag of measles, poor bitch,' Ned said as we watched

Wally's boys escorting her towards the Field Security place and the Ites trailing after like wolves.

In the next village we came to we were still a novelty and the wine was shoved through the windows at us in vast quantities. The usual Ite who'd been to the USA came and demonstrated his English and we pretended to understand him till all his cobbers were convinced he hadn't been lying all these years and really could speak English.

'He'd have been a top-sergeant if he'd stayed in the States,' said Ned.

'Why top-sergeant?' I asked.

'All Yanks are top-sergeants,' said Ned.

Just then I picked out what seemed to me a bright-looking youth and he turned out to be this joker Amedeo. According to him all the roads out of the village were blown. But he reckoned he could find a way through to his own village which was a few miles north-east of us.

'The only thing is,' Terry said then, 'I feel the call of Uncle Spam.'

I wasn't sure whether it was hangover or hunger with me but I felt pretty hollow myself. And, anyhow, I was keen to get away from one particularly unpleasant bloke in a blue suit who kept telling us he was a bank manager and inviting us to lunch. I've always maintained there must be something wrong with people who can look after all that money without spending it and it was pretty clear Blue-suit was no exception because the rest of the crowd kept their eyes on him the way a horse does when there's a fly he doesn't like hanging about. In fact, it was obvious he was one of the local Fascist johnnies and the crowd were still scared of him and wanted to see if he could make his marble good with us.

'This joker's a bit of *non buono*,' said Terry, who'd smelt him too. 'Let's get out of here into the fresh air.'

So we put Amedeo in the back with the plonk we hadn't been able to drink and driving east we came to the blown bridge.

But the plonk hadn't had time to take much effect yet and my mind kept running over the day's bad marks: a hangover, old Bandy's face when we shook hands, that crack of Wally's about base-wallopers, the poor scragged whore, the Ite from the USA and the bloody business man. A poor catch so far.

'You know, Terry,' I said, 'what say we call it a day and go home?'

'Don't be a piker, Mick,' he said. 'I know it's not been much chop so far but we're only getting started. Come on, take a pull of this plonk.'

So I knocked back a bottle and sure enough what with that and the smell of some eggs frying that Ned had scrounged, and the sun shining on the nice colours of the 1/200,000 map with the roads marked in yellow and red, I began to feel better.

On the broken bridge someone had splashed up in tar: Viva Stalin, Viva Churchill.

'Wonder why there aren't any Viva Roosevelts?' said Terry.

'Too hard to spell,' Ned said, looking up from the pan.

'Suit them better to defend their bloody bridge rather than paint it after it's down,' I said. But I didn't really mean it any more. And I'd just realized from looking at the map that the drained swamp on our right was the setting of Silone's *Fontamara*. The wonder was that they still had the heart to splash up even the names of hope.

After that pretty nearly every bridge and culvert was blown. And we weren't very anxious to go near the ones that weren't. Even as it was, creeping down into the gullies and skirting along the faces or tacking up them, we always stood a reasonable chance of going up on a Teller.

Once we came on a mule with its guts blown out but still alive. Terry got out and finished it off.

'Jesus,' he said as he put away his pistol. 'And to think we're doing this for pleasure.' So I could tell he was feeling the way I was. And I remembered he and his truck had gone up in one of the Ruweisat battles when he was an LO. He still had a bit of metal in his bum.

It wasn't so bad for Ned. He had all he could do keeping the car going and right side up. She was one of the few vehicles left in the Div. with the old desert camouflage and she had a mileage behind her that was nobody's business. Ned was very attached to her.

'One thing,' Ned remarked some time after we'd passed the mule, 'if we do go up I can always blame you jokers.'

Of course it soon turned out that Amedeo had no idea where the mines were. But he was quite happy and like most Ites he put all his brains into finding reasons for staying that way. He sat on the roof and dangled his legs in front of the windscreen. He had confidence in us, he explained.

Eventually we struck a good bit of road and were able to hit her up, keeping well clear of the verges. Every time we passed one of those little Itie farms the kids dropped everything and rushed out after us. But the old people just waved and went on with whatever they'd been doing as if they'd got to the stage of not caring who drove by in fast military cars, Germans or anyone else. They knew they'd never do any riding themselves, by this time.

Well, it all took time and it was late afternoon when I poked my head out the trap in the roof to see what Amedeo was screeching about.

'Ecco, ecco,' he was shouting. 'Castel di Goriano.'

And sure enough, a couple of miles away you could see a village perched up on top of a knoll. And very nice it looked too, so old it was the colour of the ground and sitting up there soaking the sun into itself the way a lizard does.

'He says it's Castel di Goriano,' I said, pulling inside again. 'It's really in 5 Corps territory, I should think.'

We checked up on the map and sure enough it was.

'First come, first served,' says Terry. 'The poor old pongos are probably still indenting in triplicate for mine-detectors.'

By this time we were climbing up the last slopes and had had to slow down. There were swarms of partisans all round us, banging off those Itie tommy-guns. The roof was covered in kids and Amedeo had moved to the bonnet. At the main gate we found the whole town had turned out to meet us and there wasn't a dog's chance of getting the car through. There was nothing for it but to abandon ship.

The next thing I knew was that I was being hoisted shoulder high and carried up the main street. I got my head round long enough to see that Terry and Ned were aloft too and even young Amedeo for good measure. So I didn't feel quite such a fool. Besides, I was tickled at Ned's face. You could see he was worrying his head off about the car. But I wasn't going to worry, because I'd seen a hefty partisan with a carbine sitting on top of it and it was obvious that it would have been high treason for anyone to start monkeying with it that day.

Well, as we go up the street we're pretty busy what with keeping our balance and catching the wreaths of flowers tossed up by the girls and taking a swig from every bottle that was pushed at us and kissing all the babies their mothers kept holding up to us. And there was an old woman who kept kissing me on the boot. But the other two didn't notice, thank God. They had troubles enough of their own.

As a matter of fact, once you got used to it, it wasn't at all unpleasant. Of course, we knew we were pretty phoney heroes but the Ites wouldn't have believed us if we told them and, anyhow, it's amazing how quickly you get to take this sort of thing for granted. In fact, if you had enough of it you'd always want more. That's the way old Musso went, I expect, and a good many others before him.

At the town hall things were slightly easier. All the big shots were there and they weren't bad blokes for big shots. They seemed to be under the impression one of us was General Montgomery but they weren't at all upset when we explained it was only us. They weren't weeping tears of joy like most of the people outside and they had a tendency to keep the thing rather dignified and ceremonial. But that suited us all right because we weren't very tight. And the glasses kept coming overhead in a continuous chain, which was the main thing. I haven't seen the booze flow so freely since the old days at Wallacetown pub after a Southland-Otago match.

In fact, all was as merry as a marriage bell until Terry got the notion into his head I ought to make a speech, since I had a smattering of the tongue. The idea took on like a house on fire and I must say I didn't put up as much opposition as I might have done what with the plonk and the feeling I had at the time that there was a good deal to be said for the human race. It almost seemed worth it that day, all the good cobbers that were gone, the hard backward fighting in Greece and Crete, the boredom and sweat of Maadi, and all the scares a man had had in the desert.

So the next thing I find myself out on a balcony with a great red carpet over it and the mayor holding forth explaining what was going to happen the way mayors always do. Then he bows to me and I go forward and put my hands on the balcony. And below me in the piazza is the whole population, man, woman and child, all absolutely crammed, with their faces turned up and waiting. When I saw them my heart jumped into my mouth and in spite of all the plonk I was so dry I could scarcely move my tongue.

'Give her the gun, boy,' says Terry by my side.

So I lift up my hand.

'Popolo di Castel di Goriano,' I paused and I could feel the silence go shuddering over them like the sun on a hillside and over me too and I knew I had them.

'Popolo,' I began again, 'popolo questo giorno libero.' A simple trick, after all. But it worked and I thought that one word 'free' had sent them mad. The applause went roaring up out of that narrow square and past my ear like a rocket.

Meanwhile Terry spots I've shot my bolt for the moment and am working out my next sentence and so he starts up a yell in the background: Viva il Maggiore Michele. Of course, that was all they needed – a handle for me and away they went. They like things personal.

When he saw I was ready Terry leans forward and lifts his hand: 'Silenzio per il Maggiore,' he says.

And then there was the sort of silence Shakespeare must have heard waiting for him over the centuries when he wrote the first line of one of his best spellbinders.

'Siamo venuti,' I said, 'noi, il terrore del mondo, i novozelandesi, i diavoli e cannibali, i rubatori, i negri – come vedete.' And I threw my hands out wide like Abraham and smiled my sweetest smile.

Well, give me the Ites for speed at picking up irony. They jumped to that one all the faster because the Jerries had been doing a special line for months on what scoundrels, cannibals and niggers the Kiwis were. And since Terry and Ned and I were only just a bit off white the 'negri' part underlined the nonsense of the rest.

By that time, I'd got properly into my stride and what with Terry leading the cheers whenever I stopped to think I had plenty of time to think the thing out into Latin and then work out what the Italian words must be.

'Siamo venuti,' I repeated, 'soltanto tre; perciò possete vedere come forti sono i tedeschi.'

At that there was a terrific burst of booing which had me puzzled till I saw it was the mention of Jerries that had started them off. But then I thought of a further refinement. You see, they were a bit narked because only three of us had turned up and not a battalion or so and it was a bit delicate to explain.

'E perciò possete vedere,' I went on, 'che il vostro futuro è per voi stessi.'

Of course they jumped to this immediately, too. We didn't want to overawe them but just to suggest by our fewness that now they were their own masters.

'Siete liberati dei tedeschi,' I began to develop the idea, 'si deve adesso liberarvi di voi stessi, del tyrannismo ancora rimasta, dei fascisti, e si deve fare per voi stessi uno governo di libertà, di giustizia, di ugualità, di fraternità.' By this time I was well away and that little man who sits on your shoulder and sneers when you're talking English was completely out of it. Danton had nothing on me.

'Restono cose difficili per il popolo Italiano.' That hushed them a bit. They didn't like the sound of difficult things ahead much. So I came in again with a swing.

'Ma, senza dubbio, questo popolo Italiano col suo corragio, colla sua onestà, la sua fortezza, va fare una vita piu bella, una vita chi saro conforme colle tradizioni splendidissime di questa patria, questa patria piena della grandezza passata e in questo momento gravida d'una grandezza piu magnifica, uno futuro digno del madre della civilizzazione.'

I'd got pretty tangled in my nouns, what with all those genitives, but it didn't seem to matter. The older people were all weeping and the younger all cheering. The vivas were deafening and above them came sharply the crackling of enthusiastic carbines where the partisans were grouped on the fringes of the square.

'Siamo soldati, uffizali forse, ma ciònonostante soldati, soldati semplici, come i vostri eroici partigiani.' I had to stop there again. The partisans were not at all modest and joined more vociferously than anyone in the vivas for themselves. I made a mental note of that as another useful motif to use when things got dull. Meantime I wasn't going to be cheered away from my joke.

'Non siamo oratori,' I went on, 'non piu duci.'

The allusion got them. 'Abbasso il Duce, abbasso il fascismo, abbasso Mussolini.' The roar was deep and angry. That was the first time I'd ever roused and heard the anger of a crowd.

Well, it went on in that fashion. I'd worked out the keynotes. The Jerries and Musso when you wanted rage, the glorious partisans when you wanted to cheer them up a bit, the glorious allies for terrific applause, the distant past of Italy for sentiment and the difficult future for sobriety. My difficulty now was to find some way of stopping.

Then during one particularly prolonged bit of cheering I leaned over the balcony and was watching them. As a matter of fact, I was thinking to myself that I could understand old Musso's point of view a bit better now. There was something that got you about having all those people below you there in the piazza and feeling your mind one jump ahead of your voice all the time and your voice being able to produce whatever emotion you wanted out of them. It was very exciting. And you felt it was dangerous, too. Something like taking risks with a very powerful car at top speed. At the same time you felt a certain phoneyness in your power, the way when you're shickered you know in the back of your mind things aren't really as good as they seem.

As I was staring down at them like that and trying to think of how the hell to finish without an anti-climax, I suddenly spotted the parish priest in front of the crowd and immediately I saw my end all cut and dried. I started into a peroration about the magnificence of the alliance of which Italy had now proved herself worthy, drew them into a series of vivas for Roosevelt, Churchill and Stalin and then when I'd got them at the top of their pitch, pointed suddenly at the priest and said: 'Now the time has come when the lion can lie down with the Lamb of God, the Te Deum can be sung in Moscow, and here in Castel di Goriano, as a symbol of the glorious alliance which is winning us freedom and the future, the parish priest can join with us in singing "The Red Flag."'

And so out it comes in those magnificent Italian voices: 'Bandiera Rossa trionfera', and I must admit I was so moved myself that I forgot to look to see whether the priest was singing with us. And it was a good moment to make my getaway.

'You didn't say which got up again,' said Terry, 'the lion and the lamb. Or just the lion.'

'Where's the plonk?' I said. I needn't have troubled to ask.

And that was the programme for the next hour or two except that from time to time one of us had to show himself on the balcony just so that the crowd wouldn't feel they were out of it. Then when we thought it was time we got going, the mayor wouldn't hear of it because they'd jacked up a special liberation dinner for us and the widows of all the partisans the Jerries had shot before they left were invited as well.

Well, by the time that dinner was over, and a pretty queer dinner it was, with lovely girls waiting on us and the widows bursting into tears from time to time and a stream of people coming in and out all the time to shake our hands, and gallons of plonk and more speeches, I was just about done. I had just enough sense to stop Ned abandoning his seat of honour towards the end and sneaking out with one of the women. Not one of the widows, though.

Anyhow, that settled it and in spite of all the protests we decided to get cracking. So we had a last round of speeches, nobbled Ned and made for the car.

The cold air must have got me then because the last thing I remember was thinking it was midnight and wondering how the hell Ned was going to get us first of all through the crowd and then through the minefields and wishing the partisans escorting us wouldn't fire off their carbines so much. Then I must have passed out.

The next thing I knew it was bloody cold and there was a rooster crowing somewhere and I had an iron throat. I tried to pull up my sleeping bag and it wasn't there. That brought me to and I saw we were still in the car and it was just cracking dawn.

I felt so depressed I didn't care where we were or how we'd got there. I reckon that most of the time we've got ourselves so organized that we only see as much truth as is good for us. Just the way our bodies only get as much air as is good for them. But all the time all sorts of muscles are probably at work stopping the atmosphere from closing in and squashing us. And that's the way with truth. The muscles of a man's mind are constantly engaged in keeping it back and only letting in a trickle at a time. But when he's exhausted or got a hangover, which is the same thing, he can't keep the truth out and it all bursts in. And that's what we call being depressed.

Well, that's the state I was in. The bloody truth came pouring in like water into a diver's suit. I saw that what we'd thought was good fun was deadly serious for the poor old Ites. They really believed the things I told them. And of course in theory they were true. But they weren't true, all the same.

Nothing is as simple as that. And nobody can risk being as simple as those Ites. Even after all these years they hadn't guessed what was coming to them, the steady disappointments, the gradual realization that nothing had really changed, because they were still men and women and so still vulnerable. Only it would be less easy for them now because they were rid of the enemy outside themselves, the scapegoat. They'd been reckless enough to hope and they'd have the rest of their lives for a hangover.

But it wasn't only that. I could see what was coming to me as well. I'd got a glimpse of it the day before when old Bandy went. The fact was that chaps like me had got older without noticing it. We'd never give anything again what we'd given the Div. We'd never bring the same energy to anything that we'd brought to things like the breakthrough at Minqar Qaim or the assault on Cassino. And we'd never be able to make friends again the same way or drink and laugh and die the same way. We'd used up what we had and we'd spend the rest of our lives looking over our shoulders.

Yes, that was it. The best was over with the worst. There was nothing left now except the dragging of some wretched whore through the streets in Avezzano yesterday, in Castel di Goriano today perhaps, and in the rest of the world tomorrow. Now that we knew the war was won, it was just a question of a lot more people dying for another year or two. The real excitement when you might lose was gone. And the peace everyone had felt while the war was really on was going too. A man'd soon have to start up again all the old fights with himself that used to go on in the days when there was no danger to his skin.

Terry stirred beside me and woke up.

'What the bloody hell are we doing here and where the hell are we?' I asked.

'Jesus, it's cold,' he said, 'listen to those bloody frogs. Petrol, we're out of petrol. We missed Avezzano in the dark and then when the petrol ran out we had to stop here.' He looked out the window. 'A mist, frogs, and it's pretty flat. We must be in that Fucine Swamp of theirs.'

'We're in the bloody cactus, in fact,' I said. Not that I cared much but it was a pleasure to think of something else.

'We'll be jake,' he said. 'We'll rustle up some breakfast and then make tracks up to the main road. If there's an armoured car about or a boy with a bicycle we can easily get a message back for petrol.'

'Yes,' I said.

But we didn't stir. Neither of us cared much for the thought of Wally's jokes when we passed through again.

'I could do with a drink,' I said. The muscles of my mind were doing so much work I could hear them creaking. But there was still too much truth getting by.

Ned opened his eyes. 'I saved a couple of bottles,' he said. And he pulled them out of the front pocket.

We sat there drinking in the early morning and the cold seeped into us like reality.

'Never mind, Ned,' Terry said. 'It was all that third gear work that used up the petrol.'

'Shouldn't have happened all the same,' said Ned.

'Anyhow, it was a great day,' Terry said. 'She's been a bonny war.'

'She's been a bonny war,' I said, and took another swig at the bottle.

My Enemy's Enemy

I

'YES, I know all about that, Tom,' the Adjutant said through a mouthful of stew. 'But technical qualifications aren't everything. There's other sides to a Signals officer's job, you know, especially while we're still pretty well static. The communications are running themselves and we don't want to start getting complacent. My personal view is and has been from the word go that your friend Dally's a standing bloody reproach to this unit, never mind how much he knows about the six-channel and the other boxes of tricks. That's a lineman-mechanic's job, anyway, not an officer's. And I can tell you for a fact I mean to do something about it, do you see?' He laid down his knife, though not his fork, and took three or four swallows of wine.

'Well, your boy Cleaver doesn't impress me all that much, Bill,' Thurston, who hated the Adjutant, said to him. 'The only time we've tried him on duty he flapped.'

'Just inexperience, Tom,' the Adjutant said. 'He'd soon snap out of that if we gave him command of the section. Sergeant Beech would carry him until he found his feet.'

'Mm, I'd like to see that, I must say. The line duty-officer getting his sergeant out of bed to hold his hand while he changes a valve.'

'Now look here, old boy.' The Adjutant levered a piece of meat out from between two teeth and ate it. 'You know as well as I do that young Cleaver's got the best technical qualifications of anyone in the whole unit. It's not his fault he's been stuck on office work ever since he came to us. There's a fellow that'd smarten up that bunch of goons and long-haired bloody mathematical wizards they call a line-maintenance section. As it is, the NCOs don't chase the blokes and Dally isn't interested in chasing the NCOs. Isn't interested in anything but his bloody circuit diagrams and test-frames and what-have-you.'

To cover his irritation, Thurston summoned the Mess corporal, who stood by the wall in a posture that compromised between that of an attendant waiter and the regulation stand-at-ease position. The Adjutant had schooled him in Mess procedure, though not in Mess etiquette. 'Gin and lime, please, Gordon. . . . Just as well in a way he is interested in line apparatus, isn't it, Bill? We'd have looked pretty silly without him during the move out of Normandy and across France. He worked as hard as any two of the rest of us. And as well.'

'He got his bouquet from the Colonel, didn't he? I don't grudge him that, I admit he did good work then. Not as good as some of his chaps, probably, but still, he served his turn. Yes, that's exactly it, Tom, he's served his — '

'According to Major Rylands he was the linchpin of the whole issue,' Thurston said, lighting a cigarette with fingers that were starting to tremble. 'And I'm prepared to take his word for it. The war isn't over yet, you know. Christ knows what may happen in the spring. If Dally isn't around to hold the line-maintenance end up for Rylands, the whole unit might end up in the shit with the Staff jumping on its back. Cleaver might be all right, I agree. We just can't afford to take the risk.'

This was an unusually long speech for anyone below the rank of major to make in the Adjutant's presence. Temporarily gagged by a mouthful of stew, that officer was eating as fast as he could and shaking his forefinger to indicate that he would as soon as possible propose some decisive amendment to what he had just been told. With his other hand he scratched the crown of his glossy black head, looking momentarily like a tick-tack man working through his lunch-break. He said indistinctly: 'You're on to the crux of the whole thing, old boy. Rylands is the root of all the trouble. Bad example at the top, do you see?' Swallowing, he went on: 'If the second-in-command goes round looking like a shithouse detail and calling the blokes by their Christian names, what can you expect? You can't get away from it, familiarity breeds contempt. Trouble with him is he thinks he's still working in the Post Office.'

A hot foam of anger seemed to fizz up in Thurston's chest. 'Major Rylands is the only field officer in this entire unit who knows his job. It is due to him and Dally, plus Sergeant Beech and the lineman-mechs, that our line communications have worked so smoothly during this campaign. To them and to no one else. If they can go on doing that they can walk about with bare arses for all I care.'

The Adjutant frowned at Thurston. After running his tongue round his upper teeth, he said: 'You seem to forget, Tom, that I'm responsible for the discipline of officers in this unit.' He paused to let the other reflect on the personal implications of this, then nodded to where Corporal Gordon was approaching with Thurston's drink.

As he signed the chit, Thurston was thinking that Gordon had probably been listening to the conversation from the passage. If so, he would probably discuss it with Hill, the Colonel's batman, who would probably report it to his master. It was often said, especially by Lieutenant Dalessio, the 'Dally' now under discussion, that the Colonel's chief contact with his unit was through the rumours and allegations Hill and, to a less extent, the Adjutant took to him. A tweak of disquiet made Thurston drink deeply and resolve to say no more for a bit.

The Adjutant was brushing crumbs off his battledress, which was of the greenish hue current in the Canadian Army. This little affectation, like the gamboge gloves and the bamboo walking-stick, perhaps suited a man who had helped to advertise men's clothes in civilian life. He went on to say in his rapid quacking monotone: 'I'd advise you, Tom, not to stick your neck out too far in supporting a man who's going to be out of this unit on his ear before very long.'

'Rylands, you mean?'

'No no no. Unfortunately not. But Dally's going.'

'That's gen, is it?'

'Not yet, but it will be.'

'I don't follow you.'

The Adjutant looked up in Gordon's direction, then leaned forward across the table to Thurston. 'It only needs one more thing,' he said quietly, 'to turn the scale. The CO's been watching Dally for some time, on my suggestion. I know the old man pretty well, as you know, after being in his Company for three years at North Midland Command. He's waiting to make up his mind, do you see? If Dally puts up a black in the near future – a real black – that'll be enough for the CO. Cleaver'll get his chance at last.'

'Suppose Dally doesn't put up a black?'

'He will.'

'He hasn't yet, you know. The terminal equipment's all on the top line, and Dally knows it inside out.'

'I'm not talking about that kind of a black. I'm talking about the administrative and disciplinary side. Those vehicles of his are in a shocking condition. I thought of working a snap 406 inspection on one of them, but that wouldn't look too good. Too much like discrimination. But there'll be something. Just give me time.'

Thurston thought of saying that those vehicles, though covered with months-old mud and otherwise offensive to the inspecting eye, were in good running order, thanks to the efficiency of the section's transport corporal. Instead, he let his mind wander back to one of the many stories of the Colonel's spell as a company commander in England. Three weeks running he had presented his weekly prize of £1 for the smartest vehicle to the driver of an obsolete wireless truck immobilized for lack of spare parts. The Company Sergeant-Major had won a bet about it.

'We'll have some fun then, Tom old boy,' the Adjutant was saying in as festive a tone as his voice allowed. He was unaware that Thurston disliked him. His own feelings towards Thurston were a mixture of respect and patronage: respect for Thurston's Oxford degree and accent, job at a minor public school, and efficiency as a non-technical officer; patronage for his practice of reading literary magazines and for his vaguely scholarly manner and appearance. The affinity between Thurston's unmilitary look and the more frankly ragamuffin demeanour of Dalessio could hardly explain, the Adjutant wonderingly felt, the otherwise unaccountable tendency of the one to defend the other. It was true that they'd known each other at the officer's training unit at Catterick, but what could that have to do with it? The Adjutant was unaccustomed to having his opinions contested and he now voiced the slight bafflement that had been growing on him for the last few minutes. 'It rather beats me,' he said, 'why you're taking this line about friend Dally. You're not at all thick with him. In fact he seems to needle you whenever he speaks to you. My impression is, old boy, for what it's worth, you've got no bloody use for him at all. And yet you stick up for him. Why?'

Thurston amazed him by saying coldly: 'I don't see why the fact that a man's an Italian should be held against him when he does his job as well as anyone in the sodding Army.'

'Just a minute, Tom,' the Adjutant said, taking a cigarette from his silver case, given him by his mistress in Brussels. 'That's being a bit unfair, you know. You ever heard me say a word about Dalessio being an Eyeteye? Never. You were the one who brought it up. It makes no difference to me if a fellow's father's been interned, provided – '

'Uncle.'

'All right, uncle, then. As I say, that's no affair of mine. Presumably he's okay from that point of view or he'd never have got here. And that's all there is to it as far as I'm concerned. I'm not holding it against him, not for a moment. I don't quite know where you picked up that impression, old boy.'

Thurston shook his head, blushing slightly. 'Sorry, Bill,' he said. 'I must have got it mixed. It used to get on my wick at Catterick, the way some of the blokes took it out of him about his pal Musso and so on. I suppose it must be through that somehow, in a way, I keep feeling people have got it in for him on that score. Sorry.' He was not sorry. He knew quite certainly that his charge was well-founded, and that the other's silence about Dalessio's descent was a matter of circumspection only. If anyone in the Mess admired Mussolini, Thurston suspected, it was the Adjutant, although he kept quiet about that as well. It was tempting to dig at his prejudices on these and other questions, but Thurston did his best never to succumb to that temptation. The Adjutant's displeasure was always strongly urged and sometimes, rumour said, followed up by retaliatory persecution. Enough, dangerously much, had already been said in Dalessio's defence.

The Adjutant's manner had grown genial again and, with a muttered apology, he now offered Thurston a cigarette. 'What about another of those?' he asked, pointing his head at Thurston's glass.

'Thank you, I will, but I must be off in a minute. We're opening that teleprinter to the Poles at twenty-hundred and I want to see it's working.'

Two more officers now entered the Mess dining-room. They were Captain Bentham, a forty-year-old Regular soldier who had been a company sergeant-major in India at the outbreak of war, and Captain Rowney, who besides being in charge of the unit's administration was also the Mess's catering officer. Rowney nodded to Thurston and grinned at the Adjutant, whose Canadian battledress he had been responsible for securing. He himself was wearing a sheepskin jacket, made on the Belgian black market. 'Hallo, William,' he said. 'Won the war yet?' Although he was a great chum of the Adjutant's, some of his remarks to him, Thurston had noticed, carried a curious vein of satire. Bentham sat stolidly down a couple of places along the table, running his hands over his thin grey hair.

'Tom and I have been doing a little plotting,' the Adjutant said. 'We've decided a certain officer's career with this unit needs terminating.'

Bentham glanced up casually and caught Thurston's eye. This, coming on top of the Adjutant's misrepresentation of the recent discussion, made Thurston feel slightly uncomfortable. That was ludicrous, because he had long ago written Bentham off as of no particular account, as the most uninteresting type of Regular Army ex-ranker, good only at cable-laying, supervising cable-laying and looking after the men who did the actual cable-laying. Despite this, Thurston found himself saying: 'It wasn't quite like that,' but at that moment Rowney asked the Adjutant a question and the protest, mild as it was, went unheard.

'Your friend Dally, of course,' the Adjutant answered Rowney.

'Why, what's he been up to?' Bentham asked in his slow Yorkshire voice. 'Having his hair cut?'

There was a general laugh, then a token silence while Gordon laid plates of stew in front of the new arrivals. His inquiry whether the Adjutant wanted any rice pudding was met with a facetious and impracticable instruction for the disposal of that foodstuff by an often-quoted route. 'Can't you do better than that, Jack?' the Adjutant asked Rowney. 'Third night we've had Chinese wedding-cake this week.'

'Sorry, William. My Belgian friend's had a little misunderstanding with the civvy police. I'm still looking round for another pal with the right views on how the officers of a liberating army should be fed. Just possess your soul in patience.'

'What's this about Dally?' Bentham persisted. 'If there's a move to give him a wash and a change of clothes, count me in.'

Thurston got up before the topic could be reopened. 'By the way, Jack,' he said to Rowney, 'young Malone asked me to remind you that he still hasn't had those cigarettes for the blokes he's lent to Special Wireless.'

Rowney sighed. 'Tell him it's not my pigeon, will you, Thomas? I've been into it all with him. They're under Special Wireless for everything now.'

'Not NAAFI rations. He told me you'd agreed to supply them.'

'Up until last week. They're off my hands now.'

'Oh no they're not,' Thurston said nastily. 'According to Malone they still haven't had last week's.'

'Well, tell him . . .'

'Look, Jack, you tell him. It's nothing to do with me, is it?'

Rowney stared at him. 'All right, Thomas', he said, abruptly diving his fork into his stew. 'I'll tell him.'

Dodging the hanging lampshade, which at its lowest point was no more than five feet from the floor, Thurston hurried out, his greatcoat over his arm.

'What's eating our intellectual friend?' Rowney asked.

The Adjutant rubbed his blue chin. 'Don't know quite. He was behaving rather oddly before you blokes came in. He's getting too sort of wrapped up in himself. Needs shaking up.' He was just deciding, having previously decided against it, to inflict some small but salutary injustice on Thurston through the medium of unit orders. He might compel the various sections to start handing in their various stores records for check, beginning with Thurston's section and stopping after it. Nice, but perhaps a bit too drastic. What about pinching his jeep for some tiresome extra duty? That might be just the thing.

'If you ask me,' Bentham was saying, 'he's too bloody stuck-up by half. Wants a lesson of some kind, he does.'

'You're going too far there, Ben,' the Adjutant said decisively. He disliked having Bentham in the Officers' Mess, declaring its tone to be thereby lowered, and often said he thought the old boy would be much happier back in the Sergeants' Mess with people of his own type. 'Tom Thurston's about the only chap round here you can carry on a reasonably intelligent discussion with.'

Bentham, unabashed, broke off a piece of bread and ran it round his plate in a way that Thurston and the Adjutant were, unknown to each other, united in finding unpleasant. 'What's all this about a plot about Dally?' he asked.

II

'You got that, Reg?' Dalessio asked. 'If you get any more interference on this circuit, put it back on plain speech straight away. Then they can see how they like that. I don't believe for a bloody moment the line's been relaid for a single bastard yard. Still, it's being ceased in a week or two, and it never was of the slightest importance, so there's no real worry. Now, what about the gallant Poles?' He spoke with a strong Glamorganshire accent diversified by an occasional Italian vowel.

'They're still on here,' Reg, the lineman-mechanic, said, gesturing towards the test teleprinter. 'Want to see 'em?'

'Yes, please. It's nearly time to switch 'em through to the teleprinter room. We'll get that done before I go.'

Reg bent to the keyboard of the machine and typed:

HOW U GETTING ON THERE READING ME OK KKKK

There was a humming pause while Reg scratched his armpit and said: 'Gone for a piss, I expect. . . . Ah, here he is.' In typical but inextinguishably eerie fashion the teleprinter took on a life of its own, performed a carriage-return, moved the glossy white paper up a couple of lines, and typed:

4 CHRISTS SAKE QUIT BOTHERING ME NOT 2000 HRS YET KKK

Dalessio, grinning to himself, shoved Reg out of the way and typed:

CHIEF SIGNAL OFFICER BRITISH LIBERATION ARMY ERE WATCH YR LANGUAGE MY MAN KKKK

The distant operator typed:

U GO AND SCREW YRSELF JACK SORRY I MEAN SIR

At this Dalessio went into roars of laughter, digging his knuckle into one deep eye-socket and throwing back his large dark head. It was exactly the kind of joke he liked best. He rotated a little in the narrow aisle between the banks of apparatus and test-panels, still laughing, while Reg watched him with a slight smile. At last Dalessio recovered and shouldered his way down to the phone at the other end of the vehicle.

'Give me the teleprinter room, please. What? Who? All right, I'll speak to him. . . . Terminal Equipment, Dalessio here. Yes. Oh, really? It hasn't?' His voice changed completely, became that of a slightly unbalanced uncle commiserating with a disappointed child: 'Now isn't that just too bad? Well, I do think that's hard lines. Just when you were all excited about it, too, eh?' Over his shoulder he squealed to Reg, in soprano parody of Thurston's educated tones: 'Captain Thurston is tewwibly gwieved that he hasn't got his pwinter to the Poles yet. He's afwaid we've got some howwid scheme on over heah to depwive him of it. . . . All right, Thurston, I'll come over. Yes, now.'

Reg smiled again and put a cigarette in his mouth, striking the match, from long habit, on the metal 'No Smoking' notice tacked up over the ventilator.

'Give me one of those, Reg, I want to cool my nerves before I go into the beauty-parlour across the way. Thanks. Now listen: switch the Poles through to the teleprinter room at one minute to eight exactly, so that there's working communication at eight but not before. Do Thurston good to bite his nails for a few minutes. Put it through on number . . .' – his glance and forefinger went momentarily to a test-frame across the aisle – 'number six. That's just been rewired. Ring up Teleprinters and tell 'em, will you? See you before I go off.'

It was dark and cold outside and Dalessio shivered on his way over to the Signal Office. He tripped up on the cable which ran shin-high between a line of blue-and-white posts outside the entrance, and applied an unclean expression to the Adjutant, who had had this amenity provided in an attempt to dignify the working area. Inside the crowded, brilliantly lighted office, he was half-asphyxiated by the smoke from the stove and half-deafened by the thumping of date-stamps, the ringing of telephones, the enraged bark of one sergeant and the loud, tremulous singing of the other. A red-headed man was rushing about bawling 'Emergency Ops for 17 Corps' in the accents of County Cork. Nobody took any notice of him: they had all dealt with far too many Emergency Ops messages in the last eight months.

Thurston was in his office, a small room partitioned off from the main one. The unit was occupying what had once been a Belgian military school and later an SS training establishment. This building had obviously formed part of the original barrack area, and Thurston often wondered what whim of the Adjutant's had located the offices and stores down here and the men's living-quarters in former offices and stores. The cubicle where Thurston spent so much of his time had no doubt been the abode of the cadet, and then *Unteroffizier*, in charge of barrack-room. He was fond of imagining the heavy-built Walloons and high-cheeked Prussians who had slept in here, and had insisted on preserving as a historical document the chalked *Wir kommen zurück* on the plank wall. Like his predecessors, he fancied, he felt cut off from all the life going on just outside the partition, somehow isolated. 'Alone, withouten any company,' he used to quote to himself. He would laugh then, sometimes, and go on to think of the unique lavatory at the far end of the building, where the defecator was required to plant his feet on two metal plates, grasp two handles, and curve his body into the shape of a bow over a kind of trough.

He was not laughing now. His phone conversation with Dalessio had convinced him, even more thoroughly than phone conversations with Dalessio commonly did, that the other despised him for his lack of technical knowledge and took advantage of it to irritate and humiliate him. He tried to reread a letter from one of the two married women in England with whom, besides his wife, he was corresponding, but the thought of seeing Dalessio still troubled him.

Actually seeing Dalessio troubled him even more. Not for the first time it occurred to him that Dalessio's long, matted hair, grease-spotted, cylindrical trouser-legs and ill-fitting battledress blouse were designed as an offensive burlesque of his own neat but irremediably civilian appearance. He was smoking, too, and Thurston himself was punctilious in observing inside his office the rule that prohibited smoking on duty until ten at night, but it was no use telling him to put it out. Dalessio, he felt, never obeyed orders unless it suited him. 'Hallo, Thurston,' he said amiably. 'Not still having a baby about the Poles, I hope?'

'I don't think I ever was, was I? I just wanted to make sure what the position was.'

'Oh, you wanted to make sure of that, did you? All right, then. It's quite simple. Physically, the circuit remains unchanged, of course. But, as you know, we have ways of providing extra circuits by means of electrical apparatus, notably by utilizing the electron-radiating properties of the thermionic valve, or vacuum-tube. If a signal is applied to the grid . . .'

Thurston's phone rang and he picked it up gratefully. 'Signalmaster?' said the voice of Brigadier the Lord Fawcett, the largest and sharpest thorn in the side of the entire Signals unit. 'I want a special dispatch-rider to go to Brussels for me. Will you send him round to my office for briefing in ten minutes?'

Thurston considered. Apart from its being over a hundred miles to Brussels, he suspected that the story told by previous special DRs who had been given this job was probably quite true: the purpose of the trip was to take in the Brigadier's soiled laundry and bring back the clean stuff, plus any wines, spirits and cigars that the Brigadier's Brussels agent, an RASC colonel at the headquarters of the reserve Army Corps, might have got together for him. But he could hardly ask the Lord Fawcett to confirm this. Why was it that his Army career seemed littered with such problems? 'The regular DR run goes out at oh-five-hundred, sir,' he said in a conciliatory tone. 'Would that do instead, perhaps?'

'No, it certainly would not do instead. You have a man available, I take it?'

'Oh yes, sir.' This was true. It was also true that the departure of this man with the dirty washing would necessitate another, who might have been driving all day, being got out of the section billet and condemned at best to a night on the Signal Office floor, more likely to a run half across Belgium in the small hours with a genuine message of some kind. 'Yes, we have a man.'

'Well, I'm afraid in that case I don't see your difficulty. Get him round to me right away, will you?'

'Very good, sir.' There was never anything one could do.

'Who was that?' Dalessio asked when Thurston had rung off.

'Brigadier Fawcett,' Thurston said unguardedly. But Dally probably didn't know about the laundry rumour. He had little to do with the dispatch-rider sections.

'Oh, the washerwoman's friend. I heard a bit about that from Beech. Not on the old game again, is he? Sounded as if he wanted a special DR to me.'

'Yes, he did.' Thurston raised his voice: 'Prosser!'

'Sir!' came from outside the partition.

'Ask Sergeant Baker to come and see me, will you?'

'Sir.'

Dalessio's large pale face became serious. He pulled at his moustache. Eventually he said: 'You're letting him have one, are you?' If asked his opinion of Thurston, he would have described him as a plausible bastard. His acquiescence in such matters as this, Dalessio would have added, was bloody typical.

'I can't do anything else.'

'I would. There's nothing to it. Get God's Adjutant on the blower and complain. He's an ignorant bugger, we know, but I bet he'd take this up.'

Thurston had tried this, only to be informed at length that the job of Signals was to give service to the Staff. Before he could tell Dalessio about it, Baker, the DR sergeant, arrived to be acquainted with the Lord Fawcett's desires. Thurston thought he detected a glance of protest and commiseration pass between the other two men. When Baker had gone, he turned on Dalessio almost savagely and said: 'Now look, Dally, leaving aside the properties of the thermionic bleeding valve, would you kindly put me in the picture about this teleprinter to the Poles? Is it working or isn't it? Quite a bit of stuff has piled up for them and I've been holding it in the hope the line'll be through on time.'

'No harm in hoping,' Dalessio said. 'I hope it'll be working all right, too.' He dropped his fag-end on the swept floor and trod on it.

'Is it working or is it not?' Thurston asked very loudly. His eyes wandered up and down the other's fat body, remembering how it had looked in a pair of shorts, doing physical training at the officers' training unit. It had proved incapable of the simplest tasks laid upon it, crumpling feebly in the forward-roll exercise, hanging like a crucified sack from the wall-bars, climbing by slow and ugly degrees over the vaulting-horse. Perhaps its owner had simply not felt like exerting it. That would have been bloody typical.

While Dalessio smiled at him, a knock came at the plywood door Thurston had had made for his cubicle. In response to the latter's bellow, the red-headed man came in. 'Sergeant Fleming sent to tell you, sir,' he said, 'we're just after getting them Polish fellows on the printer. You'll be wanting me to start sending off the messages we have for them, will you, sir?'

Both Thurston and Dalessio looked up at the travelling-clock that stood on a high shelf in the corner. It said eight o'clock.

III

'That's just about all, gentlemen,' the Colonel said. 'Except for one last point. Now that our difficulties from the point of view of communication have been removed, and the whole show's going quite smoothly, there are other aspects of our work which need attention. This unit has certain traditions I want kept up. One of them, of course, is an absolutely hundred-per-cent degree of efficiency in all matters affecting the disposal of Signals traffic, from the time the In-Clerk signs for a message from the Staff to the time we get . . .'

He means the Out-Clerk, Thurston thought to himself. The little room where the officers, warrant-officers and senior NCOs of the unit held their conferences was unheated, and the Colonel was wearing his knee-length sheepskin coat, another piece of merchandise supplied through the good offices of Jack Rowney in exchange, perhaps, for a few gallons of petrol or a couple of hundred cigarettes; Malone's men's cigarettes, probably. The coat, added to the CO's platinum-blond hair and moustache, increased his resemblance to a polar bear. Thurston was in a good mood, having just received the letter which finally buttoned up arrangements for his forthcoming leave: four days with Denise in Oxford, and then a nice little run up to Town for five days with Margot. Just the job. He began composing a nature note on the polar bear: 'This animal, although of poor intelligence, possesses considerable cunning of a low order. It displays the utmost ferocity when menaced in any way. It shows fantastic patience in pursuit of its prey, and a vindictiveness which. . .'

The Colonel was talking now about another tradition of his unit, its almost unparalleled soldier-like quality, its demonstration of the verity that a Signals formation *of any kind* was not a collection of down-at-heel scientists and long-haired mathematical wizards. Thurston reflected it was not for nothing that the Adjutant so frequently described himself as the Colonel's staff officer. Yes, there he was, Arctic fox or, if they had them, Arctic jackal, smiling in proprietary fashion at his chief's oratory. What a bunch they all were. Most of the higher-ranking ones had been lower-ranking officers in the Territorial Army during the Thirties, the Colonel, for instance, a captain, the Adjutant a second-lieutenant. The war had given them responsibility and quick promotion, and their continued enjoyment of such privileges rested not on their own abilities, but on those of people who had arrived in the unit by a different route: Post Office engineers whipped in with a commission, older Regular soldiers promoted from the ranks, officers who had been the conscripts of 1940 and 1941. Yes, what a bunch. Thurston remembered the parting words of a former sergeant of his who had been posted home a few months previously: 'Now I'm going I suppose I can say what I shouldn't. You never had a dog's bloody chance in this lot unless you'd been at North Midland Command with the Adj. and the CO. And we all know it's the same in that Mess of yours. If you'd been in the TA like them you were a blue-eyed boy, otherwise you were done for from the start. It's all right, sir, everybody knows it. No need to deny it.'

The exception to the rule, presumably, was Cleaver, now making what was no doubt a shorthand transcript of the Colonel's harangue. Thurston hated him as the Adjutant's blue-eyed boy and also for his silky fair hair, his Hitler Youth appearance and his thunderous laugh. His glance moved to Bentham, also busily writing. Bentham, too, fitted into the picture, as much as the Adjutant would let him, which was odd when compared with the attitude of other Regulars in the Mess. But Bentham had less individuality than they.

'So what I propose,' the Colonel said, 'is this. Beginning next week the Adjutant and I will be making a series of snap inspections of section barrack-rooms. Now I don't expect anything in the nature of spit-and-polish, of course. Just ordinary soldierly cleanliness and tidiness is all I want.'

In other words, just ordinary spit-and-polish, Thurston thought, making a note for his sergeant on his pad just below the polar-bear *vignette.* He glanced up and saw Dalessio licking the flap of an envelope; it was his invariable practice to write letters during the Colonel's addresses, when once the serious business of line-communications had been got through. Had he heard what had just been said? It was unlikely.

The conference broke up soon afterwards and in the Mess ante-room, where a few officers had gathered for a drink before the evening meal, Thurston was confronted by an exuberant Adjutant who at once bought him a drink. 'Well, Tom,' he said, 'I reckon that fixes things up nice and neat.'

'I don't follow you, Bill.'

'Step number one in cooking your friend Dally's goose. Step number two will be on Monday, oh-nine-thirty hours, when I take the Colonel round the line-maintenance billet. You know what we'll find there, don't you?'

Thurston stared blankly at the Adjutant, whose eyes were sparkling like those of a child who has been promised a treat. 'I still don't get you, Bill.'

'Use your loaf, Tommy. Dally's blokes' boudoir, can't you imagine what it'll be like? There'll be dirt enough in there to raise a crop of potatoes, fag-ends and pee-buckets all over the shop and the rest of it. The Colonel will eat Dally for his lunch when he sees it.'

'Dally's got three days to get it cleaned up, though.'

'He would have if he paid attention to what his Commanding Officer says. But I know bloody well he was writing a letter when that warning was given. Serves the bastard right, do you see? He'll be off to the mysterious East before you can turn round.'

'How much does the Colonel know about this?'

'What I've told him.'

'You don't really think it'll work, do you?'

'I know the old man. You don't, if you'll excuse my saying so.'

'It's a lousy trick and you know it, Bill,' Thurston said violently. 'I think it's completely bloody.'

'Not at all. An officer who's bolshie enough to ignore a CO's order deserves all he gets,' the Adjutant said, looking sententious. 'Coming in?'

Still fuming, Thurston allowed himself to be led into the dining-room. The massive green-tiled stove was working well and the room was warm and cheerful. The house had belonged to the commandant of the Belgian military school. Its solid furniture and tenebrous landscape pictures had survived German occupation, though there was a large burn in the carpet that had been imputed, perhaps rightly, to the festivities of the *Schutz Staffel*. Jack Rowney, by importing photographs of popular entertainers, half-naked young women and the Commander-in-Chief, had done his best to document the Colonel's thesis that the Officers' Mess was also their home. The Adjutant, in excellent spirits, his hand on Thurston's shoulder, sent Corporal Gordon running for a bottle of burgundy. Then, before they sat down, he looked very closely at Thurston.

'Oh, and by the way, old boy,' he said, a note of menace intensifying the quack in his voice, 'you wouldn't think of tipping your friend Dally the wink about this little treat we've got lined up for him, would you? If you do, I'll have your guts for garters.' Laughing heartily, he dug Thurston in the ribs and added: 'Your leave's due at the end of the month, isn't it? Better watch out you don't make yourself indispensable here. We might not be able to let you go, do you see?'

IV

Early on Monday Thurston was walking up from the Signal Office towards the area where the men's barrack-rooms were. He was going to find his batman and arrange to be driven some twenty miles to the department of the Advocate-General's branch which handled divorce. The divorce in question was not his own, which would have to wait until after the war, but that of his section cook, whose wife had developed an immoderate fondness for RAF and USAAF personnel.

Thurston was thinking less about the cook's wife than about the fateful inspection, scheduled to take place any minute now. He realized he had timed things badly, but his trip had only just become possible and he hoped to be out of the area before the Colonel and the Adjutant finished their task. He was keen to do this because the sight of a triumphant Adjutant would be more than he could stand, especially since his conscience was very uneasy about the whole affair. There were all sorts of reasons why he should have tipped Dalessio off about the inspection. The worst of it was, as he had realized in bed last night, when it was too late to do anything about it, that his irritation with Dalessio over the matter of the Polish teleprinter had been a prime cause of his keeping his mouth shut. He remembered actually thinking more than once that a thorough shaking-up would do Dalessio no harm, and that perhaps, the son of an Italian café-proprietor in Cascade, Glamorganshire, had certain disqualifications for the role of British regimental officer. He twisted up his face when he thought of this and started wondering just why it was that the Adjutant was persecuting Dalessio. Perhaps the latter's original offence had been his habit of doing bird-warbles while the Adjutant and Rowney listened to broadcast performances of the *Warsaw Concerto*, the Intermezzo from *Cavalleria Rusticana*, and other sub-classics dear to their hearts. Cheeping, trilling and twittering, occasionally gargling like a seagull, Dalessio had been told to shut up or get out and had done neither.

Thurston's way took him past the door of the notorious line-maintenance billet. There seemed to be nobody about. Then he was startled by the sudden manifestation of two soldiers carrying brooms and a bucket. One of them had once been in his section and had been transferred early that year to one of the cable sections, he had forgotten which one. 'Good-morning, Maclean,' he said.

The man addressed came sketchily to attention. 'Morning, sir.'

'Getting on all right in No. I Company?'

'Yes, thank you, sir, I like it fine.'

'Good. What are you fellows up to so early in the morning?'

They looked at each other and the other man said: 'Cleaning up, sir. Fatigue party, sir.'

'I see; right, carry on.'

Thurston soon found his batman, who agreed with some reluctance to the proposed trip and said he would see if he could get the jeep down to the Signal Office in ten minutes. The jeep was a bone of contention between Thurston and his batman, and the batman always won, in the sense that never in his life had he permitted Thurston to drive the jeep in his absence. He was within his rights, but Thurston often wished, as now, that he could be allowed a treat occasionally. He wished it more strongly when a jeep with no exhaust and with seven men in it came bouncing down the track from the No. I Company billet area. They were laughing and two of them were pretending to fight. The driver was a lance-corporal.

Suddenly the laughing and fighting stopped and the men assumed an unnatural sobriety. The reason for this was provided by the immediate emergence into view of the Colonel and the Adjutant, moving across Thurston's front.

They saw him at once; he hastily saluted and the Adjutant, as usual, returned the salute. His gaze met Thurston's under lowered brows and his lips were gathered in the fiercest scowl they were capable of.

Thurston waited till they were out of sight and hurried to the door of the line-maintenance billet. The place was deserted. Except in illustrations to Army manuals and the like, he had never seen such perfection of order and cleanliness. It was obviously the result of hours of devoted labour.

He leant against the doorpost and began to laugh.

v

'I gather the plot against our pal Dally misfired somewhat,' Bentham said in the Mess dining-room later that day.

Thurston looked up rather wearily. His jeep had broken down on the way back from the divorce expert and his return had been delayed for some hours. He had made part of the journey on the back of a motor-bike. Further, he had just read a unit order requiring him to make the jeep available at the Orderly Room the next morning. It wasn't his turn yet. The Adjutant had struck again.

'You know, I'm quite pleased,' Bentham went on, lighting a cigarette and moving towards the stove where Thurston stood.

'Oh, so am I.'

'You are? Now that's rather interesting. Surprising, even. I should have thought you'd be downcast.'

Something in his tone made Thurston glance at him sharply and put down the unit order. Bentham was standing with his feet apart in an intent attitude. 'Why should you think that, Ben?'

'I'll tell you. Glad of the opportunity. First of all I'll tell you why it misfired, if you don't already know. Because I tipped Dally off. Lent him some of my blokes and all, to get the place spick and span.'

Thurston nodded, thinking of the two men he had seen outside the billet that morning. 'I see.'

'You do, do you? Good. Now I'll tell you why I did it. First of all, the Army's not the place for this kind of plotting and scheming. The job's too important. Secondly, I did it because I don't like seeing an able man taken down by a bunch of ignorant jumped-up so-called bloody gentlemen from the Territorial Army. Not that I hold any brief for Dalessio outside his technical abilities. As you know, I'm a Regular soldier and I disapprove most strongly of anything damn slovenly. It's part of my nature now and I don't mind either. But one glance at the Adj.'s face when he was telling me the form for this morning and I knew where my duty lay. I hope I always do. I do my best to play it his way as a rule for the sake of peace and quiet. But this business was different. Wasn't it?'

Thurston had lowered his gaze. 'Yes, Ben.'

'It came as a bit of a shock to me, you know, to find that Dalessio needed tipping off.'

'How do you mean?'

'I mean that I'd have expected someone else to have told him already. I only heard about this last night. I was the only one here later on and I suppose the Adj. felt he had to tell someone. I should have thought by that time someone else would have let the cat out of the bag to Dally. You, for instance. You were in on this from the start, weren't you?'

Thurston said nothing.

'I've no doubt you have your excuses for not letting on. In spite of the fact that I've always understood you were the great one for pouring scorn on the Adj. and Rowney and Cleaver and the rest of that crowd. Yes, you could talk about them till you were black in the face, but when it came to doing something, talking where it would do some good, you kept your mouth shut. And, if I remember rightly, you were the one who used to stick up for Dally when the others were laying into him behind his back. You know what I think? I don't think you care tuppence. You don't care beyond talking, any road. I think you're really quite sold on the Adj.'s crowd, never mind what you say about them. Chew that over. And chew this over and all: I think you're a bastard, just like the rest of 'em. Tell that to your friend the Adjutant, Captain bloody Thurston.'

Thurston stood there for some time after Bentham had gone, tearing up the unit order and throwing the pieces into the stove.

Acknowledgements

IN the course of preparing this anthology I incurred many obliga-
tions. If, in what follows, there are any omissions I hope they will be
attributed to a failing memory and a filing system that has become
only the more confused with my fitful attempts to reform it. My
first and principal thanks are due, of course, to the writers themselves, alive and dead, who in those days of now forgotten stress
knew only too well how perilously brief their time for writing and
for living was likely to be. In my introduction I have tried to
indicate my admiration and respect for those editors of precarious
periodicals who tried, not altogether vainly, to keep literature itself
alive. To one of these, Mr John Lehmann, I am grateful for cour-
teous and helpful advice about possible sources; to another, Mr
Clem Christesen, who edited the Australian periodical *Meanjin*
in the relevant period, I am also indebted for advice as well as
for a long friendship; and my old friend, Walter Allen, responded
readily and constructively to my appeal for opinion and assistance.
Many other friends were persecuted by me at various times and
in various ambiences and I particularly valued the sympathetic
patience shown with my problems by my former colleague at the
Oxford University Press, Mr Peter Sutcliffe, and by Dr Godfrey
and Dr Peter Lienhardt of the Institute of Social Anthropology at
Oxford.

At the Imperial War Museum I was unhesitatingly helped by
Christopher Dowling and by the Keeper of Printed Books, Dr Gwyn
Bayliss. My one attempt to exploit a library nearer home, the Public
Library in Oxford, was frustrated by a bureaucratic rule that denied
me membership, not because my identity was in dispute but because I did not carry with me documentary evidence of my address.
I therefore found it easier to buy the books I required from the local
bookshops, where one's credibility was not impaired by failure to
carry a driver's licence or a 'rent-book'.

To resume the more congenial task of expressing positive grati-
tude: I am particularly indebted to the courtesy and efficiency of
Mrs Judith Luna of the Oxford University Press who attended at the
book's growing pains (and endured some of them) and who, among

other acts of kindness, relieved me of the invidious problem of deciding how many and which of my own stories should be included.

D.D.

★

The editor and publishers wish to thank the following for their permission to reproduce copyright material:

Kingsley Amis: from *My Enemy's Enemy* (1962). First published in *Encounter*, 1955. Reprinted by permission of Victor Gollancz Ltd.

H. E. Bates: 'There's Something in the Air', 'No Trouble at All' and 'The Disinherited' from *The Stories of Flying Officer 'X'* (Jonathan Cape Ltd.). Reprinted by permission of Laurence Pollinger Ltd., for the Estate of the late H. E. Bates.

Elizabeth Bowen: 'Mysterious Kôr' from *The Demon Lover* (first published in *Penguin New Writing*, No. 20, 1944). Reprinted by permission of Jonathan Cape Ltd. on behalf of the Estate of Elizabeth Bowen.

Jocelyn Brooke: 'The Blanket'. First published in *Penguin New Writing*, No. 29, 1947, ed. John Lehmann. Reprinted by permission of A. M. Heath & Co. Ltd. for the estate of the late Jocelyn Brooke.

Roald Dahl: 'A Piece of Cake' from *Over To You* (Penguin Books, 1973). Reprinted by permission of Murray Pollinger.

Dan Davin: 'Not Substantial Things' from *The Gorse Blooms Pale* (Nicholson & Watson, 1947); 'East is West' from *Breathing Spaces* (Robert Hale & Co., 1975). Reprinted by permission of the author.

Ralph Elwell-Sutton: 'The Deserter'. First published in *Folios of New Writing*, Spring 1940 (Hogarth Press) and later republished in *Penguin New Writing*, No. 12, 1942, ed. John Lehmann. Reprinted by permission of the author.

Graham Greene: 'Men at Work' from *Collected Stories* (The Bodley Head and William Heinemann). Reprinted by permission of Laurence Pollinger Ltd.

Eric Joysmith: 'The Crew of the Jackdaw' from *Bugle Blast* (George Allen & Unwin Ltd., 1943).

Humphrey Knight: 'The Sea and the Sky'. First published in *Penguin New Writing*, No. 18, 1943, ed. John Lehmann.

Alun Lewis: 'Private Jones' from *The Last Inspection*; 'Ward "O" 3(b)' from *In The Green Tree*. Reprinted by permission of Allen & Unwin.

Jack Lusby: 'A Flying Fragment'. First published in the *Bulletin*. Reprinted by permission of Mrs Maria Simms.

Julian Maclaren-Ross: 'I had to go sick' from *Memoirs of the Forties* (1965). Reprinted by permission of London Magazine Editions.

John Prebble: 'The Soldier Looks for his Family' from *Selected Writing* (ed. Reginald Moore, Winter 1944, Nicholson & Watson). Reprinted by permission of Curtis Brown Ltd.

V. S. Pritchett: 'The Voice' from *Collected Stories* (Chatto & Windus Ltd.). Reprinted by permission of A. D. Peters & Co. Ltd.

F. J. Salfeld: 'Fear of Death'. First published in *Penguin New Writing*, No. 17, 1943, ed. John Lehmann. Reprinted by permission of the author.

William Sansom: 'The Wall' from *The Stories of William Sansom* (Hogarth Press, 1963), © William Sansom 1963. Reprinted by permission of Elaine Greene Ltd.

H. R. Savage: 'Night Attack'. First published in *Penguin New Writing*, No. 24, 1945, ed. John Lehmann.

Norman Swallow: 'All This is Ended'. First published in *Penguin New Writing*, No. 27, 1946. Reprinted by permission of the author.

Fred Urquhart: 'The Prisoner's Bike' from *Selected Stories* (Maurice Fridberg's Hour Glass Library, 1946). Reprinted by permission of Anthony Sheil Associates Ltd.